INFORMATION PAYOFF

INFORMATION PAYOFF

The Transformation of Work
in the Electronic Age

Paul A. Strassmann

THE FREE PRESS
A Division of Macmillan, Inc.
NEW YORK

Collier Macmillan Publishers
LONDON

The Free Press
A Division of Macmillan, Inc.
866 Third Avenue, New York, N. Y. 10022

Collier Macmillan Canada, Inc.

Printed in the United States of America

printing number

1 2 3 4 5 6 7 8 9 10

Library of Congress Cataloging in Publication Data

Strassmann, Paul A.
    Information payoff.

    Bibliography: p.
    1. Office practice--Automation. I. Title.
HF5547.5.S79 1985   651.8'4   84-24737
ISBN 0-02-931720-7

*In memory of my precious son Eric,
who had the gift of understanding
what the future might bring*

Contents

List of Illustrations

Preface

This book reflects my personal experiences in making presentations and answering questions about office automation. In the last two years I addressed over 20,000 corporate executives, government administrators, office managers, technical experts, and legislators. The talks took place in just about every major metropolitan area in the world. Over 150 of these talks were organized in fairly small group settings to facilitate dialogue. My purpose was to explain the emerging roles of information technology and its effects on information work. In return, I hoped to gain insight into the concerns of the decision-makers who would influence investments in this new information technology.

The range of questions from the audiences was amazing. Even though each group was reasonably homogeneous by virtue of the way attendance was organized, the issues raised in each session covered a much wider spectrum than I had expected. The participants had a highly personal desire to understand what the emerging issues were and how to cope with the coming changes. Their questions ranged from engineering minutiae to philosophical concerns about the future of our civilization. Nevertheless, technical matters were totally overwhelmed by nontechnological concerns. Managers already know that computers are a miraculous technology. Managers were now eager to discuss what the future may bring in terms of its effect on people, rather than in terms of ever-more marvelous machines.

The lecture series confirmed my assumption that managers did not clearly see how they could take advantage of information technology to improve their operations. Even though business journals now cover topics found only in specialized computer journals just five years ago, my overall conclusion was that the decision-makers were unsure about how technology and people will ultimately fit together. The hardware and the displays of software were tangible enough, to be sure. What was shrouded in uncertainty was how the technology would affect individuals and how it would modify existing organizational relationships. The attendees at some of the most intensive question-and-answer periods rightly sensed that information technology will cause vast changes in the established power structure, in management skills required to direct people, in relationships among people in the workplace, and in government influence on our professional and personal lives.

In the absence of personal experience with information technology the safest thing for a manager to do would be to read with much greater care the profusion of articles, magazine inserts, pamphlets, and promotional materials spawned by the media. Purchasing a personal computer and learning one of the computer languages would certainly seem to be the right start for acquiring "computer literacy." The questions and answers from my audiences revealed that indeed a great deal of reading and experimenting had already taken place. Attendance at executive presentations about office automation is a highly self-selective process anyway: those who spoke up appeared to have considerable knowledge about the basic technologies, prices, and performance of equipment. What they lacked was a reasonably confident sense about what may happen when people are placed in the totally electronic office environment of the future.

Here are some of the most frequently voiced concerns: What are some of the realistic scenarios about office work after the introduction of office automation? What is known about the economic justification for investments to support the work of executives, managers, and professionals? What sort of evidence is there about the organizational changes everyone is talking about? How about signs of employee resistance? What shall we do with the unemployed workers displaced by automation? Will it be necessary to master electronics in order to hold a managerial job in the future?

I believe that all really worthwhile managerial learning takes place through personal observation, provided that there is some sort of a theoretical context within which real-world encounters can be placed. I concluded that the topics encompassed by information technology are just too varied to be brought together in any single book, or even in an encyclopedia. Besides, anything recorded today is likely to be either obsolete by the time it is published, or irrelevant to the needs of a particular manager, who must deal with problems as they occur. To understand the future implications of technology one should examine its present applications in the workplace.

Neither systems analysis nor various approaches to technology assessment seem to be of much practical value to an executive confronted with decisions about what technologies to invest in. I have come to recognize that many simultaneous approaches are necessary: a person can develop insights into complex socio-technological situations only by assimilating many perspectives.[1] Understanding grows from a gradual balancing of experiences so as to synthesize a unique solution. This approach is characterized by its emphasis on strategic factors that affect the entire business and by its emphasis on people and their motivation before evaluating the effects of technology per se. By contrast, a purely mechanistic approach defines most of the issues in terms of increased funding, acquisition of more equipment, effective procurement policies, and sophisticated computer networks.

The central concept of this book is that the most worthwhile insights into the meaning of information technology cannot be obtained from an examination of the technology itself. Understanding must begin with meticulous observation of people and organizations under conditions when information technology is or is not applied. This book, then, contains projections about the future based on present experiences, as seen from individual, organizational, and societal points of view.

The usual approach to dealing with the effects of information technology is to first examine its supply side, which includes the technology of computers, software, communications, information services, applications, databases, printers, memory devices, and so forth. For the last twenty-five years we have been preoccupied with such supply-side issues. If I may venture a guess, over ninety-five of every hundred pages of text written about office automation have dealt with these aspects. In the past this amount of attention was appropriate because the technological capabilities were the key to getting anything accomplished. As a consequence, the audience for all of this technical knowl-

edge was concentrated among the two million technologists involved
with the design, manufacture, and application of office automation
devices. The actual users of computers could absorb only small doses
of useful knowledge about computers from this literature.

As already indicated, I consider the technical aspects of information
technology to be less important than human factors when trying to
anticipate future developments. Technology forecasts are absent here
because they are adequately covered already in existing publications.
This book is directed to the many managers and users who wish to
have a better understanding of the organizational effects of information
technology before they consider investing significant amounts of their
scarce cash in further office automation. This book is also addressed
to the observers who wish to make sense of the outpour of articles
and speeches about the coming information revolution, but find themselves without an adequate treatment of what the human consequences
of this change may be. My intent is to show how information technology can alter job design, organizational forms, and social influences
in such a way that all combine to create a workplace which is much
more productive and satisfying than we have today.

This book examines information technology from its demand-side
perspective. It covers topics such as individual productivity enhancement; productivity measurement; worker attitudes; union acceptance;
training of employees and managers; privacy, legal protection, and
security; organizational design; employee motivation and the quality
of services; organizational structure of firms operating in networks;
pricing of information; preserving property rights to know-how; cen-
tralization vs. decentralization of management; how to justify investments in information technology; how to estimate the full costs of
information networks; work at home; and what to do with workers
who become unemployed because of an inability to deal with the new
office environment.

The primary concerns of managers and the educated public are
demand-side issues. They need to understand what is likely to happen
when over 400 million information workers (the currently estimated
worldwide population of "white collar workers") begin using the new
information technologies to perform a significant portion of their work.
The contents of this book, then, are directed to topics which will
affect many more individuals than would a discussion of supply-side
effects.

Right now we are about to witness an explosion of information
technology into the workplace on a scale previously matched only

by the worldwide spread of the automobile. The placement, within fifteen years, of more than 200 million electronic workstations in offices all over the world is a likely forecast. Whether this will actually happen will not be determined by technological considerations. The capacity of global information industries to supply practically unlimited quantities of equipment is well ahead of the users' ability to absorb it. The capacity on the supply side is steadily increasing. Enormous amounts of entrepreneurial capital, imagination, research, engineering talent, and marketing skill are causing cost reductions and performance improvements on a scale never before experienced. Within ten years technological capabilities will cease to be matters of concern to decision-makers in advanced industrial countries. From a managerial standpoint questions of technology will be safely delegated to between 5 and 8 million technologists, service providers, and vendor support personnel.

Information technology and information services will be commodities easily available at highly competitive prices in a global marketplace. The choices of how and when to use information technology will then be largely dictated by socioeconomic considerations. Investment decisions will be made within the framework of all the other investment choices management must make anyway. Buying information technology will not be different, in principle, from any other business decision. However, the methods of equipping the workplace with information technology will be as different from present practices as the decisions to create factories in the eighteenth century differed from the ways in which tools were acquired under the guild system in the fourteenth century.

The entire purpose of this work is to explore information technology, as seen in terms of its payoff in the workplace. My premise is that computers are the single most important technological means for assuring the future growth of society's productivity. They are therefore the single most important source of increased personal wealth as well as the basis for improvement of the quality of life in the workplace. Computers will be one of the principal foundations for a new kind of economy, one based primarily on the delivery of valuable services to consumers, rather than merely on the production and delivery of products. Computer-linked technology will be the basis for dramatic increases in the organizational effectiveness essential for prosperity, increased real incomes, new employment opportunities, and an improved quality in private life. A variety of new names have been suggested to describe this phenomenon. I will attempt not to

favor any of these new additions to our vocabulary, although I will
cover many of the topics currently discussed under any of the following
labels: Teleinformatics, Compunication, Integrated Information Systems, New Information Technologies, Office-of-the-Future, Office
Automation, Office Revolution, The Third Wave, Telematics, and Bu-
reautics. These are just a few of the terms recently suggested to describe
social change with its origins in information technology.

Individual chapters will deal with clearly observable clues to the
future. We have behind us thirty years of experience with computers
and with their effects on automating a large number of information-
processing activities. Minicomputers, office terminals, word-processing
equipment, and even personal computers have been installed in a sufficient number of organizations long enough that we scarcely need to
treat them as unknown influences. It is, therefore, reasonable to make
projections for the period down to the end of this century. Technological progress can be reasonably expected to continue at current rates
and will not be discussed much further. It will be political forces
that will ultimately dictate the rate at which the benefits from information technologies will be realized.

Information Payoff progresses from the well-known to the increasingly uncertain. Unless specifically attributed to others, all of the observations, case studies, and cost estimates are derived from my own
work as manager and consultant. The book begins with a discussion
of information technology as seen from an individual's point of view.
Chapter 1 deals with current patterns of information work. Chapters
2 to 4 cover what I have observed about the effects of electronic
workstations on the work of individuals.

When considering how people begin to cooperate electronically,
the focus of the book changes to the functioning of organizations.
The major theme of Chapters 5 through 8 is an assessment of the
economic effects of office automation on businesses, with special attention to the topics of productivity improvement and productivity measurement. Here we examine what happens when businesses start
investing in information technology as a means to superior competitive
performance. Chapter 9 covers topics which should be of particular
interest to a chief executive, a business planner, or to an information
resources manager, because in it I deal with the question of how investments in information technology can be made to support the strategic
objectives of an enterprise. Chapter 10 provides a close examination
of one of the many widely accepted myths about the consequences
of information technology. The concept of the paperless office-of-the-

future is examined in some detail; this serves as an illustration of how carefully one must examine the facts before accepting superficially plausible theses.

Next, I deal with topics beyond the boundaries of individual businesses. Chapters 11 through 13 concern matters of social, economic, and cultural relevance. The transformation of information work is discussed as a development which can be fully understood only from a historical point of view.

Chapter 14 offers fourteen practical guidelines on how to manage information technology investments. At that point it should become clear that a careful balancing of priorities among individual, organizational, and societal factors is the prerequisite for obtaining better results from new forms of information work. Chapter 15, a summary of the book, should give the reader a quick overview of the major conclusions about ways for realizing the payoff from the transformed workplace of the future.

PAUL A. STRASSMANN
May, 1984

PART I

THE INDIVIDUAL'S PERSPECTIVE

1

Working in the Office

Less than fifty years ago special respect was usually shown to those who wore white-collar shirts to work: these were the privileged group of employees. Regardless of their income they rated a superior social status because they dealt with "information" rather than with "things." To raise a child who became a professional man was the pinnacle of aspiration for most families. Nowadays, when well over half of all workers are information workers—and almost half of those are in executive, managerial, administrative, and professional positions—we certainly cannot view this area as the province of the privileged few. Information work is the largest single employment category in industrial economies.[1] We must examine the meaning of office work in order to understand the effects of computer technology used to support it.

White-Collar Work = Information Work?

Classification of workers according to occupation is inadequate. Identification of the actual amounts of information work done leads to an improved understanding.

3

I will not use the term "white-collar worker" in this book very often. Most of such individuals wear blue shirts or pink blouses anyway. Many workers so designated operate under circumstances which are close to factory conditions. They follow highly routine work patterns and make few discretionary decisions.

Neither will I use the term "office workers." As robots are introduced into the factory, the shop-floor operators themselves become information workers, since they need a great deal of know-how to operate such sophisticated equipment. When computer terminals are placed in trucks, in warehouses, in the manager's home and in the salesperson's portable attaché case, "office work" ceases to have meaning, since it implies a single sort of location.

I favor the term "information work": it supercedes the rigid classifications that prevent a better understanding of the changes taking place in the nature of work. I consider an "information worker" to be anyone who handles information rather than physically handling materials, consumer goods, or providing tangible services (such as serving food). A person may also be doing information work as a part-time activity. The term "information worker" lends itself to a more comprehensive analysis than is usually accepted at present.

Information workers constitute the majority of the workforce in the United States. Counting information workers understates the amount of information work.

The Bureau of Labor Statistics has just changed its occupational definition from the "white-collar worker" category to "information worker." The most recent information on the composition of the United States workforce is shown in Figure 1.1

Even though this new method of counting shows an increase over the number of people included in the previous "white-collar" worker classification, it is still inadequate because it enumerates only those workers who deal with information on a full-time basis. This understates the actual amount of information work performed in the economy. The current trend is to distribute information work more widely, instead of confining it to typical information occupations. For instance, automatic teller machines provide a convenient way to reduce the number of bank clerks. These machines pass on to customers much of the administrative work formerly done by clerks and tellers. In a warehouse one will find forklift truck operators spending at least a quarter of their time checking loading tickets and adjusting shipping

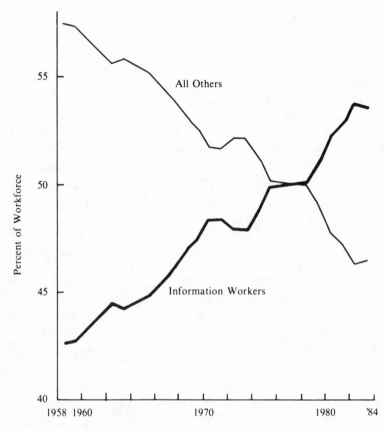

Figure 1.1   United States Information Workforce

papers. Delivery men prepare data for invoices. Lathe operators fill
out job tickets and time cards. Woodworkers in a boatyard complete
forms which include a detailed accounting for materials used and
for labor charges to be applied to job orders. An assembly worker
supervising a fully automatic robot from a control panel is not behaving
differently than an operator at the console of a large computer. Yet
government statisticians categorize all assembly workers entirely as
production workers and only the computer operator as an information
worker.[2] Moreover, I think that perhaps as much as a quarter of
the time of *all* "non-information workers" is devoted to some sort
of information work. By contrast, I do not believe that any significant
portion of the information workers' time is applied to the handling
of materials or goods. Therefore, I suggest that more than 63% of

all equivalent working days in the United States economy in 1982 was devoted to information work.

The growth of information workers is a global trend.

So far, my comments applied only to United States statistics. Examination of data from other countries reveals the same tendency to underestimation of information workers: official methods for counting white-collar employment simply enumerate the number of heads in each standard occupational category. Regardless of this built-in bias, the general tendency is the same. The fraction of information workers in the workforce is growing in every one of the twenty countries I visited during the last two years.

Information work, in terms of hours or cost, represents more than two-thirds of United States labor expenditures.

The total amount of information work is further understated by counting the number of people as an indicator of work done. The average weekly workhours expended by information workers is 10% to 20% greater than those put in by workers in other occupational categories. For example, people in service occupations—such as in food and hotel establishments—average only a 31.7-hour workweek because they are often employed only part-time. Executives and administrators are reported to average a 43.6-hour workweek. If workhours rather than people are used to estimate the amount of labor performed in the United States economy in 1982, then my estimate of information work becomes greater than 70% of the total.

Using the dollar value of wages and benefits further tips the balance in favor of information work. Information workers, as a group, receive 35% higher wage rates and more generous benefits than non-information workers. On a dollar basis I estimate that the United States economy spends at least 67% of its labor costs on information work.[3]

Consumer Information and the "Cottage Industry"

The future cottage industry will involve not only a transfer of existing office work to the home. It will deliver new, do-it-yourself consumer services which are otherwise not affordable.

Progressively more information work is extending into the home and into consumer activities. The lead in this direction has been taken by the labor-intensive financial sector, which views the home banking terminal as a solution to its escalating labor costs.[4] It is hard to tell what the net benefit of this shift will be to the entire economy after we have subtracted the hours saved by employing smaller numbers of employees in financial services and then added the increased hours spent by large numbers of consumers on self-service. My point is simply that there is a pronounced trend favoring the transfer of office tasks out of the traditional office. In the name of efficiency and convenience, the work now performed by clerical personnel in airlines, libraries, banks, government, insurance companies, and so forth will be done directly by consumers. For instance, many airlines have installed automatic ticketing machines to reduce the number of counter clerks they employ. Since only a few clerks remain (and they are largely devoted to handling inquiries), travellers find themselves lining up behind ticketing machines to do added information work.

Home computers are enjoying a boom partially because they are picking up increased amounts of work that the consumer cannot afford to have done for him by others. Spreadsheet software and checkbook balancing programs proliferate in the home market as computer owners discover that they can manage their own financial accounting. Tax preparation software is also in great demand because the government has introduced increasingly complex tax regulations that even well-educated persons cannot handle without expert assistance. The increased paperwork burdens of new tax-saving investment and pension schemes have added millions of hours of information work to consumers' ostensibly "leisure time."

Toffler's *Future Shock* and *The Third Wave* described the advent of a new "cottage industry" as the migration of information work from the offices to the home. I see the phenomenon primarily as newly created information work done by consumers who previously could not have afforded it. These new consumer activities become an extension of an already large do-it-yourself and underground service economy that avoids the payment of cash for much-needed but unaffordable banking, legal, consulting, tax preparation, vocational training, educational, and even medical diagnostic services. The areas in which I believe such self-help will grow most rapidly are vocational tutoring, personal financial advice, health counselling, and legal assistance. All of these are presently characterized by unreasonable cost and inadequate or insensitive delivery of services by the professionals concerned. This combination offers attractive opportunities for displacement by clever computer-mediated dialogue in each of the fields mentioned.

Avoiding the costly services of professionals is the primary motivation for the rise of home computing.

We can observe the elimination of information intermediaries by taking account of the increased direct availability of computerized services to consumers and by noticing what kind of software people are purchasing for their home computers. I estimate that more than 75 million home computers will be installed in the United States by 1995. On a worldwide basis there should be well in excess of 130 to 150 million home computers by that time. This fantastic amount of information processing power will permit consumers to perform service functions that are presently delivered only to a small number of privileged clients. The personal time expended by consumers in information work at home will result in an increase in the standard of living because the new services will deliver to the many what only wealthy people used to buy. To understand how information work will be done in our society we will have to pay attention to those activities in which information labor, currently available only through professionals, is being displaced by the expenditure of the consumer's own time.

When forecasting the demand for professional personnel in the twenty-first century we should moderate our projections of ever-increasing numbers of information workers by allowing for large transfers of information work from the business sector into the consumer sector. As home computers are installed in many, if not most homes, as "intelligent" software becomes available, and as network connections become easier to make, all this new information processing capability will mean an expansion of the information economy outside of the marketplace. Large numbers of professional experts should find it attractive to supplement their incomes by advising consumers on choosing among the bewilderingly specialized options. Professional services—which presently produce and deliver routine specialized work—will virtually disappear in the face of self-administrated expert know-how. Occupational counselling, preventative medicine, financial planning, equipment maintenance, legal assistance, travel advice, vocational instruction, support of hobbies—these are just a few of the new growth opportunities. I see this also as an opportunity to reduce the costs of many government services. By making automobile registration, filing of taxes, and other government functions available from the terminals of private individuals or from public buildings such as libraries, many labor-intensive government activities could be made less expensive and more convenient to the consumer. The specialists' information work will be supplanted by superior services at lower costs. That has always been the formula for advancing economic progress.

Where Are the Information Workers?

The United States is not a postindustrial economy. It is a managerial economy.

Despite different interpretations of how to account for the amount of information work in the economy, it is still useful to understand what the official statistics tell us. According to the Bureau of Labor Statistics, information workers now make up the majority of the civilian workforce.[5]

One way of looking at these occupational statistics is to combine the entire executive and managerial, plus half of the professional and clerical personnel, into an overall management grouping. Altogether this accounts for more than 25 million employees. Only half of the professional and clerical employees are included because they—about 15 million of them—can function only as part of an organization in which they act as assistants to their managers and executives. It is this grouping of the workforce that leads me to conclude that the United States is predominantly occupied with management of the economy. The symbols of our society should not be the plow, the anvil, the machine tool, or the engine wheel—although such images frequently appear on letterheads, on murals, or in advertising. The most frequent work symbols should more appropriately be the in- and the out-basket, the telephone, and the conference table. This is gradually being supplanted by an even more potent symbolic object—the visual display unit—which seems endow a manager with the power of new electronic magic.

To understand changes in the structure of information work one should observe the changing pattern in the employment of professional personnel.

To gain a firmer grasp of the directions of office automation we must understand recent employment trends, which reveal that the

fastest-growing group among information workers consists of professionals, defined here as experts and specialists.[6] The professionals'
consistent growth rate can be explained by the escalating information
needs of the managerial group, which depends upon the professionals'
advice to cope with the increasing complexity of the business environment.

Another way of viewing the professional group is to realize that
its members are increasingly in a position to become independent agents
who can price and sell their services in the marketplace. Seen in this
light, consistent growth in the number of professionals reflects their
ability to satisfy the growing market for information services offered
by the economy as small businesses grow faster than large businesses.

The key to forecasting the future roles of professionals is a solid
understanding of the economic causes for the increase of professional
personnel, whether as assistants to management or as independent
sellers of information services in the marketplace. It is interesting to
examine recent trends and to observe how occupations shifted during
this past recession.[7] While the total workforce shrank by 4.2% between
July 1982 and the bottom of the recession in January 1983, professional
and technical employment during the same period actually increased
by 3.5%! This is a good indication of the powerful forces at work
in the economy which thirst for additional professional and technical
resources in spite of severe cost pressures.

If we extrapolate the professionals' past growth rates, we discover
that they would exceed 25% of the total workforce within twenty-
five years. They would be earning well over one-third of all wages
in the economy. I cannot imagine how the society implied by such
shifts could function effectively unless the professionals deliver a clearly
identifiable contribution to economic growth. This is why the question
of how information technology can make professionals more productive is such a critical issue in all discussions concerning the future
of information work. It is necessary, therefore, to examine carefully
the activities on which managerial and professional employees expend
their time.

What Generates Office Work?

**Specialization generates office work in a bureaucracy. Relationships
among specialists rather than with customers determine how much
work will be done.**

Office work is complex, especially in large organizations. To get virtually anything accomplished, numerous steps must be completed. If there are professional specialists involved, work must travel from desk to desk. This point can be illustrated by drawing a diagram showing every step involved in the process of arriving at a decision. Whenever I have taken the trouble to chart all of the linkages between the various office activities I have always been surprised by their large number. When I show my diagrams to the managers involved, they note that they could come up with even more complex examples.

I find that the costs incurred in completing most office activities are set by relationships among managerial, professional, and technical personnel. The costs are determined by organizational structure rather than by the value of the result. Whether an engineering change notice requires 53, 223, or 423 events—such as phone conversations, copies of memoranda, or meeting discussions (roughly $1,000, $5,000 or $10,000)—is more a reflection of the procedures established among managerial, professional, and technical personnel for processing information than a function of the intrinsic scope, monetary value, or relative importance of the revised engineering design itself.

The "Parkinson Ratio" states how many internal communications are needed in order to accomplish anything of value for a customer.

Twenty years ago I started collecting flow charts depicting office events. For instance, one of my cases indicates that forty-three different forms (altogether 113 pages, counting originals as well as copies) had to be filled out in order to add a temporary employee to the payroll. In another situation I assembled eighty original forms plus 200 copies— all of them necessary to lease a single piece of industrial equipment. My experience leads me to conclude that for each organization there is a characteristic number of information transactions which are necessary to get anything accomplished. There is also a benchmark *minimum* number of coordinating steps necessary to take care of a customer's request. That benchmark can be found by examining how the best competitor is performing the function in question. Over the years, I have found it useful to estimate both the benchmark minimum as well as the actual numbers of information transactions involved for the organizations I have studied.

I have called a ratio of these counts the "Parkinson's Ratio" in honor of Professor Parkinson, whose *Parkinson's Law and Other Studies in Administration* made him known as a perceptive observer of the behavior of bureaucracies. According to my method of counting, a typical, well-run industrial organization should not require more than twenty to thirty internal communications to respond to a customer's requests for goods. In service organizations, such as banking or insurance, nonroutine customer requests for new loans, new policies, or compensation of claims should not require more than fifty to eighty internal communications. In reality, Parkinson's Ratios of three and even four times as much have been observed.

Government organizations must conform to more intricate regulations than private businesses. Citizen requests involving even the slightest deviation from procedure can easily add up to 200 to 300 communications. These are all minimum ranges. Actual Parkinson Ratios can easily run to between four and six times as high, compared with private industry benchmarks, especially if the entire system is prone to many errors. Organizations with clearly excessive Parkinson Ratios invariably react to quality problems by adding further elaborate control steps as safeguards—which only makes the initial problem worse. Paperwork commissions, congressional committees, and productivity consultants thrive on pathological Parkinson Ratio cases. Such cases list transactions in tremendous excess of what might be expected. For dramatic purposes I specially treasure a few well-documented cases of almost infinite Parkinson Ratios. Readers can readily collect their own specimens. Just look for enormous amounts of work, voluminous files—and minimal results.

The mechanism behind a high Parkinson Ratio can be seen in the schematic diagram of Figure 1.2.

Due to the specialized nature of the various administrative functions, customers such as "A" and "B" must communicate with some of the fourteen departments—"1" through "14" (e.g., marketing, shipping, billing, credit, service)—in order to get satisfactory answers. Each of these departments in turn must be kept informed and coordinated—by section management "II" through "V"—about all that is going on with regard to the customers. This generates routine communications, mostly in the form of computer reports or copies of forms. However, these intraorganizational communications expand enormously when any changes in interdepartmental relationships take place. Such common occurences as customer complaints, reorganization, changes in territories, or the hiring of new account personnel all generate profuse amounts of nonroutine messages, phone calls, and meetings to keep the intraorganizational relationships in balance.

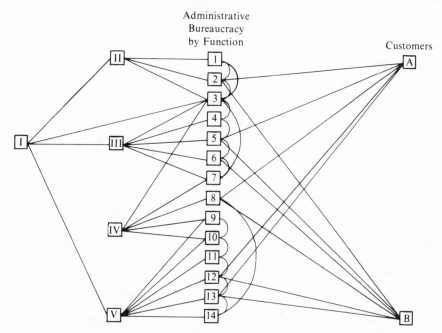

Figure 1.2 Information Flows Between an Administrative Bureaucracy and Its Customers

What Are the Reasons for Excessive Communications?

Administrative bureaucracies expend disproportionately large amounts of energy on intraorganizational relationships. Form takes precedence over purpose.

The real world of the office is full of delays, miscommunications, errors, and changes. These are costly and time-consuming events. One must submerge oneself in the flows of messages, letters, and copies in order to get a realistic view of what is taking place among those working in an office. For instance, tracking a simple four-page bulletin informing the field sales force about a minor change in pricing policy can reveal a surprisingly complex train of events.[8]

Anyone endowed with the enormous patience necessary to track all of the diverse actions in an office can estimate the total cost for delivery of a result. Because of the great expenditure of time and effort needed to gather such information, office work is rarely examined in terms of the total costs (from inception to finish) entailed in producing one of its products. Due to the large number of experts, specialists, and people contributing only to parts of an entire work process, the work elements will be classified in terms of office functions, rather than in terms of results. Secretaries will describe their activities in terms of filing, copying, and making telephone calls. Managers will talk in terms of attending meetings, writing memoranda, reading proposals, and so forth. Office work observed from such a standpoint tells us a great deal about the types of activities people are engaged in but nothing at all about the *purpose* of their work. This view of the office has its origins in the compartmentalization of manufacturing tasks. Its goal is to classify office activities into standard, isolated categories so that improvements can be made without considering the purposes of the work itself.

Efficiency analysis can lead to increased amounts of office work that does not need to be done at all.

The industrial engineering approach offers attractive solutions aimed at increased office efficiency within the limits of an existing work organization. It is just about the only approach that is simple and relatively easy to use in situations where the presence of too many organizational boundaries prevents full disclosure of the cost of work. It is much easier to analyze in detail the cost per photocopy in the marketing department, or the cost of typing in the pricing section, than to explore what it would cost to deliver an entire proposal. Besides, lowering photocopy cost and reducing time spent on typing makes simple technological fixes possible; these are usually preferred to making changes in *how* people work. The result of pursuing this incremental approach to office automation may well be increased efficiency in doing work that does not produce any net gain for the organization or its customers.

The prevailing method for analyzing office work favors the reduction of work processes into the smallest observable components and then building an understanding of what is going on by trying to reconstitute the whole out of the pieces. Typically, time sheets are given to office workers. The sheets list office events classified according to any one of a dozen standard categories. The workers are then asked to report what they are doing in terms of very small time intervals. It is thus possible to discover with great accuracy, for instance, how many unsuccessful phone calls have been attempted. Such information can be valuable in justifying the installation of a telephone switching system employing the latest technology. Studying the amounts of time consumed in standard office activities will also be useful when management has only a vague idea of what employees do with their time. If, however, the analysis is carried out in an environment where office workers have even the slightest suspicion that the data may be used to set output targets or to reduce manpower, the information will be virtually useless.

Detailed time studies of office work have limited value and even then only in limited situations.

A few years ago a number of organizations published studies which showed how much time was expended by managers in attending meetings, reading memoranda, and making phone calls. The fact that some of these activities, such as searching for information, could be handled much more efficiently by electronic means was used as a justification for office automation. The arithmetic of such computation is impeccable: a 15% improvement in even a small fraction of an expensive, labor-intensive activity will generate savings sufficient to pay for the annual costs of new electronic equipment.

Although what I call the "reductionist approach" is the most frequently used method to assess the advisability of investments in information technology, I do not think that seasoned managers are really buying all of its conclusions. Office productivity and management responsiveness are not necessarily improved by installing office equipment which speeds up individual office functions. If a secretary types 300 lines of mostly useless text per day it does not follow that replacing the typewriter with a word processor capable of generating 3,000 mostly useless lines of text per day will be an improvement enhancing the profitability of the firm.

If we wish to understand why office work takes place, how it functions, and how it contributes to the success or failure of an enterprise, detailed examination provided by the reductionist approach will not serve as a useful initial step. There is something to be learned about how a frog jumps by dissecting a frog and examining its muscles under a microscope. But if we are interested in what makes frogs jump, a frog should first be observed as a living organism. Analogously, office work should be first observed in its entirety, as a medium for delivering superior services to customers. Dissecting it into detailed work steps should be done as the last part of a long sequence. If the order is reversed we will end up with useless pieces rather than with an understanding of how people can become more effective.

Office Work Is a Reflection of Relationships

Office work is the outcome, not a cause, of organizational design.

In the same way that industrial technology provided the means for improved production, so information technology should be viewed as providing the means by which management may improve the organization of the enterprise. The first approach in examining office work should be at the level of organizational design. Administrative procedures determine how much information work will be done. The geometry of the organization chart, the levels of management review, and the layers of specialists explain more about the presence of information workers than a minute examination of their detailed activities. Having a position within the framework of the organization defines and legitimizes one's efforts. This fact is confirmed by our continued adherence to the ancient concept of *holding* an office. With the title of the office comes office space, secretarial assistance, and the need for additional support staff. Tenure of an office position means that others must route information to its incumbent. Except when the office is producing rigidly defined paperwork it is extremely difficult to define the results expected from it and what customer needs it must satisfy. Within large organizations an office is not defined in terms of results, but in terms of jurisdiction and power. Its costs are dictated by its charter, budget, appropriation, expenditure authority, grant, funding, headcount, or any of the many other ways that dictate the scope of an organization in the absence of customer feedback. Without an earned income the costs of an office are likely to be independent of the value of the work which needs to be done.

The costs of doing office work are a unique reflection of organizational design. They are as individual as fingerprints.

In the pricing-policy bulletin example mentioned above, all of the costs and all of the events were determined by the management style of the organization making this minor policy decision. All of the events—holding meetings, making photocopies and phone calls, writing drafts and so forth—were traceable to the organization's highly diffused method of arriving at a decision. The cost of making the pricing-policy decision described in this case was unique. Another organization would most likely have a very different process for making the same sort of decision. This is why companies find it so difficult to make administrative cost comparisons with others—even for the most elementary office functions, such as the cost of processing an invoice or the cost of placing an employee on the payroll. Individual organizations will distribute the total work involved in preparing an invoice or in drawing up a payroll check in dissimilar ways across departmental boundaries. Unless the organizational designs are closely comparable, attempts to make cost comparisons for isolated functions, such as personnel, finance, auditing, market research, and data processing, will be misleading. For instance, the fact that one organization spends 5.6% of sales on research and development and another organization spends 7.1% of sales on research and development is irrelevant. The first organization may include development engineering in its budget, while purchasing most of its component technology from others. The second organization may support all engineering costs, including a large amount of proprietary development of parts manufactured by others. I have seen organizations that claimed great efficiencies because they decreased their costs of data processing from 3.5% of revenue to only 2.8% of revenue, as compared with a competitor's 4.7%. In fact, they were overlooking the shift of costs from centrally held budgets—where they were counted—into the hands of the users, where they showed as indirect expenses.

What some writers call organizational culture is, among other things, an expression of how an organization distributes its costs of management. Different cultures and different organizational structures will have office costs that are not comparable at any level defined only by an internal organizational chart. Therefore, information technology investment projects will not have comparable effects except when they are judged in terms of external results and on an individual basis, company-by-company.

Limitations of Industrial Engineering Methods

The closer one examines the details of office work the less one knows what is going on.

Office costs have different characteristics from production costs. The physical properties of products can be rigorously compared. It is hard to do that with information activities. By specifying standard manufactured components it is possible to obtain competitive bids from suppliers. Bureaucratic organizations resist having parts of their office work subcontracted to others: office work is just too much a reflection of idiosyncratic ways for managing affairs to make such subcontracting attractive. Whereas consumers indirectly impose limitations on the variety of manufactured products, there are no obvious limits to the complexity of office procedures. This is why office organizations have a tendency to employ their own people to do everything, to achieve what is called a high level of vertical integration. All of the built-in incentives reinforce the motivation of modern management to enlarge its scope and to add more manpower in response to the tremendous variety, complexity, and uniqueness with which information processing is done.

Managers of information workers will push for the highest possible degree of vertical integration in all of their activities as the only means by which unique work results can be assured. Vertical integration in the office environment means a high level of self-sufficiency, tending to include all conceivable expertise within the organization itself. Excessive vertical integration in manufacturing, if associated with high levels of poorly utilized capital equipment, is always accompanied by reduced efficiency and by financial losses. No wonder that excessive vertical integration in the office environment leads to an enormous waste of manpower. The behavior of people in such an organization becomes so specialized and so ingrown that an outside observer finds it hard to understand why certain activities are taking place. In due course even insiders become confused by the baroque complexities of internal procedures which define which expert will perform what task. Internally integrated and completely self-sufficient organizations have a tendency to become isolated from the external world, as more and more communications are directed towards internal coordination. This phenomenon can be frequently found in giant corporate headquarters and in large government agencies because they tend to reward inward communications at the expense of all other forms. In such extreme settings insights derived from examination of the isolated details of office events can yield only misleading conclusions.

After years of experimentation, I found that the traditional methods derived from industrial engineering for breaking up office work into minute events and then subjecting them to mechanization, have only trivial applicability to office work. At best, this approach may apply to less than one-tenth of the total workhours expended in the general office, on highly structured tasks, performed by personnel earning less than one-fifteenth of total payroll dollars. Furthermore, such tasks must be sufficiently standardized to be easily comparable to the work done by others. Very little office work meets such criteria.

Information technology offers new means for organizing office work. Automate only after you simplify.

Investments in office automation should be associated with an exploration of completely new ways of attaining business objectives, rather than just reducing the costs of old ways of doing things. This is why I strongly emphasize techniques originating in strategic planning and in financial analysis before resorting to office work-analysis methods.[9] Unfortunately, neither strategic planning nor financial analysis has as yet acquired adequate tools for dealing with information costs, by contrast with their refinement in treating production costs. As a consequence, the approach of top management to problems that concern information expenses can be compared with the application of a permanent tourniquet to stop a hemorrhage. Such a drastic measure stops the bleeding, but it may destroy an essential part of the body. Value analysis, predicated upon a strategic understanding of the role played by information work in the competitive functioning of the enterprise, should always precede studies of detailed office activities.

One should not undertake the automation of office work until organizational studies have shown that office communications have been stripped down to their essentials. One should not automate obsolete patterns of how people work.

Structured vs. Unstructured Work

The nature of unstructured office work varies enormously.

Office workers recognize the ever-changing character of the office scene. This makes them wonder how useful it will be to install computers to do work which is so hard to describe and certainly difficult to program. The problem concerns misunderstandings about the nature of office work and about the characteristics of computers.

Let us first examine the straightforward approach to the programming of office work which has prevailed in the automation of well-ordered tasks. Computer automation is the outgrowth of punch-card processing. This activity placed the handling of information in ordered sequences by subjecting it to a factory-like process with a totally programmable and linear logic, as Figure 1.3 illustrates.

Computers which process bank checks, insurance policies, purchase orders, inventories, and manufacturing schedules are all programmed using fully definable logic for manipulating numbers, records and files. For instance, if one wishes to send out invoices it would be unthinkable to do that by means of a computer program that cannot handle every conceivable error or exception. But managers know that their people do not spend most of their time making computations and tabulating data. By far the most valuable, and certainly the most expensive, resources are devoted to such person-to-person communications as meetings, making phone calls, and negotiating. In these situations events

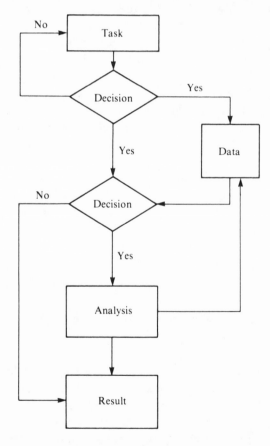

Figure 1.3   A Computer Programmer's View of Office Information Flows

take completely unexpected turns because people are engaged in actions which are unpredictable as to their outcome.[10] The programmer's logical flow chart is the wrong model for portraying what actually goes on most of the time in an office environment. A chart tracing all information-handling events would certainly exceed the entire wall space that surrounds the people who are engaged in even simple information work. Anyone trying to draw a diagram of every logical step encountered in a typical office situation would consume more time to do it than the events actually take, because conditions continually change. The employment of more programmers than office workers is the likely outcome of an attempt to construct an all-inclusive computer system. To describe all of the information work, even in a small business, is not practical. The idea of rationalizing all office work by means of a comprehensive computer program is an unreasonable objective. Only through the enforcement of rigidly regimented procedures of considerable simplicity—which would be ill-adapted to our ever-changing environment—could a computerized model of the workplace be expected to function. The caricature of an organization's information processing logic in Figure 1.4 is much more realistic.

The diagram describes what happens in offices where work cannot be ordered according to a precise system. It is difficult to imagine how programming a routine like that shown in Figure 1.3 could be of much use. The "logic" of this situation is just about as unpredictable as that of the typical office, with its results generated by various meetings, reactions expressed in hurried phone calls, and in notes casually scribbled on draft copies of a proposed document.[11]

The principal challenge to information technology is how to deal with unstructured and unpredictable office work.

When we recognize how difficult it is to systematize office work, we can begin to ask better questions. What is the specific economic purpose of various office work functions? If we do improve office productivity how will we know that we are better off? If we automate office activities and avoid all of the overlapping communications, are we not in danger of eliminating some of the safeguards found in redundant messages? Can office automation actually be damaging, since it supresses the informal system that will always remain outside of the automated environment? For instance, if we somehow succeed in writing a program that will mathematically determine the "best pricing policy," how do we make sure that everyone will fully understand

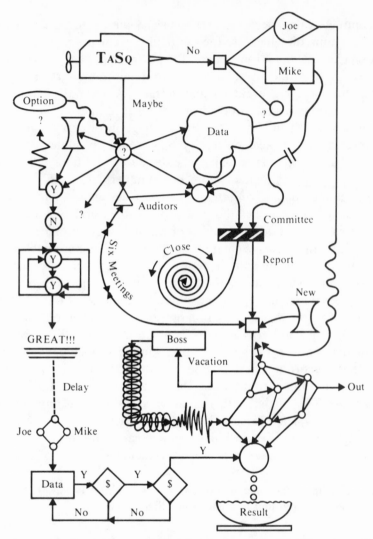

Figure 1.4 A Manager's View of Office Information Flows

how to apply the program's results? Is it possible that what appears to be wasteful communication is actually a learning experience that is essential before people can commit themselves to a new method? All of these questions have led me to conclude that one should not automate what one really does not understand. The danger is that mechanizing a few easy steps in a chain of relationships among people may damage the performance of the entire system. One of the characteristics of a productive organization is that the way individuals are linked together is of greater importance than what any individual does in isolation.

Partial improvements in office work through computerization can reduce flexibility and make everyone worse off.

For example: I was given the job of decentralizing customer billing inquiries because the central office computer could not handle all of the work. Due to budget limitations only the most sensitive portions of the customer inquiry system were to be automated. This required developing new software for seven decentralized computers. Meanwhile, the marketing organization was considering the introduction of a new marketing program. At the end of one year of programming, testing, and training, the computerized customer inquiry system started to work. Just then the new marketing program was installed—as a centrally administered effort. The partially completed customer inquiry computer programs and the new marketing scheme clashed. The rigidities of computerized methods reinforced the conflict and caused further delays. The net effect was that after one year of hard effort by all concerned, everyone was worse off. Costs were up, the confusion in resolving inquiries increased, and customer satisfaction declined.

Here is another case of how an attempt to streamline management through computerized processing yielded disastrous results. Once there was a controller who did not like the cumbersome, labor-intensive methods needed to handle special contract conditions for a diverse group of equipment dealers. As a way of cutting administrative expenses, the controller assigned all small-dealer accounts to a handful of distributors whose standard pricing terms could easily be handled by means of a fully automated system. Administrative expenses came down, to be sure. But profit margins came down even more dramatically. The distributors used their powerful purchasing leverage in negotiating with the firm and extracted unreasonable pricing concessions.

The lesson is that computer systems are increasingly being called upon to deal with applications that cannot be easily isolated from other activities of the business. The secondary effects can be far more potent than the cure attempted for a local defect. Just as a medicine that gets rid of your headache may damage your kidneys, computerization has ceased to be a simple remedy whose effects can always be localized.

Management as an Information Processing Function

The nature of office work is elusive and automating it is not a matter of simple conversion to programmed logic. Office systems must be viewed as part of a much larger managerial context. How then does one approach the construction of a theory about how to proceed with computerization?

This question is a natural one, but it is too abstract to be of much practical use. Historically, the primary focus of free-market enterprises has been to produce goods at a profit and to increase output. Management—which in my view includes office support personnel as well as research and development staffs—was always sufficiently small that it was not a critical cost factor. The classic model of work assumes that an enterprise ought to have most of its resources in production, that is, in human and capital resources that fully concentrate on the delivery of physical goods to customers. Information work was merely the cost of coordinating simple production processes; it was treated as a sort of tax to be levied on operations. This tax was designated as "overhead" for accounting purposes. Most economic theory recognizes land, labor, and capital as resources; it does not explicitly tackle the role of those special resources that deal with information as a critical element for delivering superior economic results. Figure 1.5 presents a diagram of this simplistic classical view of organizational design.

Underlying this concept of organization is the idea that the informa-

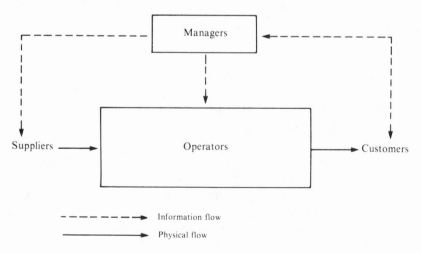

Figure 1.5 Traditional Concept of Information Management

tion processing needs of a small management team are best served by employing specialists such as labor relations negotiators, patent attorneys, compensation experts, and market research analysts. The environment—suppliers and customers—is close enough for management to understand what is going on. For the firm's internal working, procedural standardization is the rule. Through standardization of procedures, management practices, and operating methods, uncertainty is eliminated, so no added personnel is needed to deal with it. It is standardization that makes it possible for narrowly defined specialists to function precisely and with little special coordination except when rules are to be changed. It is this concept of total procedural standardization which has so far propelled the quest for machine-programmed automation of office work. The data processing executives of the 1960s and early 1970s were always talking about integrated management information systems as their ultimate objective. What they really wanted was to bring order into the office through totally programmed standardization. For a short while, this agenda fitted pretty well the organizational concepts to which senior management subscribed.

Standardization and mechanization were the dominant management ideas of the first half of the twentieth century. They were concepts which worked most effectively when markets were either controlled or were dominated by a scarcity of goods. Standardization was seen as a means for reducing production costs. This meant that fewer decisions, fewer products, fewer exceptions, and fewer changes in the marketplace were desirable. Standardization also worked well when customer needs were more predictable; when product choices could be limited; and when customers could be approached most effectively through the mass media and through mass distribution. All of these assumptions about optimizing management performance began to unravel in the 1970s. The prevailing views about the roles of information work had to be revised. Therefore, the assumptions underlying the design of computer systems had to change as well.

As global competition increased, as government intervention intensified, and as the pace of technology accelerated, enterprises had become much more complex. The inclination to employ specialists and experts as a way of dealing with new problems led to an explosive growth of staff support groups which, in turn, necessitated the creation of additional layers of management. Business began adding large numbers of professional, administrative, and technical workers in staff positions; there they were closely identified with management, since their primary task was the handling of information, rather than direct involvement with the delivery of goods or services to customers. A diagram which expresses the concept of the modern organization more accurately than the classic model can be drawn as represented in Figure 1.6.

Writers about cybernetics have pointed out what issues need to be resolved in order to make sense out of the vast quantities of information found in contemporary organizations.[12] No control system can respond effectively to stimuli unless it can also discriminate among the choices to be made as a consequence of all of this information. This, then, is the explanation for the enlargement of finance, marketing, legal, personnel, and other staffs since 1950. In the absence of a management theory for dealing with nonstandard and increasingly uncertain market conditions, additional manpower and computers were thrown at the problem of excessive information in the hope that somehow the interaction of competing staff groups would be adequate to deal with the tasks at hand. The accepted doctrine of how to organize was adopted from eighteenth-century political concepts of countervailing powers; no attempt was made to design enterprises by systematic experimentation. The political approach to balancing power between plants, divisions, laboratories, and corporate staffs fed the demands for ever-increasing numbers of information workers, who in turn employed computers to magnify their influence. Information technology

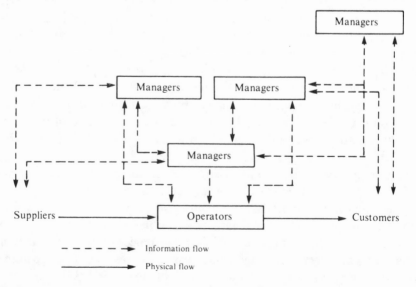

Figure 1.6   Information Flows in a Modern Organization

in the 1960s made it possible to organize the excessive amounts of information work created by the enormous growth in internal communications among information workers.

Guiding Information Work

The guiding principle of the approach to designing information work should be not inward-looking but customer-oriented. When studying the patterns of information work the relative importance of external vs. internal communications should be carefully analyzed for evidence of internal congestion. Which fraction of a firm's communications is for external use and which is produced exclusively for internal consumption should be thoroughly documented. In studying the work patterns in a home-office organization the following profiles of information transactions were observed:

1. Most work remained within the organization. Ninety-three percent of all transactions flowed internally, whereas only 7% went to suppliers and to customers.
2. Task output revealed a similar pattern. Ninety-four percent of all transactions could be found in the same office, on the same floor, the same campus. Only 6% travelled to another city.
3. Most information was obtained internally. Forty percent originated in the same office. Forty-two percent came from the same campus site. Only 4% of information came from other parts of the organization, 4% from customers.
4. Only some 10% of all information was newly generated. The rest was reformulation of already existing data, in a variety of forms, to meet internal staff needs.

I admit that the above statistics may be an extreme example of introversion. But when these results were shown to several office automation groups they confirmed that their own studies always uncovered a much larger fraction of internally consumed data than had been thought possible. It is characteristic of unproductive organizational designs to foster passing information back and forth among the internal information workers while customer and supplier inquiries remain ignored. It is also evidence of successful information work if customer and supplier requests for increasing amounts of administrative, technical, and training support are handled to the satisfaction both of the receivers and of the providers.

Office work has become the dominant economic activity in the United States. It accounts for a much larger portion of time and cost than the most frequently used statistics indicate. We can also observe the beginning of a trend to extend office work into the home as a way of increasing consumer convenience and as a means for shifting the costs of routine clerical work to the user. Information work at home will also reduce the consumer's costs for engaging professional services. One of the primary causes for the expansion in the number of information transactions is related to the way professional specialists are employed in decision making and in consultations. Most office work requires an unexpectedly large amount of variety and adaptation in order to accomplish nonroutine tasks. Faulty organizational design and organizational complexity are among the causes of growing information-handling costs. An ever-increasing fraction of the total value (or of the final price) of all products is attributable to information activities.

2

Findings from Experiments with Office Automation

The fastest-growing application of information technology involves office automation. This is viewed as distinct from other computer applications, such as data processing, robotics, scientific instrumentation, home computing, and telecommunications. This chapter will explore how the work of individuals is changed when their activities are automated.

I will illustrate some of these changes by examples drawn from carefully observed experiments in which automated has been compared with unautomated work. The results of automation are evaluated by contrast with already existing good practices. I have not biased the analysis by selecting inferior operations as bases from which to show spectacular gains.

Patent Attorney Case

The test program in the office of patent attorneys is a good example of how to organize office-of-the-future projects while at the same time checking up on their economic results. This case deals with two separate groups, each doing the identical kind of work. The test group consisted of three secretaries and four attorneys. Each person was equipped with an advanced text-processing terminal which permitted easy interconnection among all participants. Text and files could be shared with great ease. The test was run for a period of six months and required participants to keep track of their time.

The control group was also made up of three secretaries and four attorneys. They had already achieved a good level of efficiency by means of three electronic memory typewriters, each of them operated by one of the secretaries. Both the control and the test group had equal office conveniences, such as telephones with advanced features and excellent copying, microfilm, and dictating equipment. Working conditions were identical.

The new equipment was made available to the test group in a manner which illustrates the proper general approach to starting up an advanced automated office:

1. Identical workstations with full-page visual displays were installed for the secretaries as well as the attorneys. These workstations were placed near the desk where each person worked. The equipment had enough local and removable memory for each individual to regard it as his or her own. The software permitted all participants to give their devices limited but nevertheless important individual characteristics for handling office communications.

2. Shared facilities, such as expensive printers and large electronic files, were easily accessible. Of particular value was a high-quality laser printer which performed the dual function of generating book-quality paper text and of acting as a remote-access copying machine. In addition, a high-performance communications network made it possible not only to share all of the electronic files within the site, but also to connect easily with all other workstations and electronic files, including an office 200 miles away.

The test explored the effects of geographic separation on cooperative work. Since patent and licensing activities are needed wherever research and development staffs are located, an important aspect of the test was an evaluation of whether office automation encouraged the continuation of geographic decentralization. If it did not, locating the attorneys at a single location might be necessary to achieve improved productivity.

Before the project began, it was important to limit the scope of the activity to be studied. Otherwise data gathering, data evaluation, and ability to manage the program would quickly get out of control. The focus was on five critical elements of work, leaving lesser activities for follow-up experiments. The key elements were: (1) communication and coordination, (2) document creation and editing, (3) filing and retrieval, (4) legal research, and (5) time management and scheduling.

Because a large amount of coordination was necessary between the two sites, the delay involved in passing documents back and forth turned out to be crucial to the entire experiment. The use of electronic mail, compared with mail sent by courier, improved information handling (measured by time elapsed) in the sending and receipt of documents. The average document delivery time for the control group was twenty-one hours. The average delivery time for the test group was less than one hour. Not only did the average delivery time improve, but also the predictability of arrival gained. A range of between eight and forty-six hours prevailed for the control group. By contrast, delays for the test group never exceeded two and a half hours.

From a workflow standpoint, improved predictability in the delivery of messages has unusually favorable effects on information systems involving sequential work.[1] For example, the test group tended to spend much less time on the phone to follow up on the progress of projects. Quick turnaround of documents also made it possible to reduce dependence on the phone or on frequent face-to-face meetings. Incoming phone calls for the test group decreased by 45%, while outgoing calls decreased 27%. The saving of telephone time was forty-seven minutes per attorney per day. This gain resulted in more attention available for new work.

The statistics did not reveal any change in the frequency or in the length of person-to-person or group meetings. The test group observed that meetings were now used more to broaden the quality of substantive conversations with the research people, rather than to reconcile different versions of legal text.

It is also interesting to note that even though the total time spent by the secretaries on office work did not change, there were changes in the work patterns:

1. Unproductive document revision and retyping was reduced from 22% to only 15% of total time.
2. Secretaries assumed some of the telephone activity previously handled by the attorneys, increasing their share from 1% to

12% of total time spent on the telephone. This was a source of improved job satisfaction because it stimulated increased social contact, which is always viewed as a more desirable form of office work than typing or filing.

3. Output, as measured in text pages, increased enormously—by 200% to 250%—while the time applied to typing decreased from 19% to only 15% of total time.

The reasons for these shifts can be explained by the following important factors:

1. Time spent on revisions of documents came down appreciably because the attorneys personally inserted many of the lesser changes directly through their own keyboards. Revision time for a complex patent document decreased from an average of 133 minutes to 61 minutes.
2. Turnaround days for documents decreased, permitting much better utilization of time, reducing interruptions, and streamlining workflow. Completion time for drafts of complex patent documents decreased from twenty to seven days.
3. Many more technical and legal reviews were conducted. This is why the output of pages of text reported by the test group increased so enormously without a corresponding increase in the amount of time.

The directly measurable and immediately available savings were considerable: 11% more hours available, per attorney; 13% more hours available, per secretary. There were numerous other, more intangible benefits in terms of output quality, job satisfaction, and responsiveness to business needs. These, in the opinion of management, were sufficient to justify the entire additional expense for the office automation equipment.

It was gratifying to listen to the reactions of the attorneys and of the secretaries in the test group. They emphasized the *qualitative* improvements, not the economic savings. What mattered most for the attorneys was their enhanced professional status. Their greatest satisfaction came from an improved ability to keep up with a large volume of cases and their clients' favorable reactions to the improved quality of legal support. Here are some of the attorneys' comments at the conclusion of the test: "The system has changed my way of doing business." "Making changes while the client was in the office and then giving him completed work is a new way of life." "The system placed more control in my hands."

The principal satisfactions for the secretaries derived from their upgraded social and economic status, achieved through increased personal contact. They were favorably motivated by the acquisition of new skills that command higher compensation. Being party to an experiment and having new opportunities to make decisions increased their job satisfaction. Here are some of their comments reported at the conclusion of the test: "I have more time now to find out what is going on in this place." "I talk about my machine at parties. My job is more interesting. I see my way now how to upgrade my job." "Moving text around on the screen and seeing the result makes me feel that I am accomplishing something."

Perhaps the simplest way of understanding what happened to the test group can be explained by tracing the job steps performed by the control group. For instance, drafting an initial patent application required twenty-one separate office tasks when done within the control group. The test group shifted the creative work, including insertion of new paragraphs, to the attorneys, while relying on the secretaries to use electronic files for extracting routine text. The secretaries' role changed to a supporting, review, and editing role. Total reliance on the electronic medium until the end product was printed on paper eliminated more than half of the workhours. I found that in the initial patent application draft, fourteen separate job steps disappeared completely. Such changes in the patterns of workflow created favorable side effects which influenced how participants responded to the experiment. The roles of the individuals under the test conditions were sufficiently changed to warrant the conclusion that, from their point of view, a transformation of work had taken place.

Records Management Case

The objective of this test was to manage the records, documents, correspondence, visual graphics, and teaching texts generated by a group of professionals developing materials for classes in which new technical skills were taught. The entire educational process requires a great deal of flexibility because the curriculum is subject to rapid change.

It will be useful to describe here what I mean by records management in the context of an electronic network. Records management is one of the capabilities included within the broad category of office automation. All text and graphics—even sketches on slips of paper—are managed, created, changed, disseminated, and stored electronically. In the test case, the economic advantage of records management came from sharing expert and support personnel among a large group of curriculum developers. For instance, the electronic network allowed the smooth handling of all correspondence and artwork through a central group rather than through the scheduling of support people to complete discrete projects. The development of teaching materials involves the participation of many review staffs and requires constant revisions. The curriculum developers and the instructors had encountered many difficulties when correspondence and documentation was done by a shared support organization. The professionals' work patterns and workload demands were not only individually different in style and form, but were also subject to sudden peaks in demand for secretarial and graphics services. These peaks also tended to coincide. Uninterrupted and direct access to an electronic network capable of handling the teaching materials in gradual installments eliminated the need for sudden, large amounts of work.

Electronic records management depends on text processing, which, in turn, requires specialized training and long experience before one has sufficient expertise to complete major projects, such as a teaching manual. This fosters a separation between the professionals' creative work and the specialized services performed by the support people. The key element in this test case was to determine the extent to which work could be accomplished directly by the professionals without too much extra training and to discover how work could be passed most smoothly back and forth between the professional and the support staffs. The technology chosen used graphic commands which were largely self-explanatory and thus made it possible to perform complex editing, filing, and text distribution functions with relative ease. In this way, the teaching professionals could deal with text that would have greatly enhanced instructional value as a consequence. The electronic medium was expected to deliver information in a format that would help students to recall standard patterns of instruction. This test was run for a period of twelve months; at peak times it involved over twenty-five professionals and between six and eight support personnel.

A network capable of performing all of the above tasks was put into place as a pilot test while a conventional control group remained in place. The highest payoffs came from providing the teaching staff directly with superior means for preparing and revising graphic exhibits and visual aids.[2]

It was interesting to observe how dependent an educational process can become on high-quality visual forms when convenient means for producing graphics becomes available. Even though the preparation of visual displays showed the highest savings, cost comparisons of the pilot vs. the control groups did not adequately reflect the effectiveness of the new electronic methods in improving the teaching process. Managing the records electronically made it possible to apply proven patterns of text and graphics to new teaching tasks. The direct involvement of the curriculum designer with the creation of commercial-quality artwork was facilitated by easy access to standard diagrams and illustrations. Complex formats, such as tables comparing features of various technical options, were also embedded within the software. In this way the instructor could call for a format and then just fill in the applicable information. This convenience fostered a more creative environment and brought about a rethinking of how to best mix the verbal, graphic, and written media in order to achieve the desired teaching objectives. Essentially, the role of computer technology was to hide the technical details of graphic and text design within the software logic of the workstation and thus make it possible even for an average instructor to become a creator of superb teaching aids.

Additional savings were realized from the ability to connect the local network at the curriculum development site with other networks. Most of the gains were realized by speeding up reviews of the technical contents by engineering experts. Agreements about administrative details involved in classroom teaching of sales personnel could also be negotiated much faster with marketing managers.

This case demonstrated the feasibility of saving 50% or more in the cost for specific work items. Moreover, the simplification of the entire text preparation process caused a transformation in the way teachers and their support staffs worked together. The students' appreciation of teaching quality showed marked gains. Management regarded the results of the experiment not only as proof of greater cost efficiency but also as a demonstration of qualitative improvement far more valuable than the costs of the technology.

Semiconductor Circuit Design Case

So far we have dealt only with cases in which the final result of office work was not fundamentally altered by the introduction of electronic technology. Higher quality, faster turnaround, and cost improvements resulted from changed methods of doing the job, but the basic outcome of the work remained unaffected.

In the present case we will observe a development which foreshadows the kind of change that will ultimately dominate the electronic workplace—new work relationships with radically different ways of achieving economic goals at vastly reduced costs. For an example of how workstations with "intelligent software" can transform work, I have chosen the complex area of circuit design.

A diagram of the tasks involved in designing and manufacturing semiconductor circuits would describe a time-consuming process involving over 100 processes performed by thirty to forty separate organizations. If time is available and designs are reasonably mature, it is advantageous to invest large amounts of money and effort to produce a custom LSI (Large-Scale Integration) circuit. The lead time for such an effort would be in excess of nine months, the design costs at least $50,000. Test time would consume about six additional months and cost more than $20,000. One would then end up with a low-cost electronic package at about $5 per circuit, if produced in large quantities.

If designs are not mature, or if time is limited and production needs are low, a more conventional approach employing standard assembled components can be used. This can be done quite speedily, in around six to ten weeks, with design and testing costs in the $6,000–$12,000 range. The disadvantage of this method lies in the high costs of assembly and in the error-prone quality control process. In limited quantities, each circuit would cost about $500.

If one could redesign the costly workflow for producing a LSI circuit and place most of the work with just a handful of people, then very significant cost reductions and lead-time improvements would be realized. One could end up with many of the cost advantages of LSI and at the same time enjoy the rapid lead times which are obtained when assembling circuits from standard components.

LSI circuits based on computer-aided design and computer-aided manufacturing are starting to transform the circuit-making business. The computer contains not only electronic logic design, but also intricate rules related to the design of the surface of the silicon chips, the sequencing of manufacturing steps, the drafting of logic diagrams, the validation of electrical connections, and the simulation of expected circuit performance. The net effect of such an approach is to reduce the number of specialists' activities by around 50% and to eliminate about one-third of the distinct organizations that were needed to work the entire process.

One of the technical approaches to such job restructuring is known in the electronics industry as the Mead/Conway method for LSI design.[3] It provides the best of all possible worlds: conventional component lead times of less than ten weeks, development investments of less than $10,000, and unit prices comparable to those for mass-produced LSIs. The really revolutionary change inherent in this method of manufacturing is the effect it has on the relationships between designers, manufacturers, and customers. A different approach to the division of labor is now possible. The availability of standard design languages embedded in graphics workstations offers automated mass production of customized items at mass-production prices, with few assets tied up in inventory. Mask-making, fabrication, and component manufacturers can receive electronically encoded designs which incorporate detailed manufacturing instructions for computer-controlled robots and tools. By eliminating most of the cumbersome activities preceding the manufacturing process, automated manufacture of totally individualized products is possible. This will completely change the economics of the design and production of microcircuit-based devices. Ultimately, one-of-a-kind silicon chips (the technological basis for totally personalized machines) will be available at an affordable cost to virtually anyone needing them.

Public Agency Case

I have gathered voluminous information about reductions in office work which can be achieved through office automation. For various types of office tasks it is possible to construct tables similar to industrial engineering estimates of potential improvements through acquisition of factory tools. For instance, the speed of simple arithmetic can be improved by 65% using a programmable calculator as compared with one which is manual. Typing original text on a word processor has only a 23% improvement potential, vis-à-vis more traditional typing, since the job of text entry by means of a keyboard soon places an upper limit on what is achievable. Computerized graphics for simple charts has about a 40% advantage over cut-and-paste methods. A computerized search of reference data from a magnetic file can be done about 37% faster electronically than with a mechanically inserted microfilm cartridge.

Such standard task estimates are not very useful in predicting the overall cost reduction potential in a particular situation. The actual results obtained from the application of electronic equipment to specific job conditions will vary a great deal from case to case. To demonstrate the great range of possible outcomes when office automation is introduced, it is interesting to see what happens to office tasks after the establishment of electronic office systems.[4] The work example analyzed was the time needed to complete a routine expense request requiring a budget amendment.

Office automation resulted in a variety of changes in people's work patterns. For instance, 36% of office tasks remained the same because certain legal procedures limited what changes could take place. Most of the productivity gains came from tasks which were completely eliminated. Around 39% of the original office tasks fell into this category. Some of the office tasks disappeared because software dispensed with the need for manual help. Some tasks vanished because electronic mail eliminated most of the need for the physical handling of documents. When I examined the job relationships in the electronic office and compared them with the original situation, I was surprised by the many improvised rearrangements of work: they made this case unique. This is why efficiency studies based entirely on average results, even from similar cases, cannot predict the outcome of a particular situation very accurately.

Another reason for the difficulty in estimating expected savings in this case can be traced to the sources of cost reduction. Perhaps as much as 70% of the dollar savings came from improvements over the previously ineffective efforts by professionals and administrators in dealing with the proposed budget amendment. The improvement came from people whose adaptation to the new work patterns could not be anticipated. Morale and a positive attitude had a greater effect on the final outcome than did technology.

I have found that if a comparison between conditions prior to and after automation is needed, the most useful approach for evaluating office productivity gains is by tracking changes in the total cost for delivering an identifiable work product, such as such as purchase orders, customer proposals, or engineering change records. To gather such information systematically, one must classify work into its components. Actions such as "analyze," "write," and "draft" represent events that can easily be identified by office personnel. This is essential if we want employees to gather information about their work and then engage them in discussions about ways to improve what they are doing.

In this case the improvement in work time expended was 33%. What is most interesting is the total rearrangement in workflow which evolved to deliver the final result. There were office tasks such as editing, completing, and distributing whose amount of time contracted by 50% to 90%. There were also tasks such as organizing, drafting, and typing for which the automated approach was substantially more time-consuming than the manual method it replaced.

Comparing the old and new work patterns provides insight into the complexity of implementing a new office system. The results in this case suggest that there had to be a great deal of cooperation among the people involved in the budget preparation process before a net gain of 33% could be realized. Some individuals had to consent to increase their workload and to assume new functions so that there could be a reduction in the work of others. Professional and managerial personnel ended up doing some work that traditionally belongs to clerical and secretarial employees. Clerical and secretarial personnel enlarged the scope of their activities and ended up with office work that previously was restricted only to higher ranks.

The careful rebalancing of work, when changing to an automated office, can be also observed when elapsed time is used as a measure of how much has been accomplished. In this case I have observed a 36% schedule improvement to deliver a budget proposal: what previously took thirty-four days now takes only twenty-two days. The speeding up of the entire process is unequally distributed. For instance drafting, typing, editing, and distributing are now completed two to three times faster, while meetings and organizing efforts take much longer than before. The overall gain in elapsed time for getting a job accomplished is impressive. But it does not reflect qualitative improvements derived from having much more time available for improving the entire effort through better organization. When one introduces office automation, many gains can be made just from rethinking and restructuring work rather than from automation itself or the speeding up of output it makes possible. Large improvements can be obtained by removing inexpensive obstacles. I believe that in this case a substantial part of the savings came from relieving the pressure of deadlines on the managers and allowing them time to make changes that had little to do with information technology per se.

One of the most important questions about the effects of office automation concerns work habits. Is productivity gained by means of speeding up work, thus creating increased nervous tension? Are some of the gains due to people working longer hours due to surveillance from a machine? None of the evidence gathered in this case or in any of the other similar cases has suggested anything of the sort. As a matter of fact, the interviews with employees indicated the contrary. As missed deadlines become less ominous, more psychic space became available for personal contacts and for a more relaxed approach to managing work relationships. My findings show that there was no change in the total amount of an individual's time devoted to work before and after office automation.

The cases selected in this chapter illustrate some economic and behavioral effects of office automation. The most valuable lesson gained lies in a greater respect for the intricacy involved in successfully introducing information technology into the workplace. Office workers are a delicate element in an ever-changing environment, an element which must be continually re-balanced as electronic machinery is brought to bear on inefficient office work. Gains achieved during the gradual evolution of a more automated office depend on the ability of organizations to encourage new work roles for individuals.

3

How Information Technology Changes Work

The application of information technology can be viewed as another stage in the long evolutionary process of acquiring new means to overcome man's unaided capacities. Whether or not a specific tool is used by man depends upon the interaction between needs and costs. Information technology is declining in cost just when the burden of unproductive information-handling labor is expanding. Will the lowered costs be sufficiently attractive to stimulate an increase in the uses of the new tools? This chapter explores what is known about the patterns of acceptance of information technology. It also deals with issues which influence the arrival of the automated workplace.

Roles of Supporting Personnel

Reduction in the routine workload for support personnel should be anticipated so that their contribution can be enlarged.

In the electronic office a large share of document creation, document distribution, and data analysis are either automated or shifted directly into the hands of managers and professionals. This relieves secretaries, typists, and clerks of many repetitive tasks which presently require very little thought. The resultant changes in the flow of work makes possible new work relationships which can make better use of the support personnel's talents. Planning how to take advantage of these new opportunities should be a sine qua non before initiating an office automation project. Designing for success increases its likelihood.

With more time available to the supporting personnel, it is possible to consider job enhancement for the secretary and the clerk, especially in areas which require personal contacts. A great deal of work presently done by administrative and professional personnel—such as legal research, retrieval of financial reports from databases, summarizing operating information, generating management reports, analysis of competitive bids, client billing, and similar tasks—can be completed by properly trained support personnel. Clerical support people can do work such as dealing with routine customer matters, that is much closer to the objectives of the business. Such transformations will not happen without giving a great deal of thought to the transition. The economic benefits of information technology are derived from its effect on the productivity of work. When office automation projects are conceived, even more attention should be given to the planning of how work will be rearranged than is devoted to technical matters. A pattern for such rearrangement of work should be designed into the project from its inception as a prerequisite for economic success.

Benefits

More output is not necessarily better output.

Automated equipment creates labor savings: a marked increase in efficiency, measured in terms of physical output. There will be a strong temptation to generate more letters, issue invoices in greater detail, or print detailed reports in order to demonstrate success in the use of automation. Producing increased quantity just because it is easier, however, is a good way to wipe out potential benefits. Work tends to expand to fill the capacity of equipment and people unless management anticipates how to harness the new resources to new purposes. I have found that it is much more profitable to apply savings in time to work that was previously left undone rather than just to do more of the same.

The most remarkable business benefits are realized from planned *quality* improvements in areas such as customer service. Excessive emphasis on cost reduction is likely to obscure opportunities to achieve quality gains. Concentration on tangible procedural improvements may cause one to overlook the potential for larger changes which benefit the entire business.

Case studies show that most of the benefits from information technology are derived from improvements in intragroup communications rather than from acceleration of an individual's work. A critical minimum number of connected workstations must be present before a group can try out new approaches to organizing work. Standalone products improve efficiency to some extent, especially for isolated staff jobs involving lengthy computations, but it is necessary to develop information networks on a substantial scale before one achieves major improvements in office communications. I doubt most of the claims about benefits obtained from a proliferation of personal computers, without network connections and without access to shared resources. It is known that managers and professionals spend more than half of their time in communicating with each other. It follows that they need equipment that enhances their communications if the information technology is to be of much value.

Due to the complex interrelationship among behavioral, organizational, economic, and information-technology factors, investments in this area are high-risk propositions. Expectations of immediate gains should not be set too high and resources should not be overcommitted. Aiming for excessive initial gains just to sell the project will increase risks beyond anyone's ability to comply. It will, in fact, assure failure. The realization of benefits from information technology projects is paced by changes in organizational behavior which can be realized only in very gradual, small steps. Success will come when the organization discovers that it has reached a few safe initial objectives, and that on a second or third try it can achieve previously unattainable performance levels with very small additional effort.

Communications Patterns

Improved communications permit improved organizations.

Rapid turnaround of written messages by electronic mail stimulates a gradual transfer of general office communications from conversations to keyboard entries, to the Visual Display Unit (VDU) screen, and to the high-speed printer.[1] This new form of communicating across time zones and between remote sites opens new organizational opportunities for getting work accomplished on a decentralized basis. Placing thousands of people in a single building is no longer the only way that intraorganizational communications can be encouraged. Electronic conferencing, supported by text- and voice files, offers opportunities to increase manyfold one's effective contacts with any individual on the network.

Sharing formal and informal communications concerning a temporary task among all participants allows much greater flexibility for an organization to deal with problems. The electronic communications medium encourages the creation of temporary, problem-oriented groups as contrasted with the present approach to organization, which depends on permanent, procedure-oriented groups.

The existence of communication links among various organizations makes it possible for professional and managerial people to belong to several project- or interest groups, both within their own organizations and externally. An active manager or professional can reasonably expect to receive electronic messages on five to ten networks and to belong to more than twenty interest groups. His personal computer can scan the traffic on all of these channels. I have tracked the highly unstructured nature of professional and managerial work and observed the frequent interruptions in their work. Shared network files, properly set up, will serve as a collective memory, allowing each participant to join in the exchange of communications when it is convenient rather than when dictated by physical presence.

The electronic medium changes the message.

I have witnessed the shift in the proportion of communication from the verbal to the electronic medium by observing what happened when electronic mail was introduced. Not only has the relative share of voice vs. written words changed, but the total volume of messages has increased enormously. The gain was achieved entirely through increasing use of the "written" message. This creates problems for individuals who have learned to use the give-and-take of the verbal medium to adjust their own thinking quickly. The general imprecision and ambiguity of two-way verbal conversations makes it possible for people to avoid unpleasant topics and to divert direct questions.

Written communication is more explicit and excludes the powerful nonverbal signals that are present in discussions, in arguments, and especially in confrontations. All leaders I know have exceptionally well-developed verbal and nonverbal group-manipulation skills. They use wit, contingent statements, probing questions, and the force of physical presence to get their point of view across to others. The written electronic communication, however, alters the way such persuasion can be presented.

Electronic mail is also easily distributed and copied, which means that a phrase which may be perfectly innocuous in a private and informal exchange can suddenly be broadcast to a large number of individuals who do not understand its context. I have found this to be true especially of witty remarks—which are fine as a way of breaking up tension in a meeting, but which may appear to be destructive sarcasm when placed in a public electronic file.

Electronic mail does not fit in with most current top-executive habits.

I suspect that the formality of written messages accounts much more for the executives' reluctance to use the keyboard than their presumed lack of typing skills. The written medium seems to suit much more the quantitatively oriented, analytic, well-organized person who usually ends up in a staff position.

The traditional senior executive is usually prefers to use informal personal conversations and meetings to receive information.[2] Except in unique situations, it is unlikely that a personal electronic workstation could be of much benefit to someone who is conditioned to using the face-to-face approach. The executive will certainly not attempt to read a voluminous report on a visual display screen: that is just too inconvenient compared with a portable, bound report printed on paper. Office automation for the executive suite is to be avoided as a leading application except for terse messages or for the receipt of urgent communications at the executive's home.

Access to business networks from the home greatly increases the value of the electronic medium.

The capability of a network to provide access to electronic mailboxes, even from inexpensive home computers, enhances the value of the new electronic environment. The office is a difficult place for generating creative thoughts or for serious concentration on documents. In the long run I see the role of the office building as emphasizing the socializing needs of the business. The purpose of getting people together in a building will be much more to stimulate inspiration, cooperation, motivation, and the sharing of complex experiences with members of a team than actually to complete creative work. This is why conference rooms, recreational and meeting facilities may become much more important in the future office architecture than is currently the case. Rush-hour commuting delays can be avoided and family life improved, since the electronic medium makes it possible to keep in touch with associates at the office. I have replied to an urgent query from Japan ahead of the time when it was sent (due to time zone differences) because I was able to handle the inquiry from my home. The flexibility gained in handling office problems from one's home has promoted a favorable employee attitude towards office automation. There are also cost advantages when terminals are available for the employees' home use. In addition to improving morale, most of the training costs can be shifted to the employees' own free time. For all practical purposes the unfavorable effects of the employees' absenteeism is eliminated. Many professional, secretarial, and clerical functions can be performed at home since a major portion of these employees' really productive work is performed in isolation anyway, while completing information-intensive tasks. This will be of great benefit to young mothers, to individuals with health problems, to people with other disabilities, and to an increasing number of retired knowledge workers who possess an enormous accumulation of experience but who do not wish to subject themselves to the strains of commuting to a full-time job.

I am convinced that equipping employees with office workstations for home use will result in the employees' devoting more actual time to productive work than can be expected at the office, while simultaneously increasing their job satisfaction.

The Importance of Leadership

The faster we go, the further ahead we need to look for signs to guide us. Identifying the right signs—that is leadership.

New applications of technology and the desire to acquire the latest equipment follow imitative patterns. Management should recognize these tendencies when embarking on information technology ventures.

In the absence of strong leadership, which means the leaders will personally adopt the new electronic environment, little success can be expected. By leadership, I also mean a strong sense of purpose and a vision that the leader articulates about how the results to be obtained from the technology relate to the purposes of the business. If such leadership is lacking the whole point of the venture will become muddled: relationships among the various participants in the effort will be full of conflict and will stimulate counterproductive behavior. The teamwork needed to deliver good results will be diffused into disjoint acts by isolated individuals.

By leadership I do not mean only inspired messages from top management published in the employee newsletter, but also the acting out of intentions by personal demonstrations of new computer applications under working conditions. All successful computer technology projects are carried on the shoulders of a handful of enthusiastic and dedicated operating managers (rather than technical experts), who can articulate what the fundamental objectives of the system are, regardless of how many figurehead administrators come and go. These managers provide the continuity and safeguard the integrity of information systems. Nowadays, the life cycle of major network systems investments ranges from seven to twelve years, while the frequency of corporate reorganizations seems to be descending to less than two years. Consequently, long-term operating managerial leadership is essential for sustaining the effective use of the electronic environment.

But clarity of the operating objectives of information technology projects is not sufficient to assure success. The long life cycle of these investments requires that technical integrity of the networks and the databases is maintained. In the background of all successful computer projects there is always a handful of dedicated technical managers who hold the system together and who seem to know how to make the computers function even under the most adverse conditions. One of the most important purposes of management is to create conditions which will motivate this group of people and which will safeguard the accumulated know-how located in the heads of a few technical leaders.

There are two kinds of technical leaders. One type is made up of "techies"—those who know where the technical faults are and how to get around them. The second type consists of the "technology brokers"—leaders without much technical training but with much organizational know-how. They blossom into positions of leadership because they understand the precarious connection between the organization's realities and the fragile computer systems that support it.

In one system for which I was responsible, a telecommunication device used to fail frequently. Even with ample spare parts the vendor could not keep it from malfunctioning at critical times. Our "broker" knew of a backup phone link through which marketing people could connect during emergencies. The "broker" made a deal with marketing to incorporate the bypass. Since this had not been planned, the users could be instructed only informally. This simple fix saved everybody much pain until a new telecommunication vendor was found. Meanwhile, the "broker" carried the most valuable part of the system's documentation in his head and was glad to share it with whomever he considered to be his friends.

Without a few knowledgeable and practical spirits who preserve the continuity of management and technical leadership, chances are that even lavishly funded projects will not deliver the expected results.

Attitudes

Introduction of information technology is an emotional experience.

One of my most unexpected discoveries was the extent to which emotional bonds are formed between frequent network users and their personal computers. When one individual had to give up a personal computer, I heard reports about unusual disturbances in his work relationships. A professional psychologist likened them to drug-addiction withdrawal symptoms. The person in question exhibited anger and diminished effectiveness; he made irrational efforts to get the machine back. Augmentation of a person's information-handling capabilities by means of a workstation may set the stage for a dependency of ever-increasing intensity.

When it comes to the acquisition of additional hardware or to the purchase of enhanced software, I am convinced that emotionally involved computer users cannot be trusted to make the right decisions. They make exaggerated claims in order to enlarge the supposed power of their machines. They exhibit a form of compulsive acquisitive behavior. The sales forces of computer manufacturers are specially trained to cater to such tastes. How equipment and software add-ons are procured and how individuals acquire a dependency on a preferred vendor can be explained only by psychology, not by economics.

Dominant male roles requiring the delegation of office minutiae to female secretaries were challenged in many office network experiments. Typing of general correspondence has usually been identified as a female occupation. Tradition-oriented managers have resisted the acquisition of typing skills as a threat to their status, especially when they found out how poorly they were doing. One good way to overcome such attitudes is to find a high-status male in the organization who will start typing some of his own messages. In the absence of similar initiatives office automation may spread only among certain restricted groups, in which psychological barriers to change have been removed by accident or by insufficient secretarial support.

Workstations permit managerial and professional personnel to do their own electronic filing. It is essential for managers and professionals to devise their own electronic filing schemes and to perform the electronic analogue of traditional paperwork-filing chores. The ease with which electronic file indexing, keying, retrieval, and message entry is performed has made this shift less onerous. Tradition-oriented secretaries find such increased involvement on the part of their managers a reduction in their responsibility for files which are still predominantly paper-based. After all, the etymology of "secretary" implies "keeper of secrets." Knowing where everything is located is the key to secretaries' sense of importance. Such ambivalence will persist until all filing becomes totally electronic and automatic. It may also help if managers start working with secretaries on upgrading their work assignments, so that a decrease in filing responsibilities is not seen as a job threat.

Language

The computer medium is not only reshaping business communications but also business language.

The way one thinks about work is noticeably influenced by interaction with computers. Not only do network participants become insiders with a sense of elite group membership, but they also acquire an argot, slang, or special phraseology that emphasizes their distinctiveness. Some of it is rather contrived, but most of it is derived from the rich experience that the electronic network offers. Network commands, which were originally devised as labels to identify and execute office tasks, become recognized as precise and unambiguous statements comprising a richer repertoire than that available in ordinary office conversations. As a result, verbs and nouns originally improvised by some designer have become transplanted into everyday language, describing a wide variety of office transactions. The net effect is that computerese and all sorts of acronyms have entered into ordinary office talk. The problem is that different organizations will give different meanings to identical words. To outsiders, conversations become incomprehensible. To insiders, this adds a warm feeling of belonging to a chosen clan and compensates for other defects of the impersonal computers.

Disputes and differences of opinion should not be entrusted to the electronic medium. A sentence, once entered into the computer network, is unforgiving. It can magnify differences and intensify emotions, especially if people of higher rank are included on the distribution list. Arguments can escalate and damage personal relationships. The antidote is restraint in the use of extreme claims and the relaxation of management's insistence on receiving copies of all correspondence.

Something should be said about the writing style most suitable for electronic mail and for electronic conferencing. The conventional corporate and government interoffice memorandum is expected to have a weighty, official tone. Pompous sentences are preferred. Personal references or any expression of emotion is to be scrupulously avoided. If the electronic message is to be used as a major supplement to verbal exchanges, it simply cannot persist in using the dull verbiage of official communications. Expressions of individuality and even occasional irrelevancies should be encouraged in lengthy electronic exchanges. What seems to work is to write as one speaks rather than as one usually writes in official announcements. I do not know why, but receivers of my electronic messages delight in receiving text that has occasional spelling and typographic errors. Somehow, it makes the exchange more human and serves as evidence that it is conveying a personal communication. I am now less careful in editing informal messages because they seem to reinforce the conversational nature of many of my electronic contacts.

Universal access to shared printing facilities, especially if sophisticated composition software is used, produces output of high visual quality. The appearance is far superior to anything encountered in ordinary office situations. It is startling to receive a totally insignificant message that seems fit for inclusion in a formal report. People will just have to become aware that even accurately plotted three-color graphs may contain completely misleading information. Carefully tabulated sales projections, itemized in great detail, can be meaningless even if generated by an elaborate computer model. In the electronic medium, sensitivity to content is a more highly prized skill. Discrimination on the basis of appearance is no longer advisable.

Too many managers write poorly. This is due to the fact that most managerial experiences have been visual and verbal. An avoidance reaction may develop about using an electronic workstation, not because it is complex, but because the user's writing skills are minimal. One solution is to use software aids which look up correct spelling. One can also use software which checks up on the construction of sentences and which analyzes the clarity of an entire paragraph. Using the secretary as an editorial assistant or sending electronically important text to a professional editor may alleviate this problem.

Misuses and Abuses

Information technology's long list of advantages is matched by an equally long list of potential disadvantages.

Theology has been preoccupied with arguments about the nature of good and evil. One view states that they are a matched pair, and that it all depends on human action which way the balance will tilt. I have a similar perspective on information technology. For every wonderful advance I can record a possible loss. On balance, we have been gaining for the last few decades. We are lacking carefully documented case histories that would portray both the misuses as well as the successes of information technology. Computer journals and all vendor literature are devoted to euphoric tales about great achievements. Few indeed are the blemishes analyzed. The trade literature contains practically no adequately documented cases about electronic systems that failed. It is almost as if medical journals contained only articles about healthy people. At the other extreme one can find articles—almost entirely from the labor movement—that describe only incidents of abuse.

Management is entitled to learn not only from advertised successes, but also from misuses and abuses, about how an information technology project has actually failed to achieve its objectives. After all, the medical profession learns mostly from people who are not healthy. Presently, there is a distinct reluctance to pursue stories about disappointing computer projects because events become quickly shrouded in technical details. In my entire career I have never found a single case in which technology itself was the primary cause of failure. Ultimately there are only people-caused failures, even in situations when it is alleged that machines have malfunctioned. There is no reason for management to abstain from careful scrutiny of failed information technology investments, especially if this may provide experience for preventing future damage to the organization.

Junk Mail

Electronic junk mail travels faster and better.

The new computer networks exist without much central control over the content, form, or dissemination of messages. As a result, the systems may be abused by the dissemination of irrelevant information. Automatic distribution lists, which are an integral part of any good electronic mail system, exacerbate this condition and help to generate enormous quantities of electronic junk mail, which overloads disk files and unnecessarily occupies high-speed printers. It is very easy to generate a tenfold to thirtyfold increase in the amount of information received by an individual when he becomes involved with the electronic medium and gets onto all sorts of public distribution lists. Central authorization of access to distribution lists may remedy some of the excesses, but it will create restraints on information flow—thus eliminating most of the advantages of easy interconnection between people. If authorization restrictions are imposed, which is frequently the case, people will often request access to everything lest they miss something of value. One needs to be very careful when attempting to regulate electronic information because one deals here with conflicting influences. Some people find that receiving large amounts of electronic mail is emotionally satisfying as a compensation for their loneliness in large office complexes.

As a remedy for excesses and abuses it is necessary to price network usage at commercial rates, as a direct cost to the user. Applying overall budget limits is a much more effective way of restraining unreasonable usage than exercising direct control.

Personal Privacy

Preservation of privacy is essential to obtaining a personal commitment to use the computer as a means for communication.

Issues of computer privacy, security and individual trust are no different than what we have had all along with paper-based information, except that these issues are now becoming more pervasive because the volume of communications is increasing very fast.

The shared electronic file, easily created and easily accessible to a peer group, is one of the essential prerequisites for a well-functioning electronic office. These advantages, however, also create problems in preserving privacy and in maintaining organizational control. For example, in one case a private directory of recommended restaurants and of wines supplied by an acknowledged gourmet enhanced feelings of good fellowship and brought a friendly feature into the office network. As a further step, the shared file was opened for contributions by users to reflect actual experiences with particular meals and with individual wine purchases. A problem arose when the file became a sort of anonymous bulletin board which introduced commentaries about less legitimate endeavors.

In another case, a word-of-mouth electronic mailbox became the depository of anonymous, devastating criticism of management actions. Some of the alleged facts were wrong, but some disclosed company-classified data. A variety of measures are possible in such situations, including the creation of a central audit trail which would account for the origin of all network messages. With dozens of interconnected networks and hundreds of distributed electronic files, such solutions are easier to propose than to install and administer.

Unless the electronic files are explicitly locked by passwords or even by encryption, all network information is accessible if one knows where and how to look for it. In order to protect the organization from losses of confidential information, and to guard individuals against invasion of privacy, electronic network security and protection must be of a much higher order than with conventional paper documents, letters, or telephone traffic. Users of networks also need to realize that a central authority could surreptitiously install software that permits surveillance of all transactions. So far—except in financial and government installations—I have not seen network security measures and the need to protect personal privacy become an impediment to the introduction of information technology.

Some critics of the electronic age insist that privacy and security matters will emerge in the forefront of concerns within the next ten years. I do not think they will. These concerns serve as a justification of a long history of government commissions, consultant reports, and regulatory proposals. With sufficient amounts of money for expensive equipment and with some inconveniences to the users, privacy and security matters will remain manageable. Meanwhile, people will continue to keep really private and confidential data in their locked file cabinets and to mail really confidential documents by one of the courier services.

Employee Dissatisfaction

Poorly managed organizations are likely to have more complaints about computers than are well-managed organizations.

There is a rising chorus of objections to the introduction of computers in the workplace. The Visual Display Unit (VDU) has been singled out as a device that causes psychological stress, creates eye strain, damages eyesight, produces muscular discomfort, leads to backaches, forms skin rashes, possibly induces birth defects, emits dangerous radiation, fosters emotional disorientation, and stimulates a sense of anxiety. Whether VDUs indeed cause actual physical damage is something that should be clinically investigated. The National Research Council (NRC) report on "Video Displays, Work and Vision" has shown that some of the most adverse allegations were not factually supported.[3] Since the release of the NRC report, the arguments have shifted to more subtle influences, which will require time-consuming and expensive studies before we have convincing proof—one way or the other—as to the alleged harmful effects.

The arguments concerning VDUs have recently changed direction. Whereas once the anti-VDU partisans called for proof that VDUs were not harmful, they now require a demonstration that they are harmless. There is clearly a big difference between these two ways of conducting a dispute. Positive harm is always easier to demonstrate, even though the causes of the harm itself may not be so easily understood. Proof of the *absence* of any causal relationship between VDUs and whatever effect is under study requires large-scale and long-term occupational epidemiology studies—which nobody has funded so far. Until such research has been completed, we can expect that poorly designed or incomplete studies will continue to be misused by both sides to the dispute.

There is also the question of who should bear the burden of proving harm or harmlessness. It makes sense to say that the office-equipment vendors should be fully accountable for testing their VDUs for electronic hazards, such as emission or radiation. (Incidentally, all current equipment meets or exceeds government standards in this regard.) But this has not stopped the complaints about VDUs. The problem is that the placement of computers in the workplace is not just a technical matter.

The introduction of office automation entails a complex socioeconomic disturbance which will generate all sorts of psychological side effects, such as occupational stress. Whenever employees are excessively distressed by such a change, it should be of foremost concern to their management, especially since such a situation is bound to be highly counterproductive. I know of stressful office situations, with incredibly low worker morale, which employ VDUs. I know of stressful office situations, with incredibly low worker morale, which do *not* employ VDUs. I am also acquainted with very pleasant working conditions where people actually enjoy doing the same office tasks on VDUs as encountered in the demoralized shops which have the same equipment. It takes more than simply installing VDUs to get either effect. Who, then, should have the responsibility of making sure that the introduction of information technology does not heighten employee dissatisfaction? Clearly, this is a management responsibility. There is a long list of reasons why operating VDUs is not as convenient as handling paper. Uncomfortable furniture, high noise levels from impact printers, dangling wires, poor lighting, strange office procedures, fear of technological unemployment, and the hostile language embedded in most terminals are good reasons why already bad employee relations will invariably worsen when computers enter the picture. Furniture, noise, lighting, and unfriendly machines can be improved by paying attention to them and caring enough to fix them. There is a price to be paid for introducing information technology. Some of the expected economic gains must be reinvested in improved employee morale. The remedies are not technological but managerial.

One of the most frequently proposed remedies for problems arising from the introduction of information technology is government regulation. The highly personal and individualized characteristics of the electronic environment make it inconceivable to me that meaningful legislation could be written. I have observed totally futile efforts on the part of corporate staffs to write procedures that would cover such simple matters as the acquisition of microcomputers, furniture standards, or the introduction of "quality circles" to improve the reliability of work output. I do not think that any useful government regulation can be drafted in this area except to deal with situations of demonstratable neglect of the employees' well-being. Attempts to do anything more would be ineffective. The acceptance or rejection of information technology is a matter influenced entirely by highly localized conditions and by individual relationships on the job. These cannot be regulated by high-level generalizations.

The sign of a truly revolutionary technology is that it is misused to serve nontechnical purposes.

There are other parties to the employer–employee relationship which will influence whether or not information technology is viewed as an abuse or as a benefit. Organized labor is interested in computerization issues as a way to stimulate unionization of information workers. For instance, I believe that the claim VDUs are a health hazard has been an effective way to overcome the traditional reluctance of many information workers, engaged in routine office work, to consider collective bargaining. State legislatures presently have a backlog of regulatory bills attempting to deal with an accumulation of such complaints.[4] The entire situation is characterized by much legal confrontation and by a minimum of solid research dealing with specific complaints. Lurking in the background, I find a totally different agenda, which deals with the regulation of, and bargaining about, work relationships. Put succintly, "Ultimately technology is not just a question of machines and systems, but of power and how power is allocated. . . ."[5] The misuses and abuses of technology could develop into an increasingly adversarial confrontation between employers, employees, unions, and regulatory bodies. The regulation of mere technical details involved in running an automated office may end up being offered as a substitute for the resolution of more real conflicts.

The alleged hazards of using a VDU have become a proxy for addressing other office automation issues. Society has often used symbols in this way.

Meanwhile, the installation rate of VDUs is proceeding at an accelerated pace. Anecdotal surveys can prove that VDUs are either well accepted or disliked.[6] I have been to offices that were so arrogantly managed that it was no wonder that employees seized on the introduction of new technology as a new bargaining opportunity. I have also visited well-managed offices where employees competed to acquire and operate a VDU in order to improve the quality of their worklife.

Poor work design and poor work organization will guarantee that information technology will be abused. Good organizations will thrive in their use of computers and will find methods for chanelling established work habits into constructive courses.

Support and Other Important Details

Big information systems failures grow from many little failures.

In a survey of "advanced systems" users, which includes some of the most sophisticated office network technologies presently in use, the following four areas of dissatisfaction ranked significantly higher than any other concerns: (1) promptness of response to requests for maintenance; (2) quality of instruction and of documentation received; (3) response time of the computer; and (4) arrangement of equipment, furniture, office lighting, and office space.[7]

Only the third of these top concerns dealt with the technology itself. Inexperienced managers assume that after spending much money for the computer devices and for planning their physical installation, other sources of dissatisfaction can easily be removed. Such is not the case.

The users of a widely shared office system need to adopt procedures and set up an organized approach for taking care of small but important details. For instance, coordinating requests for maintenance calls, providing printer-inking ribbons when the supply is depleted, correcting paper jams, replenishing paper supplies in printing stations, and unplugging complicated cabling when moving furniture are just a few of the hundreds of annoying details which need to be handled. The conventional office, with only a few electromechanical devices, is much more stable and more easily maintained than the electronic environment which requires many more elements to function faultlessly—in fact, to function at all. Technical experts tend to underrate the crucial importance of these little nontechnical details.

Most office automation planners avoid providing the additional manpower needed to support even a few dozen workstations. Such help should be provided generously from the very inception of any program. After experience is gained and people find all sorts of short-cuts, one can always decrease the amount of support. Unfortunately, precisely the opposite approach has been followed by naive experimenters. In order to justify the new equipment, budgets are shaved on the assumption that everything will work. I have seen $16,000 systems placed on $400 desks which were uncomfortably high and in front of $125 chairs that guaranteed bodily discomfort to anyone expected to sit in them for hours, gazing at a fixed screen. The excessive glare of overhead fluorescent fixtures was not remedied because any changes in illumination were controlled by another department. Only when office workers are ready to reject the technology is the required support grudgingly provided. Starting office automation projects with such negative experiences is a liability which is very hard to overcome.

Balancing Discipline and Innovation

Big information systems failures arise from an imperceptible drift towards chaos. Unless continuous action is taken to the contrary, all information systems tend towards disorder.

Successful office automation installations must provide for all sorts of central guidance to keep the necessarily decentralized activities from drifting into chaos. For instance, security passwords must be handed out and registered, shared peripherals on the network must be assigned network addresses, billing identification for cost accounting must be set, common methods for electronic labelling of magnetic media for archival storage must be documented, individuals must be assigned standard names for directory purposes. There are at least twelve possible ways of addressing Paul Strassmann on the networks I belong to. Some sort of central organization has to see to it that the sequence of last name, first name, initial, location, organization, etc., follows a scheme that is uniformly intelligible. Similarly, telecommunications links must be classified to allow for alternate routing of messages, information-retention schedules must be chosen, procedures for relieving files of excess information must be set up, network congestion must be tracked as usage grows, fallback actions in case of failure must be programmed. This list could go on for pages, depending on the architecture that has been chosen for the network and the extent to which responsibility has been decentralized.

For office automation to work on any large scale at all, it is essential to arrange things according to a deliberate design that will provide the necessary order and cohesion. A telecommunications complex linking even dozens of workstations requires a network administration organization that will plan, monitor, and regulate the electronic flows. Unfortunately, very few organizations pay much attention to these needs in their exuberance to get started on the way toward the office-of-the-future. It is represented by equipment vendors as instant, plug-in technology. In fact, the devices one buys are more like the materials one purchases for constructing a house. Just having furniture, kitchen appliances, and a supply of lumber does not produce a home. A design is needed, even if it does not specify precisely where everything will be ultimately located. Similarly, information systems must be planned at the right level of detail so that they will ultimately reflect a balance between order and adaptability. The role of the chief executive in guiding the overall information architecture of his firm is at least as important as the direction of how the various operations will be organized.

Contest of Power

Taking care of the politics for managing technology is the most important act in guiding office automation.

Much of the private conversation among professionals in the information technology field has to do with stories about power contests for control between the data-processing centralists and the enthusiastic people who finally wish to be liberated from the heavy hand of computer bureaucrats. These tales have by now become the legend which has made quite a few office automation efforts an intense personal contest rather than a technical design issue. The resolution of these conflicts is comparable, on a historical scale, to the feuds between shepherds and farmers. The outcome is just as predictable. The highly organized computer people will end up running the networks, even though in the process of acquiring this power their role will change. Introducing office automation, then, should be viewed not only as a change in the way individuals work, but also as a process in which centrally directed expertise is used to influence the acceptance of information technology. Without an understanding of the political contests between central network control and decentralized adaptation to business needs, an executive observer will have a hard time understanding which of two equally plausible arguments should be favored. Both central control and decentralized responsiveness must be carefully balanced to achieve harmony with the way that the organization distributes political power in its other functions.

One of the principles of international politics has long been the dictum that trade follows the flag. I find that the most practical way of resolving the disputes between the big computer centralists and the microcomputer autonomy-seekers is not to listen too much to technical arguments but to follow the maxim that system design should follow organizational design. If the chief executive really believes in decentralization of authority, then distributing the responsibilities for systems management is in order, and vice versa. At this point of development, information technology can deliver equally effective solutions regardless of organizational choices. One should bear in mind, however, that systems architectures have a very long life—if only because they represent a very painful accumulation of knowledge and habit. If one does not like one's apartment, it is relatively easy to move out and find something more suitable. Information systems are not like a property, however; they are much more like a family. It is extremely costly and painful to change the architecture of an automated information system to which an organization has become accustomed.

The time required in the planning cycle for information systems strategies now exceeds that of the product planning cycle, the plant capacity planning cycle, and most likely also the research and development planning cycle for almost every case I have examined. The time has come to take short-term, "expedient," organizational politics out of the information technology planning cycle and incorporate it into the overall strategic planning discipline, since such planning is one of the longest lead-time investments an organization will have to make in managing its transition into the electronic age.

Training

Training, training, training: these are the top three priorities to changing work in the automated office.

High-quality training in the acquisition of new skills is the absolute prerequisite for obtaining productive results from information technology. Substandard technology can produce satisfactory results if superior training has been given to users. However, superior equipment will not produce much if user training is deficient. All comparisons of the relative effectiveness between trained and untrained staffs attempting to use computers show that office automation is primarily a social and only secondarily a technological phenomenon.

The electronic medium should not only convey messages but also help people to discover their powers.

A superior information system includes a capability to train people to use it. Users do not progress uniformly in acquiring new skills. Nor are their needs predictable. In the absence of practice, people forget what they have learned. Using computers requires continuous retraining and reinforcement. A superior information network includes the option of switching rapidly from working into learning and back again.

Computer manufacturers have the incentive to add tutorial features to their systems because this materially reduces their own support costs. I find that the most revolutionary recent developments in information technology are not new semiconductor chips but the availability of interactive tutorial software integrated with application software.

"Learning to use a computer is much more like taking up a musical instrument than following instructions how to use an electrical appliance, such as a toaster." [8] This distinction is not well understood, which leads to a socially induced computerphobia. Nobody can be expected to sit down at a piano and be able to play the latest songs without much experience. The myth of instantly usable computers operated with utmost ease by six-year-olds is sufficient to damage the ego of any office worker. A long-lasting learning inhibition can be inflicted if, after the first thirty minutes of unsuccessful fumbling with the keyboard, a person is still erasing his initial attempts to communicate with the machine. If such an experience takes place in public, this individual will find every suitable pretext for avoiding the machine again. It will simply be too embarrassing to admit that he could not perform as he was so (mis)guided as to expect.

I have often noticed that technical experts will deny that learning how to use computers is a frustrating and time-consuming effort. All exclusive societies have rites for scaring away the uninitiated. It is a perfect setup to be able to place your manager in front of a terminal which you can operate with the greatest ease after many weeks of making every conceivable mistake. You win on two counts: first, the manager will walk away with the conviction that you are brilliant; second, he will not try to learn anything that diminishes your position.

People who need instant success in everything they do must be warned that learning how to operate an electronic workstation is a frustrating process. Practice is necessary to achieve even a minimum level of competence. The size of the training budget and the length of time for gradually building up experience to acceptable levels should not be underrated. Unfortunately, everybody benefits from de-emphasizing the necessity of investing in learning. The supplier will tell you his product is incredibly easy. The technologist will suggest special training is not necessary, because that leaves more of the budget for hardware and for prepackaged programming. Organized labor will avoid the training to keep expectations of achievable output down. Because it is very difficult to document payoffs from training, management will be reluctant to spend money on it and may try to save money on a project by cutting back on all intangible start-up expenses.

"Computer literacy training" is one way of coping with the obvious need for education in this area. For instance, a fashionable training organization offers executives instruction in programming (in BASIC, in operating systems (MS-DOS), and in database management.) The entire experience is sprinkled with lessons about semiconductor logic, binary memories, and local area network protocols. Although such training is interesting as general education, it is without practical value. Half of the attending executives were extremely poor typists and would have benefited far more from typing practice—which is essential for using any electronic workstation. Most likely, none of the executives will ever have to program anything. Training makes sense only as a means for getting people started in directly experiencing the technology in a personally useful application. General education may be introduced subsequently. For instance, electronic conferencing may be the single most important, and perhaps the only practical application for an executive to know well. Training executives how to handle and store network messages is a useful way of starting them off in experiencing the electronic age. The child's painstaking process of acquiring "literacy" is an inappropriate analogy for introducing a user to information technology. The education of an information technologist is not the right model for someone who just wants to benefit from computer applications.

When all of the influences of information technology on changing office work are finally weighed in the balance, training to build up an individual's experience and confidence will always come out as the decisive variable. A realistic assessment of the training investment must always be made if office automation is to succeed.

In trying to show how automation changes work, I have covered a variety of instances showing how office work interacts with automation. The point is that information technology is very much a human, social, and organizational phenomenon. This perspective is essential for gaining an understanding of the conflicting influences which shape the use of information technology at every step of its evolution. The value of information technology can be expressed most saliently in human and social terms. For the proper study of information technology, one should first study how the people involved are affected by it.

4

The High-Performance Individual

Information technology operated by high-performance people delivers excellent results. If operated by indifferent or even hostile individuals it is a liability. What does it take to create a favorable environment for the electronic age?

Attributes of High-Performance People and Systems

Before an organization can boast that its computers are operated by highly motivated employees it would be useful to reach some agreement as to the defining characteristics of such a situation.[1] Management should watch for the following indications.

People will continue to be enthusiastic about the system a year after adoption.

Listening to employees talking in the cafeteria and in the elevator is an excellent opportunity for sampling morale. Favorable public conversations about a system which persist long after the initial installation are a sure sign that the information technology has captured people's imagination and that it keeps delivering new and worthwhile experiences. It takes at least a year to sort out excitement over a novelty from permanent changes in attitude brought about by more productive jobs.

The operator will develop a personal involvement with the equipment.

I always look for small clues expressing individuality as a sign that high-performance individuals are occupying the office. If operating instructions in a person's own handwriting are placed near the equipment, this indicates that the machine may be becoming personally acceptable. I look for items taped near the keyboard with all sorts of reminders. A personal touch is also apparent when identical workstations are placed in ways which reflect individual preferences. Shades, screens, stands, holders, even fuzzy little toy animals identify machines whose users consider them their own. Asking a serviceperson what is wrong with a machine during a maintenance call reveals personal concern. A vendor can recognize a high-performance individual if he constantly requests information about hardware and software features. A personally involved user will also own a collection of manuals and locally invented instruction sheets describing how the machine operates.

External controls are seen as irrelevant and interfering.

Highly motivated individuals will master the technology and will develop their own procedural and stylistic shortcuts. They will resent uninvited interference from experts, especially those lacking relevant experience. They will express contempt for consultants, headquarters auditors, vendor representatives, or anyone else who comes to check up on what is being accomplished. If visitors perform their checking without prior consultation, this will be seen as a personal affront. Extra hostility is reserved for time-and-motion-study personnel, especially if they collect statistics not available to the operators. If an outsider gains information by means of hidden surveillance, e.g., by means of remote computer monitoring, defensiveness deteriorates into hatred. However, great hospitality and friendship are extended to visitors who try to help overcome lingering technical problems. These sentiments are not exclusive to high-performance workers. The marked difference is found in the more overt way these people react to such situations.

The electronic office enhances the activities involved in job socialization.

High-performance office workers expect that electronic equipment will enhance their social contacts, not inhibit them. Removing personal secretaries from the proximity of their bosses to a word-processing center operating under factory-like discipline has been the basis of a large number of economically justifiable records-management projects which, nevertheless, failed because they did not consider the inhibiting effects on social contacts. Even key-punch operators, who have the most rigidly controlled occupation in the office hierarchy, rebel when the supervision of keying is transferred to the control of a computer because the programmed instructions do not tolerate various little social conveniences in the way a human supervisor would.

In an another example, equipment designers did not realize that a shared laser printer becomes a natural gathering place for people coming to pick up their printed documents. Unless convenient equipment controls, adequate floor space, and temporary storage for finished pages are provided at such a printing station, social contacts will be inhibited and people will find even minor technical problems, such as an occasional lack of supplies, a cause for for highly vocal complaints.

I am always pleased to see references on electronic networks to personal events such as birthdays, engagements, parties, outings, personal appointments, health, food, and items for sale; business references about systems failures, maintenance fixes, software changes; even news about hurricanes. Such messages are a healthy sign that the network is used to communicate about matters of personal concern, which is essential to its effective functioning.

Learning takes place by example.

It takes only a relatively small amount of training to get a person to make limited use of even a very sophisticated computer application. This minimum represents only a small fraction of the full potential. Formal training is the best way to acquire these initial skills.

Subsequent expansion in the uses of the system grows gradually with increased ability to handle added office tasks—an ability which may be acquired after the initial training is long forgotten. I do not think that lengthy attendance in classes offering comprehensive training for all possible work conditions is effective. People differ greatly in their needs and in their learning abilities. The most useful approach to learning how to use information technology comes from a sort of ongoing apprenticeship, in which an experienced helper imparts knowledge as it is needed. Such tutoring can also be accomplished by means of programmed learning, and can be assisted by means of well-written manuals. Nevertheless, at critical times the user still needs to turn for help to someone he or she respects. Immediate, action-related, and bottleneck-removing assistance are the principal means for passing on good computer skills.

The presence of high-performance individuals can be detected when a great deal of informal training is continually taking place in the workplace rather than in the formal classrooms. In high-performance organizations almost everyone alternates between learning and teaching roles. Organizations with high-performance people frequently use tutorial meetings, where people train as a group. Such meetings seem more effective than elaborate training institutes which high-performance individuals attend only on rare occasions. Peer-group training is not only more effective but also much less expensive. Besides, nobody learns better than the person who teaches others. Creating and then maintaining such an environment is a critical factor for sustaining high-performance people in satisfying jobs.

Learning is a continuous experience.

To maintain a steady growth in the productivity of high-performance individuals, continuous education must take place. People should constantly be challenged to think about making improvements. This requires the adoption of the idea that one learns in order to do better what one already knows how to do well. It presumes that many things are in place:

1. There is enough security in the work group so that people are not afraid of working themselves or their colleagues out of a job.
2. People are willing to make their knowledge available through the electronic network to support everybody's learning experiences.
3. Applications software and personal database software are read-

ily available, so that the high-performance individuals can rapidly accumulate knowledge developed by others.

4. People have a tolerance for exploratory inquiries. Even brilliant
individuals may ask "stupid" questions as they search for answers.

5. The person who does the job should know more about it than
anybody else. Know-how is distributed as needed, rather than
hoarded by experts in order to require consultations with them
in every case.

6. There is an electronic "bulletin board" for reporting about learning experiences, so that the same mistakes need not be made
repeatedly. New versions of software incorporate the latest improvements in expertise and are used as one of the means for
accumulating collective learning. In this way knowledge can
gradually be transformed into information capital that can be
effectively shared rather than wasted through the expense of
repeated errors.

7. Communications networks are available that allow high-performance individuals to make the most of their own information
technology choices. This adds diversity to learning and makes
the sharing of unique accomplishments possible.

**Users exhibit a consciousness of tradition about the information sys-
tem.**

High-performance individuals reinforce morale by recounting
events about the origins of projects and about all sorts of difficulties
in achieving results. A visitor is treated to stories which, on the surface,
are irrelevant except to those immersed fully in their work. In one
laboratory I am always told about the time when the chief engineer
disconnected the power source during a critical customer demonstration. In another organization potential customers are given an
elaborate explanation about the origins of the commercial name of a
product which is derived from their president's unmentionable noctur-
nal experience ten years ago, but which everyone still recalls with
glee. From anthropology we know that a tribe's sense of identity cannot
survive without legends. When I visit a new site and listen to all
sorts of computer tales drawn from recent local experience I know
that a high-performing group is operating there.

High-performance users discover unpredictable new capabilities.

It continually amazes me to discover what high-performance people can do with systems which were originally designed to serve completely different purposes. I know that I have run into a high-performance environment when I am told how the organization avoided buying expensive equipment by managing to do the same job with available devices of greater simplicity. One of the principal reasons why personal computers have penetrated the office and laboratories so rapidly can be traced to a similar phenomenon. The early personal computers made it easy to expand the circuitry and to add software. When these devices became available at a relatively low cost, the creativity of high-performing individuals blossomed forth. The unprecedented growth in microcomputer applications is due to the strong attachment to them on the part of high-performance individuals who have found it attractive to channel their unused imagination into these highly adaptive and instantly responsive machines.

High-performance users will add to and elaborate upon the initial features of their electronic systems.

Under favorable conditions users will invent a variety of conventions, shortcuts, signaling, and filing methods which will improve the capacity of their system to do new work. Such small inventions are a sure sign that the technology has captured the imagination and creativity of people who thus become high-performance individuals.

If every display in the entire department is identical and if a procedure manual describes everything that is done, then the heavy hand of regimented control can be suspected. Any excessively controlled environment will repel high-performance people; those few who remain will apply their energies to bypassing the system.

High-performance people will extract from electronic systems levels of performance that the designers might have considered unfeasible.

High-performance technology evolves when the manufacturers find ways of harnessing the talents of their high-performance users to influence product design. Information technology is never pushed to its limits by the development engineers themselves because successful vendor organizations play it safe, launching their products without excessive risks. It is the users who stretch the equipment in ways in which product planners could not imagine. One can spot high-performance users when one finds them addressing well-reasoned recommendations to the equipment suppliers.

High-performance people develop new applications and find new uses for old applications.

Counting product improvement suggestions is a sure way of locating high-performance people. Experimentation and a continuous stream of small, qualitative improvements are the best signs of strong employee commitment to excellence. Many years ago I was responsible for operating a central billing system which was so complex that even minute changes could be made only in carefully staged modifications grouped six to eight months apart. All improvements were preempted by emergency changes dictated by central financial management. As a consequence, high-performance people diverted their energies into more responsive efforts, such as costly time-sharing applications which bypassed the central systems. An information system on which hundreds of administrative people depend every day cannot tolerate a one-year lead time between suggestion and implementation. The exodus of its high-performance talent left the central billing system in a condition of permanent disarray.

The great attraction of decision-support software, of inquiry languages, and of decentralized databases comes from their easy adaptability to local experimentation and from their rapid responsiveness to small incremental improvements. High-performance individuals will migrate to workplaces where they have access to time-sharing terminals, to personal computers, and to information centers: they are unwilling to remain working where their ability to make improvements is limited by cumbersome procedure.

High-performance individuals will find their computer work aesthetically pleasing.

The adjectives "beautiful," "neat," and even "sexy" are sometimes applied to computer applications. This serves as a clue that creative and imaginative thought has been applied to finding a particularly clever solution. Aesthetic experiences do not always call for color displays, high-resolution screens, or laser printouts. Aesthetic experiences in the use of computers arise when a person discovers something worthwhile, or when a job is completed more efficiently by applying imagination to it. This sense is more like what one feels after finishing a good, competitive game than like the experience of finally cleaning up a messy office. Observing a pleasant relief of tensions, a surprise and enthusiasm upon completion of a task involving information technology, one may surmise that a high-performance individual found an aesthetically satisfying resolution to a problem.

The design of an information system to serve high-performance workers differs from the design needed by others.

Culture, education, and background have conditioned people to overemphasize one preferred method of communication over another. I know accountants who deal only with columns of numbers. To these people any graphic representation of the trends conveyed by these numbers is not at all useful. I know marketing people who can recall only spoken words, preferably as rephrased by themselves. They will disregard the identical information if it is presented in a book. Then there are artistically inclined individuals whose perception of the world is stimulated only by color, shape, or music. They will be largely oblivious to names, numbers, or printed messages. It matters a great deal whether a system is designed for people with a numbers-, artistic-, or verbal bias. So far only high-performance people who can channel their work through numbers, graphics, and text are supported by office automation technology. The inadequacy of the present technology to deal with verbal communications is a major hindrance to serving most of the information-handling needs of high-performance executive and marketing people.

In a similar fashion significant differences can be found in how people deal with business information. Some clerks can pick up scraps of conversation, recognize the key phrases in a thick report, and then come up with the right answer. These are high-performance office workers. In contrast, there are others who can solve only those problems for which they can follow a precise procedure. If any sources of information are incomplete, or if their instructions do not fit the situation precisely, they cannot deal with the situation at all. When designing office information systems it makes a big difference whether they are to be used by high-performance workers or not.

Computers serving high-performance workers differ from others in their technical features.

High-performance individuals employ a broad range of formats in the use of their electronic workstations. Symbolic, procedural, analytical, and numerical information are mixed into text, graphic, and pictorial forms. The pattern on such screens will be adapted to individual situations, rather than using a limited number of techniques, such as menus, tables, or pie charts. Such workers are likely to be the first to use color screens. If their machines include a small speaker they will experiment with instructions explaining how to generate audio signals, thus overcoming the absence of sound, which is one of the major current limitations of computers. High-performance workers will always be at the leading edge of computer technology and will demand the greatest possible number of technical features. This is why it is very important for a manufacturer to know who his customers are. The manufacturer's research and development laboratories, which are likely to be strongholds for high-performance personnel, are just about the last place where product planning should be done—except when the products are destined for other, similar laboratories.

The educational needs of high-performance workers differ from those of others.

High-performance individuals detest attending formal classes to learn about a new software package. They expect the software to possess just enough indicators to allow them to search for the right instructions. The do not actually remember computer instructions except for the ones needed to get them started, since they insist on having all options represented visually as they go along. Such individuals do not study computer manuals: they just keep them for reference as a last resort, when everything else fails.

The high-performance individuals will be inclined to start utilizing the retrieval capabilities of computers for changing their approaches to acquiring new knowledge. They discover quickly that recognition from clues and from prompted symbols is a vastly superior cognitive process to having to remember specific instructions. Phone numbers of friends, appointment schedules, bibliographies, follow-up checklists, customer contacts, promises, proposals, and so forth will gradually be placed in their electronic files—becoming, as it were, indispensable extensions of themselves. Such a symbiotic existence will become apparent when an individual suddenly asserts an irresistible need for a portable computer and for telephone access to his electronic files at all times.

The low-performance individual views the computer predominantly as a tool for doing arithmetic fast and for typing repetitious letters. The machine remains a separate entity, completely apart from his person. By contrast, the high-performance individual will embrace the powers of the workstation and of networks as means to self-enhancement.

High-performance users develop a very personal way for evaluating performance.

The number of insurance policies processed per day will not satisfy a high-performance individual as a measure of accomplishment. Programmers will scoff at lines of code per month as a reflection of their skills. The sheer number of design drawings generated by an engineer on a plotting device will not be appreciated as an adequate indication of the value of the designs. Good people will not accept simple production counts as a measure of performance.

Such people are a source of continuous irritation to supervisors wishing to impose standard quantitative measures as a way of simplifying their management job. High-performance individuals can be spotted by their advocacy of personalized approaches to evaluation of their performance. The chances are that exceptional people will impose much tougher goals on themselves than anyone else would dare to propose. They can also be recognized because they venture to suggest qualitative objectives related to the purposes of the entire organization rather than just to their own work. Computer-monitored clock times or automatic counts of items processed through the computer may be useful as one of the measurement standards, provided that the high-performance individuals do their own checking—or that they participate in the setup of the monitoring schemes.[2] Computerized monitoring without employee agreement discourages high performance.

High-performance people redesign their jobs. Their career growth takes place through *work enlargement*.

High-performance individuals use information technology as a means of doing new tasks by means of aids incorporated in their software. This allows them to apply specialized know-how that otherwise would require them to pass work on to experts or to subject themselves to extensive training.

One of the primary objectives of information technology is to eliminate boring and low-wage jobs so that people can gradually be repositioned to perform work which increases their value. High-performance people can act as the catalyst which sustains the chain reaction involved in upgrading their own work while creating opportunities for others to move up as well. The standard of living is not increased by employing people to do work which can be done less expensively by other means. For instance, the full cost of a person actually entering data on a key-punch is close to $20 per hour. No wonder so many organizations export such work to low-wage countries. Yet computerized optical scanners make it possible to do the identical work for about $1 per hour—far below the total costs from any low-wage country—while creating new jobs commanding wages much higher than those of key-punch operators. Our entire history of economic and social progress has followed the pattern of high-performance labor generating increased value, thus allowing everyone to advance by making obsolete labor which nobody could afford anymore.

There are some who see high-performance individuals as the leading edge which will ultimately eliminate most office activities by means of automation. In order to protect jobs, they propose that the currently unrestrained thrust for increased productivity should be confined, so that high wages would prevail even for unaffordable office work. Given such a policy, it is clear that high-performance individuals would have to be constrained first. This restrictionist view is based on doubts as to whether sufficient new amounts of high-value work can be created to yield an improved mix of high-value occupations. We must recognize that the fact that high-performance individuals are an important means for stimulating gains through job restructuring has begun to cause deep anxieties. Superior performers may not be welcome in some organizations—and could become undesirables under certain restrictive conditions. Clearly, seen only from the standpoint of a high-performance individual, their personal perspective how organizations should utilize their talents is inadequate. The high-performance information worker, then, represents a serious challenge to the hierarchical organization, which stifles attempts at work enlargement through position descriptions, departmental charters, job classifications, and procedure manuals. The successful introduction of information technology will tend to magnify the conflicts between high-performance people and the traditional organization unless the hierarchy recognizes that electronic networks offer new options for maintaining unified goals while maximizing the contributions of their high-performance people.

In the electronic age, the work of the high-performance individual becomes more abstract as it gains in global scope.

The physical environment of concern to the hunter was highly localized, but his personal experience while hunting was very rich in sensations and relationships. The physical environment of the farmer extended beyond his village perhaps only to the nearest town. The physical environment of concern to industrial man evolved to include the national state, while his factory experience became totally confining.

The physical environment of the information worker is highly artificial, yet physically not restrictive—no matter where he may find himself on the globe. He takes similar elevators to spend the day in similar offices and then sleeps in similar hotels. Work becomes an abstraction in the form of the interoffice memorandum, the electronic financial transaction, the slide presentation and the computer conference. All of these are symbols which may have no relation to real events. The order clerk may never see the supplier or his factory. The dispatcher may never get to know any of the drivers or the pilots. The executive may never observe customers using his products. There may be ten intermediaries between the banker approving the loan and the person who misuses the money he receives, creating an uncollectible debt.

The high-performance individual who is successfully attuned to the electronic workplace possesses a conceptual outlook which is extremely rich in information and may encompass the entire world. Such a person is also likely to be psychologically somewhat distant from physical reality. The opportunities for gain as well as misuse are thus greatly magnified: the high-performance individual may use the same work style for fraud as for constructive achievement. This is why one of the primary tasks of information-age organizations is to devise institutions that diminish the remoteness and the estrangement of their high-performance individuals from the people they are to serve. I think that the ultimate outcome of this desired direction will be to place high-performance individuals in small teams which have well-defined and tightly connected personal relationships with their immediate customers. Information technology and electronic networks make this objective feasible.

The ultimate evolutionary step of the high-performance individual is to create an object in his own image: an abstract-symbol manipulator, which might also be known as the "intelligent" computer. High-performance computer people are emotionally attracted to "artificial intelligence" and to "expert systems" as a highly satisfying way of achieving a kind of immortality for their thoughts. To channel all of this creative

energy into constructive uses will require a less abstract workplace—
placing high-performance people in positions which allow them to
deliver valuable services directly.

———————

It is not the suppliers of information technology who deliver the
results from automation. In each organization there is a group of
individuals—the high-performance people—who are the agents of
change. It is they who facilitate the transformation which takes full
advantage of computers. This chapter has tried to find out more about
the characteristics of these innovators and about how to understand
them better.

PART II

THE
ORGANIZATION'S
PERSPECTIVE

5

The Economics of Office Work

Installing information technology in the office environment involves a much greater expense than just buying a workstation to be placed on a desk. Extensive resources are required to support an electronic workstation before it can be put to productive use. The most costly elements of such support are not technological but organizational. This fact has far-reaching implications for the ways that information-technology investments should be managed.

The Economics of Information Technology Tools

Computer technology is like the energy crisis in reverse: Imagine suddenly paying \$.35 for something which used to cost \$350 ten years ago and \$35 five years ago.[1]

Authors of just about every popular book on computer technology include graphs showing declining costs of semiconductors, reduced expenses for computer memory and astronomical increases in computer processing power. Such dramatic reductions in cost are unprecedented.

Their scientific and engineering causes are well understood. What is not adequately appreciated is the value of all of these inexpensive technologies. As in the case of cheap coal or ample oil, which lay useless for the first 40,000 years of man's history, the issue is not whether a cell of magnetic memory costs $.001 or $.000001. The only valid way of looking at the economics of information technology is in terms of its utility. The declining costs of information technology are only relevant insofar as they enhance the value of other resources. Since computers cannot be consumed, they do not have any intrinsic worth, regardless of price: They are just metal, glass, and plastics.

There has been an academic debate for a number of years whether information is an economic "good" in the same sense as land, labor, and capital, or whether it is something completely unique, since it does not behave like any of the other factors of production.[2] The matter can be resolved by taking a pragmatic view. When it comes to making decisions about information technology, I will always consider the competitive market price to be the final arbiter. This is why I will not discuss semiconductor costs any further. Even though falling technology prices are a welcome development, the critical variable is management's ability to use the new equipment to extract economic benefit. It is fallacious to reason that cheap computer power automatically makes it desirable to use a great deal of it. Investments in information technology must meet the same criteria of justification as any other investments. The demand for increased productivity, the need to restore falling profits, and the desire to improve responsiveness to customer needs are the driving forces behind office automation.

Payoffs are realized by managing the benefits. Costs are important, but secondary.

The most frequently used reasoning to justify purchases of information technology goes as follows: (A) Labor expenses are high and getting higher. (B) Computer expenses are low and getting lower. (C) It then follows that one should trade the expensive commodity— i.e., labor—for an inexpensive commodity (in this case, computers).

On the surface, this simple reasoning leads to apparently inescapable conclusions. Let us examine the argument a bit closer by analyzing its lucid representation in the accompanying table.

The central message is that a rapidly declining payout ratio makes the purchase of information technology increasingly attractive. At 11% of labor cost in 1990, it should be much easier to achieve payoff from

Payout Ratio for Workstation (dollars/year)

	1970	1980	1990
Technology Cost	$ 9,100	$ 8,600	$ 5,600
Labor Cost	$10,000	$20,000	$50,000
Payout Ratio	91%	43%	11%
Capability	Dumb Terminal	Microcomputer	Desktop Mainframe

Source: R. I. Benjamin, "Payout Ratios Measure Rapid Change in I.S. Role," *Information Systems News,* May 16, 1983, p. 27. Used by permission.

an investment than in 1970, when the payout ratio was 91%. Interestingly, the threshold of financial pain for making office automation investments is not lowered primarily by the 38% reduction in the annual workstation expenses—from $9,100 to $5,600. It is the increased inclusion of expensive professionals and managers in the labor cost, against which savings are counted, which makes the entire proposition so attractive. The payout ratio improves because the labor costs considered eligible for automation are up by 500%. If we consider the lowered technology costs as the supply side and the potential displacement of more expensive managerial and professional labor as the demand side of the payout ratio, it is clear that the investment decision on the use of information technology is dictated primarily by our ability to manage the demand side. Payoff becomes a matter of managing the realization of benefits rather than simply cashing in on lower computer prices.

It is ironic that when one observes how information-technology projects are managed, it is the supply side which always receives the most intensive attention and voluminous documentation.[3] As a general observation I would say that an office automation proposal of a hundred pages spends over ninety pages discussing technical matters and devotes only a part of what is left to an explanation of the expected benefits and how the savings would be delivered. Management's attention to the investment proposal is usually apportioned inversely to the costs and risks involved. Technical matters, consuming the most time, deal with relatively tangible purchases, with costs that can be defined and controlled. Benefits, covered by a few general statements full of hope about the effects on large labor costs, deal with intangible expectations which cannot easily be defined.

Management should not merely ask how information technology will operate. Supply-side matters are secondary. Management should examine how changed patterns of office work can be expected to deliver the promised benefits. Demand-side matters are what count from now on.

A Workstation for the Knowledge Worker

What sits on the desk represents just the down payment.

The economics of providing a workstation to managerial and professional personnel are far more complex than making a simple decision concerning the purchase of an electronic appliance or a machine tool.

Less than 20% of the total first-year cost of equipping an administrator or professional with a workstation involves equipment expense. In this case equipment depreciation includes five-year amortization of an $8,000 device, plus maintenance charges. Since an $8,000 device is not fully adequate to support the office applications needed by administrators and professionals, the personal workstation must draw on such shared resources as departmental files and high-performance printers. The individual must also have access to communications controllers in order to communicate with others in the building or outside. Costs are also incurred in purchasing such items as paper, local magnetic storage disks, print wheels, and cabling.

For a workstation to be useful, it must be in contact with other people as well as other networks. Telecommunications expenses of at least $1,500 include not only telephone line and instrument charges, but also the rental of access devices, access charges to networks, and costs for using electronic mail services. Computer-time charges for central computation and for central database services are included, even though these can easily exceed the $200–$600 per person per month that I have estimated.

Software purchases are estimated at only $1,000 per year in Figure 5.1, which assumes large-scale purchases shared among network participants. This figure is highly conservative. It is software, not hardware, that generates economic payoff. To create the environment favored by high-performance people requires open-ended experimentation with a variety of applications.

The estimate of first-year workstation technology costs of $6,000 is, then, understated. There are many organizations that reduce initial office automation costs by providing only limited capabilities—they buy very simple data terminals or underpowered, standalone micro-

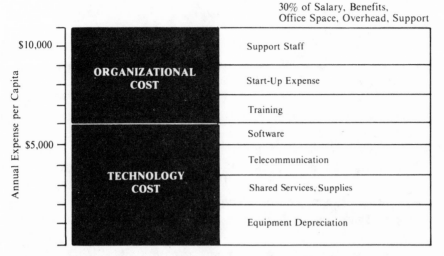

Figure 5.1   First-Year Cost of Workstation for Administrator, Professional (1981–83)

computers. If, however, major improvements in the productivity of managerial and professional employees are expected, then the $6,000 technology expense is at the low end of the range (for 1981–83 technologies) and could well be closer to $10,000–12,000 per person if all shared network costs for central computing are fully allocated to each advanced user.

It takes high costs in low-tech to make high-tech equipment function at all.

All of this presumes that no unusual expenses are incurred in improving office illumination, in rewiring the site for additional electric power, in increasing the amount of air conditioning, in providing improved acoustics in the office to reduce the noise generated by the new equipment. If the workstation is installed in a typical manager's office with a standard desk, chances are that none of the furniture will be suitable for any extended stay in front of the VDU. A few years ago I found that the only place I could install my new and expensive wide-screen terminal was to place it on top of my marble-topped rosewood credenza. After a few weeks I wore off the stripes on my pants around the knees and had to start doing exercises to relieve my aching back. An additional allowance of anywhere from

$2,000 to $20,000 per person may have to be made to take care of the necessary office space and office furniture improvements.

Dollar estimates in information technology proposals are often considered not comparable with each other.

I have reviewed many budget proposals justifying investments in computer technology. They are usually backed up by elaborate feasibility studies to give them credibility. At least 80% of the cost schedules of these studies are devoted to the elaborate examination of features of computer equipment that will account for less than 20% of the total cost. For instance, equipment components are priced with great precision according to every stock item contained in the vendor's catalogue.

Shared services are given minimum attention, since they are considered to be fixed expenses. When considered at all, they are treated as an estimated percentage factor applied to the costs of the purchases. Software and telecommunications estimates are rounded off to the nearest large number.

What receives the least analysis are the largest costs: those directly related to making the technology function and deliver its benefits. Office automation projects are dominated by user costs, or what I will call organization costs.

Except for out-of-pocket fees, like those paid for consultants, training, travel and so forth, organization costs are disregarded because the time of the people who are expected to use the technology is seen as a fixed labor expense. Including such costs would presume prior knowledge of the extent of the user's involvement, and the degree to which the business would be disrupted. There are even deeper-lying biases involved in the way office automation investment estimates are prepared. Computers, terminals, programming, and software can be isolated and classified within the conventional accounting system as one-of-a-kind investments. People, however, are regarded as an "ongoing" expense. One does not mix investment numbers with expense numbers, especially if the entire project is compartmentalized into different organizational units. The net effect is that most managements will probably never find out the full actual costs of an information-technology project. Public-sector accounting and fiscal-appropriation practices guarantee that full information-technology costs will remain unknown.

Organizational Costs

Technology is inexpensive and is getting more so. The people using it cost the most money.[4]

In Figure 5.1 I understated the $5,000 organizational cost for the first year of placing an administrator or a professional in a computer networking environment. The estimated number is based on the assumption that perfection will prevail and that the project will succeed exactly as planned. What contributes to the higher organizational costs which prevail in the real world?

Initial training, which could take an average of between three and six days, plus supplemental on-the-job training—extending over a period of more than a month to acquire operational competence—can easily add up to $1,500 per person. The initial training cost includes the salaries of the trainees as well as the costs of the trainers and of the training facilities.

Start-up expense is conservatively estimated at $1,500 per person; it covers a broad range of costs hidden in general overhead and those incurred by lowered productivity while making the transition from the old methods to the new electronic environment. This latter item includes inefficiencies in serving customer needs by new and unfamiliar means; job interruptions caused by a lack of familiarity with new procedures; time spent in meetings with the peer group to negotiate changes in the handling of work; general management counselling and resolution of personnel questions affecting employee morale. The allowance of $1,500 is likely to be the lowest estimate that is acceptable for a well-run organization.

$2,000 per person is budgeted for external support staff activities. The introduction of electronic workstations requires the involvement of consultants, central staffs, and all sorts of project-support personnel. Virtually unlimited amounts of staff time can be consumed in computerization of managerial and professional work. Organizational studies, methods analysis, security reviews, audit verification, and temporary assistance during conversion always seem to be needed to assist in the transition from manual office work.

All this adds up to a sum of $11,000 per capita in first-year organizational and technology costs to bring a typical administrator or professional efficiently into the electronic environment. This sum exceeds 30% of the average annual wage and salary costs for such personnel.

Just to break even in the first year, in other words, we would need to improve each individual's productivity by at least 30%. Productivity improvements of 30% for administrators and professionals are hard to measure; therefore, it is hard to know if they have been acheived. This does not even consider any of the obvious risks, such as runaway organizational costs obliterating favorable economic returns. This is why short payback periods are desirable for all initial office automation investments.

From a risk-management standpoint, then, organizational costs are by far the most critical investment item. If a computerization project gets out of control, its technology costs are always controllable and cannot exceed a well-defined limit. Under adverse conditions the organizational costs are not so easily controllable. Organizational costs do not have a recognizable upper limit. In the event of a failure, such as in the case of a major job dispute, organizational costs will exceed technology costs by a large margin. Damage to customer service may be the greatest expense of all—one that will never show up explicitly in any investment analysis. Organized labor is becoming keenly aware of this. It is learning about the negotiating leverage that mismanaged office automation projects can provide.

One of the most constructive ways to assist in proper planning of computer projects is to make available data about elements of organizational expense, based on past experience. For instance, the costs of systems support for "hand-holding" and for technical assistance can be determined from carefully monitored test installations. Realistic training-time estimates are mandatory. There is a great deal of information that ought to be made available by pooling data about training experiences under a variety of conditions. Such benchmark information should be of great value to organizations contemplating major information-technology investments.

Most importantly, the risks of runaway organizational costs due to technical system failures cannot be tolerated. This is why information-technology managers who are risk averse will usually prevail. In this environment a company which is conservative in technical innovation but respected for its dedication to quality service will receive the higher market share. Conservatives in the information-technology race will outlast even high-performance risk-takers. Given enough attempts, the game of "Russian roulette" becomes a deadly certainty. In other words, if service to customers is affected, the economics of information technology is unforgiving to even small failures.

My greatest concern is with the risks of runaway organizational costs due to management failures—failures in the proper direction of information-technology investments. Management cannot delegate this task to information-technology proponents, neither to their own computer experts nor, certainly, to the equipment vendors. I am dismayed to see how often executives have become imprudent gamblers with computer projects on the mistaken assumption that spending money in this glamorous area will somehow deliver favorable results. The high-risk element comes from their failure to get a full accounting from their people about all of their exposures on the benefit side of the investment. I believe that the time is coming when the investment conservatives will gain confidence that even this strange new electronic world is manageable. This discovery will evolve from painful experiences which prove that the fundamentals of good management apply as much to the economics of information work as to the economics of manufactured products. The principles of using investments to generate improved results should not be compromised by blind faith in the miracles of information technology.

Organizational Learning

The cost of any labor-intensive activity will tend to rise faster than the general rate of inflation. Only accumulated experience in making good use of capital investments (rather than avoiding them) can compensate for this trend.

Due to heavy initial organizational costs, the benefits from most investments in information technology can be realized only in the long run. One way to avoid the wait for the long-term results is not to invest at all. There is always a temptation to defer the acquisition of information technology in order to take advantage of the well-advertised declining prices of computer circuits. According to this theory, the current trend of a 50% unit cost reduction for semiconductors every time their production volume doubles should lead to an almost risibly shrunken cost of hardware. Actually, this is not true, because computer systems also contain electromechanical components, such as keyboards, printers, and disk drives. Systems also include software. None of these decrease in cost as rapidly as semiconductors. These trends are noted in Figure 5.2.

Totally conservative reasoning, advocating indefinite deferral of investments in information technology projects, is simply fallacious.

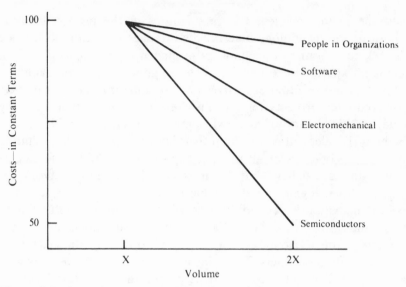

Figure 5.2   Experience-Curve Effects by Activity

As a matter of fact, such an approach will worsen the overall investment economics of a given concern, since the contribution of components, such as memory and logic, represents less than 5% of the total
cost of a system. Inflation in labor costs is clearly a factor of vastly
greater importance.

The economics of the various elements making up a $10,000 per
capita budget reveals not only the overwhelming importance of organizational costs (made up entirely of labor expense), but also the important differences in how varying rates of cost decline will influence
the payoff from an office automation program.

The shrinking importance of semiconductor costs will continue
to determine the capability of workstation devices. My Master's thesis
was completed in 1955 on a computer with the then-unbelievable storage capacity of 200 binary circuits. By 1960 I graduated to machines
whose memory was bought in 16,000-unit increments. In 1970 I considered the purchase of one million characters of memory a merely routine
decision. This book was written on a personal computer with the
computing capacity of the entire data center I managed in 1968. The
50% cost-decline curve doubles every year because competition in
the semiconductor business is both worldwide and intense. Every year,
demand for improved capacity to get the jobs done doubles as well.
There is not much to be gained from waiting.

Some cost reductions can be realized by waiting for electromechani-

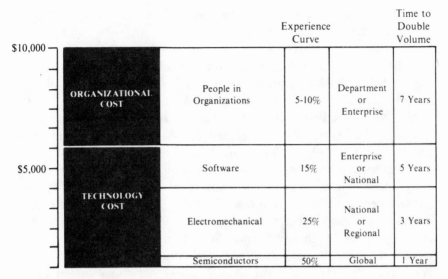

Figure 5.3   Experience-Curve Effects on Costs

cal component and software costs to come down 15%–25% every three to five years. None of these gains in technology will offset inflationary cost increases suffered while procrastinating.

What matters in realizing a long-term payoff from information technology are the gains from people who have learned how to work more effectively. This takes a long time to accomplish. The gradual decline in organizational costs can be measured by the equivalent of the components' learning curve. I call it the organizational learning-, or organizational experience curve. The key variable in information technology projects is the length of the implementation schedule— the time needed until net savings start flowing. Time is the critical ingredient of success. One should never procrastinate in getting on with organizational learning unless labor costs are declining dramatically.

The organizational-cost learning curve is inherently flat—perhaps not more than 5%–10% per year—because learning experiences are usually confined to isolated organizational units, such as to departments or plants. It is difficult to double experience if one starts small and remains small. Occasionally a project with a national or even an international scope is proposed as a way of accelerating the payoffs. These giant projects succeed only under the most unusual conditions. The essentially small and local scale of office automation projects dictates that the approach to implementation be slow and gradual.

Management's primary mission is coping with organizational rather than with technological issues.

The rate of decline in organizational costs is also low because we are dealing with changing interpersonal relationships, with altering the division of labor, with reassigning office tasks, and, frequently, with a subtle redistribution of power. In order for the first year's new organizational costs to be minimized, organizational learning must proceed without substantial organizational conflict.

Inflationary labor-cost increases have equalled or exceeded realistically achievable targets for organizational learning. To escape the squeeze between labor-cost inflation and the limitations isolated organizations experience in transforming themselves, I advocate greater learning investments in the workplace. Such capital would help overcome the effects of small-scale office automation by rapid sharing of experience from already-successful sites. I think that the solution to the problem of accelerated organizational learning lies in person-to-person contacts by means of electronic networks, in electronic conferences which allow the people with experience to share their knowledge with novices, in on-line tutorials, and in on-line user support, rather than in the more traditional forms of classroom education.

Under no circumstances should projected future declines in information technology costs be given as an excuse for deferring profitable office automation projects. If the projects are proceeding too slowly, management should see to it that big doses of organizational learning modelled on previous patterns of success—not just technology—are injected into the process.

Unit Costs vs. Per Capita Costs

Reduced unit costs of technology do not necessarily result in reduced per capita costs.

My estimate of the expenses incurred in the first year of automation did not include any elements which will increase with time. For every reduction in workstation prices there will be a corresponding increase in the use of remote services. Increased experience generates a greater transaction volume. Information volume has always grown as costs have come down. The costs of processing the increased volume have exceeded the cost reductions realized from better science and engineering. I foresee no change in this phenomenon.

I do not trust current projections showing that the total costs of information technology, per person, can be expected to decrease. As a matter of fact, a tenfold growth in information-industry revenues over the growth in information-worker population is a sign that per capita expenses for information technology are growing very fast. This should not discourage purchasing agents from buying less expensive personal computers. I do not wish to suggest that computer-center managers should lessen their zeal in fine-tuning their processing capacity for handling increased volumes of transactions at lower per unit costs. Better information processing power, at lowered prices, will continue to be available. But per capita costs of information technology and associated organizational costs will gain steadily; fifteen years from now they may exceed one-third of the payroll dollars paid to their users. There will be no reduction in the total expense of information technology as a result of decreased unit costs for electronic components.

How to Improve Organizational Learning

If information-technology use is not learned adequately, the technology itself has only the negligible value of its materials.

Creating an environment in which high-performance individuals flourish is certainly the right goal for an innovative organization. Large reductions in training expense can be realized.

Geographic and organizational limitations to sharing know-how is the reason why it takes so long to double experience. Learning time can be dramatically reduced by an organizational design which balances decentralization with efficient use of shared resources. Shared databases, creation of industry-wide cooperative projects, global division of labor, and the relaxation of regulatory interference are just a few of the many ways in which the free flow of information about successful experiences can aid purely local efforts.

Misplaced emphasis on locally developed technology may decrease its overall effectiveness. For instance, many schools, with their limited budgets, have purchased personal computers in order to offer modern teaching tools for their pupils. Little effort was given to training teachers or to changing the curriculum so that the computer equipment could be absorbed into the existing educational process. Teachers were left on their own initiative to find out how the computers could be usefully employed. It takes a great deal of experience and time to integrate computer techniques into a traditional curriculum. Enthusiastic dedication is of course desirable, but it is insufficient of itself to achieve good results. For instance, numerical methods employed in mathematics may have a great bearing on teaching physics. Without the necessary sharing of experiences and without adequate resources to invest in a new, coordinated teaching program, the introduction of improved methods will be unnecessarily delayed.

At the other end of the spectrum, a few countries concentrate exclusively on electronics—disregarding their backwardness in business applications, their inadequate workforce training, and their severely lagging productivity. There are several countries which are pursuing a determined and costly effort to build up their own fully integrated national computer industry. In the absence of a sufficiently large domestic market—and given the glut of international competition in this area—demand for some of these technologies is very small. The time needed for such countries' experience curves to double will be so extended that they may never catch up with their foreign rivals. While forcing locally-made computer products upon their domestic industry at inflated prices, and devoting precious talent to the achievement of this single-purpose technical objective, such nations pay little or no attention to promotion of user application-sharing and computer-installation knowledge. This policy has produced small, exorbitantly expensive domestic industries, shipping overpriced computers to public sector organizations which are notorious for lack of know-how in applying information technology effectively. Instead of concentrating exclusively on developing an independent supply of hardware, such countries could well have made more balanced investments in improving their domestic computer applications. Greater gains would have come from the improved productivity of their information workforce by spending modest funds to promote the sharing of applications knowledge and from management training.

Organizational learning is also improved by giving employees incentives to acquire knowledge on their own, rather than under complete company control. Sending employees to classes, especially if this is done entirely on the company's time at a company training center, is about the most expensive, least effective way of promoting the desired learning. For the convenience of educators, courses tend to be offered only in standard modules so as to attain the right student/instructor ratio. As in the tale of Procrustes, laggards will be painfully stretched and potential overachievers will be cut down to size so as to fit the standard teaching plan. Scheduling economies (based on classroom capacity) will also dictate that learning takes place in the company of total strangers.

Organizational learning involving the application of information technology takes place best within the work group. One of the lasting favorable impressions I gained from my many visits to Japan is the presence of a blackboard and a table in the corner of most offices. The entire section which gathers there frequently is not necessarily receiving a pep talk or having a conference. More often than not, they are just deeply engaged in a brief and ongoing training exercise—including all of their supervisors.

The use of computers is a technical skill only to a very limited extent. Increasingly it is a shared organizational capability. I do not know of a better way of speeding up organizational learning than to have people who work together learn together as well. This, of course, should not exclude opportunities for individual remedial learning, or for individuals to pursue their own work enlargement ambitions through supplemental education. I consider the recent wage settlement between the Communications Workers of America and the American Telephone and Telegraph Company a noteworthy milestone in labor–management relations.[5] It provides for a sizeable, jointly administered education fund to give workers technical training of a sort not necessarily related to their existing jobs. The effect of the new fund should be far-reaching, because it pays only for direct training costs. The workers' own education time is not compensated.

Organizational Learning vs. Individual Learning

The system should fit people, not the other way around.

Frequent efforts are made to reduce organizational learning costs through standardization of all means of communication. There are equally valid reasons to enhance individual learning through customizing the devices which a person uses. I have seen many examples of the forced approach to uniformity which claim the sharing of learning experiences as their objective. There is a high price to be paid for such standardization, because the pace of business is just too fast to tolerate uniformity for everyone. For people to be productive—at the peak of their potential—greater adaptation to their personal style in the handling of information is required.

The need for variety in meeting rapidly evolving business needs can be seen in the enormous diversity of manufacturers' products. So far there has been no standardization in the ways various computers present themselves to their users. No vendor can truthfully claim universal desk-to-desk workstation compatibility in communications.

The purpose of shared learning is to reduce the costs of people, not the costs of computers.

A personal computer is and should remain uniquely and permanently atuned to the habits of its user. Every person will develop his own habits: how to communicate, which buttons to use, and how to advance from one application to another. From time to time I watch people who have the same personal computer as I do. In many important details their machine is really a reflection of how they apply it and how their software library evolved. An information worker should certainly not have to change all of these acquired habits whenever a change in technology takes place. Imbedded within each machine should be software which performs the necessary translation from local, highly individualized attributes to the standards necessary for an organization to function as a coherent whole. Experience sharing should not be forced as a means to minimize the costs of technology. The purpose of sharing organizational learning is to reduce *organizational* costs. Since the value of a person's accumulated knowledge in dealing with information technology normally exceeds the price of a personal conversion device, the emergence of special computers acting as personal interpreters may well be next on the agenda. Such machines would make it possible for people to preserve their own idiosyncrasies even in an externally standardized electronic environment.

At present much is heard about the need for an industry-wide compatible microprocessor which would allow the use of an extensive library of application programs. The assumption is that the technical costs of installing a new application will be lower when dealing with a computer whose operating system can use widely available software. This emphasis does not recognize that by far the greatest expense in using a microcomputer lies in the gradual modification of a user's behavior: adapting computer routines to his job and adding new applications to an already-existing repertoire of personal skills.

Soon microcomputers will have adequate computing power to handle all application programs regardless of which operating system they have been designed for. The principal problem will not be with the internal logic of the system, but with the way the computer presents itself to the user and vice versa. A user should not have to apply completely different commands to search for a word in his own text file or to locate it in a central library. The access procedures to a global network should not be different just because each service has been designed for different purposes. A person of low verbal accomplishment should not have to use the same instructions to operate a software package as a person with a sophisticated command of the language.

The key distinction among microcomputers of the future will not be their processor, their operating system, or their internal language, but the characteristics by which they maintain the link between their master and his electronic world. The term "portability of applications" nowadays means the easy technical transfer of application codes from one machine to another in order to preserve the software investment. In the future, "portability" will mean the easy transfer of a person's acquired habits, as well as his language patterns, from one machine to another. The purpose of such portability will be to preserve a person's acquired capacity to deal with the electronic environment. Competition among computer manufacturers of the future will shift from computing features to the ease with which individuals will be able to compound their computer-accumulated learning, over their entire lifetime, without losses due to changes in the underlying technology. In the same way that individuals develop a personality over a lifetime, users will acquire and cultivate a personal "computer shadow." It will represent the style in which they have learned to carry on electronic communications. The "computer shadow" will consist of individualized codes and instructions that will be the users' interface with the electronic world wherever they may go.

If organizations are to share experiences electronically, the individuals concerned must have a common language.[6] Database specialists, telecommunications protocol administrators, and software librarians are the prime agents for accelerating the distribution of such information. To create the right environment for sharing organizational learning, new standards for access to information sources are necessary. In the same way that present efforts to achieve network compatibility rely on layers of codes to separate electronic signalling from electronic addressing, it will be useful to devise a completely new set of procedures to separate information about individual linguistic habits from electronic pulses carrying the message itself. Electronic networks of the future will have to mediate between people who come from different cultures and who possess different levels of skill in coping with electronic messages. Our present level of concern about man–machine communications across different applications- and skill levels is quite primitive, in my opinion.

In the future we will discover that managing organizational costs has become the dominant cost element in all computer projects. Technology costs will be dealt with as a virtually residual detail.

Pilot Programs and Organizational Learning

Experience is not valuable to others if they cannot make use of it.

Pilot programs, test installations, and experimental sites are popular methods for making cautious investments in computers. A small amount of equipment may be scattered to a large number of sites. A variety of applications can thus be tested and a range of technical solutions tried out. The most frequent reason given for this approach is financial limitations. A more realistic view is that managers are worried about how much trouble they may be getting into.

Arguments can be mustered on both sides as to the merits of scattered experimentation as compared with a concentrated attack on a significant business problem. There are just too many intraorganizational imponderables to decide upon an approach valid in all cases.

Small may be beautiful—but breaking things up can also diminish the potential for growth.

If the prevailing management style is to partition learning among small, isolated enclaves, then the economic gain from the cautious approach could be minimal. Each site then has to build up its own cumulative learning. Unless individual sites are promised sufficient funding to rapidly expand upon any successes they achieve, the experiment will have limited value. Even within the separate offices, high start-up costs could not be amortized over a larger base. Only if central management arranges for careful evaluation and rapid dissemination of the results from these small, experimental installations, can the principal benefits of the cautious approach be realized. I doubt that it is worth the effort in any case. I am also opposed to isolated experiments because they may actually decrease the overall experience level in an organization. Turnover among expert personnel is uncharacteristically high after the completion of isolated pilot projects. A unique achievement makes a person more attractive in the volatile job market for expert technical personnel, whereas it takes a long career to compound organizational learning before someone can be expected to manage a major information-technology project. I suspect, therefore, that many small-scale pilot programs are proposed by people with a stronger allegiance to technological learning than to organizational learning.

On balance, I favor well-focused, concentrated and well-funded office automation projects that have initially limited local objectives— but which can be rapidly expanded once they prove successful. Such projects ought also to be abandoned quickly if they do not deliver the desired results. The primary objective of such projects is, after all, to upgrade people rapidly, thus making them much more productive. When we see seasoned executives promoted into top information-technology positions, it is because in deciding between managing technology or managing organizational costs, the latter deserves to win.

Not enough is known about what works and what does not work to make automation decisions with confidence.

Consultants, academicians, and industry associations can make valuable contributions to reducing everybody's organizational learning costs through well-documented studies about what actually happens when information technology is installed. Considering the fact that the current total spending rate for new installations exceeds $50 billion per year in the United States alone, one could reasonably expect that there would be a great deal of factual information readily available about patterns of experience with successful and unsuccessful office automation projects. The reason such documentation is so scarce can be found in the reluctance to consider information technology as anything different than just another tool for mechanizing work. Given this attitude, it is safe to carry out only isolated observations of cases in which the technology has worked as expected—which can be only of limited value to someone attempting to improve the functioning of an entire organization.

I am convinced that carefully designed observations of what goes on in offices during their transition to a more automated environment are needed to cope with nontechnical workplace issues for which we presently do not have satisfactory solutions. For instance, we need to know more about the influences that result in employee fatigue. We do not know much about the relationships between typing skills and thinking processes when working on a VDU rather than on paper. We need to know more about methods to minimize errors when using a VDU. It would be of great value to understand under what conditions employees can be encouraged to train themselves. I have a long list of unanswered questions: they remind me that even after a lifetime spent in installing information technology I really cannot reliably predict how it will interact with people and with their organizations.

It is striking how much more needs to be known about how people relate to computers before the risks associated with investments in information technology will decrease. Until better insights are gathered, organizational costs will remain high. Until these organizational costs become more manageable, the rate of information technology acceptance will have to be revised downward from present euphoric extrapolations of short-term trends.

Sociology in Relation to Organizational Costs

Some organizational costs associated with the introduction of information technology depend on social factors and, therefore, lie outside management's influence. Low levels of literacy, hostility on the part of organized labor, confrontational styles of employee–management relations, counterproductive rules imposed by government regulation, and legal protection of unproductive jobs are examples of such social limits to what can be accomplished through the use of information technology. The chances are that these external factors will gain in prominence when economic growth slows down; they will retard the replacement of office labor by means of capital investments in information technology. From the perspective of the manager and of the systems analyst, the justification of office-automation technology investments should be seen as a more challenging problem than can be provided by construction of simple payoff ratios. Business economics in the electronic age will be much more demanding and will call for inclusion of cost factors and risk assessments that current computer feasibility studies neglect.

The economics of office work is dominated by labor cost. When introducing information technology, organizational expense becomes the largest element. This should dictate how the investment is made. The primary role of management is managing organizational, rather than technological, costs and risks.

6

The Efficiency Approach to Productivity

You cannot measure what is not defined. You also cannot tell whether you have improved something if you have not measured its performance.

Office productivity is currently one of the uppermost concerns among United States corporate executives. As indicated in surveys by the American Productivity Center, enhanced office productivity is seen as a means to improve profits and enhance quality of service. Improved efficiency can also help managers to deal with ever-increasing information workloads. When executives were asked about the major problems encountered in implementing productivity projects, they emphasized that productivity was very difficult to measure, especially when the objectives were qualitative.[1]

The session on white-collar productivity at the White House Conference on Productivity concluded that productivity measurement, as applied to office work, was one of the most perplexing and difficult issues.[2] Moreover, participants agreed that the lack of an understandable and workable approach to productivity evaluation inhibited the pursuit of information-technology investments.[3]

Work Efficiency

Many approaches are under study to arrive at a generally accepted methodology to evaluate office-automation investment proposals. Innumerable documents on corporate standard procedures exist in policy manuals. They include carefully designed forms for the computation of return-on-investment ratios. Elaborate attempts have been made to design procedures to measure productivity improvements realized after office automation equipment is installed. Unfortunately, these approaches work only when information handling is closely comparable to factory operations. In most cases such approaches merely produce mountains of useless data.

The reason this data is virtually useless touches upon the fundamental issue of what productivity really means in an office setting. In simpler situations productivity is defined in terms of the ratio of output to input. In office automation studies this is still the preferred formula, regardless of how the analysis is performed. Applying such a simple approach to all office work causes misconceptions about productivity.

Output is normally defined in tangible terms—pieces of paper, numbers of invoices, bank deposit receipts, or telephone calls. Input is defined in easily understandable terms such as workhours invested, numbers of inquiries needed to produce a desired result, number of employees, or aggregate costs. To capture all of these variables, various work-measurement methods are applied. These include counting pieces of paper, using accounting data, stopwatch studies of work, sampling events in the office, observation by television, computer monitoring of keystrokes, video recordings, reports by the operators, and the use of predetermined time standards.

There is a growing number of consultants engaged in this sort of work because the demand for more facts increases in proportion to the growing size of office automation budgets. It is hard to tell which of these methods is most popular, though I am convinced that the use of accounting information, originally obtained for other purposes, is by far the preferred source of information about office work. The precision attributed to accounting data and its easy availability somehow combine to obscure its inapplicability.

The output/input approach to the evaluation of office work has merit when an office function remains essentially unaltered after the installation of an electronic system. It also works if both the output and the input variables remain consistent over the duration of an automation project. It is difficult to maintain such consistency, however, because it goes counter to effective automation objectives—which aim to transform the work rather than to accelerate it.

Consider the following example, in which manual invoices combined all items. When computers were installed, separate invoices were produced for refrigerated and unrefrigerated goods in order to simplify warehouse handling. The reported productivity, measured in terms of invoices per person, increased by 80%. Upon close examination, however, most of the reported gain was due simply to changes in administrative procedure.

Office automation alters perceived product quality. The composition of outputs as well as inputs changes, too. It reallocates costs from direct labor expenses to overhead and to capital expenses.

The quality of output, as seen from the customer's standpoint, should remain comparable to previous levels, facilitating consistent output/input computations. For instance, in one case, computer-aided handling of customer complaints reduced the reported productivity, as measured in terms of inquiries handled per day, because so many follow-up calls were eliminated.

Simple output/input efficiency ratios give conflicting signals if the relation between direct costs, overhead costs, and capital expenses is not held constant. An automatic telephone call-handling computer will vastly decrease the number of hours needed for telephone operators. *Their* efficiency will therefore increase. However, this does not consider the increases in overhead costs and in capital depreciation costs. For many years the annual report of one of the largest telephone companies in the world tabulated the history of its productivity gains in terms of long-distance calls per operator. Over a period of twenty years, such statistics looked very impressive, unless one bore in mind that it took more than $100 billion to accomplish the automation involved. When the labor productivity gains were tempered by the related costs of capital investments, the improvements in productivity were deflated to more modest gains.[4] Adjusting labor productivity improvements for the contributions of capital to productivity showed the wage claims made by organized labor to be less realistic than they first appeared to be.

When the electronic environment is fully working, the office will never be the same as before.

If none of the variables entering into output or input are altered in composition, in quality, or in cost structure, then a decrease in input (e.g., reduced manhours) or an increase in output (e.g., more paper) will be *correctly* reported as an increase in productivity. All of this sounds obvious, except that it seldom applies to real situations.[5]

Why then are output-over-input efficiency measurements the favored method to evaluate office automation projects?

Industrial-Age View of Efficiency

The machine, not the person, is the scarce asset of the industrial age.

The underlying assumptions about what "productivity" is go back to the industrial-age model of what a person, aided by a machine, does. Figure 6.1 highlights the factory bias one still detects in every misapplied office automation effort. It is also presented here so that one may recognize the eighteenth-century origins of much current criticism opposing the introduction of information technology.

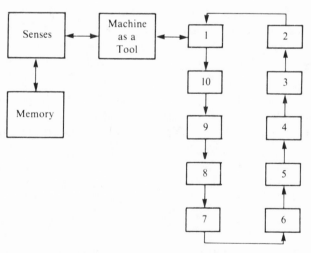

MAN	MACHINE	WORK
• Limited Capability	• Limited Function	• To Be Structured
• Efficient via Routine	• Overcomes Physical Limits	• Simplified Complexity via Sequences
• Remove Uncertainty		• Choices Predefined

Figure 6.1 Industrial-Age View of Optimizing Work Efficiency

According to this view, a human being has an inherently limited capability for handling complexity. Besides this, the handling of complexity requires information which is a manager's, not a worker's, prerogative. A person's superior coordination of eye and hand are what wages will purchase—until improved machines buy it for less. A person's brain is not a valuable asset per se under such assumptions, because the engineer designs into the manufacturing sequence everything which needs to be done. The employee's thinking is only useful insofar as it retains simple procedural instructions. Eventually, even that is dispensable when the automated machine can be programmed to do the same thing.

A person attains increased output through the performance of routine tasks. Total managerial direction and predefined procedures are necessary to obviate questions about what is to be done. Tight controls are the only way of extracting error-free production. People are seen as an extension of the machine because this view makes it possible to plan their ultimate replacement. Such a bias is based on the assumption that machines will always be potentially more efficient than people. Even though machines are usually more expensive than labor, machines represent accumulated capital, whereas labor is an ongoing expense. The design of work with an eye to automation is thus an evolutionary step in the progression towards automation, whenever that becomes affordable. Because it will become affordable—and even necessary.

Machines perform only those limited work functions that technical development allows to be done economically. Real efficiency comes from the machine's ability to speed up output and to overcome human limitations. A computer, for example, completes rapid calculations or sorts punchcards. To accomplish specialized work, specialized machines are designed by specialized people. The production process is then paced by devices performing specialized functions. Individual machines are also easier to justify financially, because each step in the production sequence has well-defined inputs and outputs which are needed if engineers are to compute expected gains in productivity.

Work is typically designed to fit a tightly controlled environment. All work options are sequenced and simplified; choices are predefined or preprogrammed. To justify a new machine, only a stopwatch and a production output count are needed. Accounting information gives precise answers to investment questions. With all variables thus under control, it is possible to compute the rate of productivity with a minimum of ambiguity. No wonder this orderly approach has such an immense appeal!

Clerical tasks have been conceived, designed, and analyzed precisely in this manner to evaluate productivity gains and to justify office automation. The designers of such operations are usually pleased with their accomplishments. They have delivered productivity improvements beyond expectation in paperwork-processing environments. They are proud of what they have done: their managements will approve requests for added computers. Obviously, a self-fulfilling prophecy is involved here. Productivity can be easily measured when work has been deliberately defined so that it can be fitted into a scheme which may work in a factory but certainly does not apply in most office situations.

How Measurement Biases One's Point of View

In order to understand the factory methods used to measure office work I examine below a number of examples and their limitations.

There exists a department that generates invoices. It reports a 10.4% year-to-year increase in the number of invoices and accomplishes this with a 3.2% increase in workhours. A 6.9% improvement in productivity is claimed.[6] The department's manager presents this to management as a sure indication of progress. I have seen dozens of similarly reported "productivity gains" widely commented on and rewarded. There is a fallacy involved in this method of reporting, because other variables—not necessarily under the department manager's control—may have a bearing on the actual productivity gains. (Wage inflation is a good example of such "forgotten" costs.)

For example, consider the facts exactly as given above, except that I will compute productivity by dividing units of physical output by total direct costs. I get different results. Instead of a 6.9% productivity gain I have to report a 0.7% loss.[7] No wonder executives are cautious when reviewing claims about productivity gains.

Luckily, it happens that in this case I know a great deal about the accomplishments of the invoicing department. I do not trust the simple output/input production ratios; I take a much broader view of the entire situation. The value of the invoicing function lies in its effect on cash and on how customers are affected by faulty billing. I define the productivity of the invoicing department in terms of its value to the business. This analysis reveals productivity gains of 77%

for the situation described above, but presented in a different perspective.[8] A small amount of money was invested by the sales department in training the sales force to handle customer complaints about billing and to settle invoice adjustments. As a result, significant improvements were realized in the costs of receivables, in debt write-offs, and especially in the time devoted by the sales force to unproductive billing matters. Such changes are then included in the evaluation of improved performance.

These three examples of productivity analysis reveal that different approaches can shed a completely different perspective on the same office situation. Depending on the way one approaches the computations, the results could be plus 6.9%, minus 0.7% or plus 77%. External costs as well as capital costs have a significant effect on the output/input ratios. Reported productivity results, then, depend largely on one's point of view in analysis.

Unit-Cost Approaches

Productivity claims can be made faster through clever rearrangements of accounting costs than by any other means.

Comparing the total unit costs of an office transaction, such as cost-per-invoice, cost-per-paycheck, and cost-per-purchase order has some merit as a technique for productivity measurement as long as the activity measured remains constant from one time period to another. In such a case we have a secure statistical basis for comparative improvements. I have installed a number of such productivity-tracking systems to evaluate the results obtained by the substitution of data-processing expenses for direct labor costs.[9]

One should not overstate the validity of unit-cost data. The unit cost of a payroll check, for instance, will depend on how one defines what is involved in processing it. Is the cost of the personnel department in signing up people included? How about the time spent in preparing and approving timecards? Are the supervisor's costs for handling discrepancies generated by the computer covered as well? Is the full cost of tax reports and of union deductions included in the unit cost? In the absence of complete information, unit-cost improvements may masquerade as productivity gains, whereas in fact, they may simply be unprofitable rearrangements in the way work is compartmentalized.

Unit costs can be manipulated through reallocation of overhead costs. Large office automation projects always increase the shared overhead costs in the absence of a full cost allocation for the newly added activities. Depending on how shared programming staffs, data center operations, auditing, input control, and telecommunications expenses are allocated, one can arrive at completely different conclusions as to the definition of real unit costs. Under normal operating conditions, highly automated applications entail large fixed expenses for labor and equipment. Costs do not increase or decrease in simple correspondence with changes in the volume of work. The term "unit cost" ceases to have a fixed meaning.[10] It can be changed at will by arbitrarily changing the amounts of shared costs allocated to it. Much of the office politics that center on information-technology projects is simply a struggle over who will end up controlling the distribution of shared expenses.

Staffing Ratios

When in doubt, management will always choose meaningless simplicity over "useless" complexity.

Experienced executives try to avoid having too many untrustworthy productivity ratios. They search for simple numbers which approximate suspected relationships between input and output. Such figures, if available, offer welcome relief from the morass of easily manipulated cost data.

Counting heads—categorized according to a personnel classification scheme—then dividing this count by another number taken from financial reports, is held in high favor as a productivity indicator. Many consultants and industry associations use this method for survey purposes and to make elaborate productivity comparisons. This technique is also the method preferred by financial analysts with only a few hours available to evaluate budget proposals. Executives favor it as a touchstone to determine where manpower use is excessive.

The result is surveys of how many lawyers are employed per thousand employees, how many personnel per billion dollars of sales, how many programmers per computer. At a more refined level this approach involves thorough data gathering, providing ratios such as numbers of secretaries per manager, size of warehousing management staffs per thousand shipments handled, and so forth.[11] In each case, an effort is made to find paired relationships that would serve as a substitute measurement of output (in terms of manpower served, purchasing dollars, square feet maintained, etc.), and which could meaningfuly be correlated with the staffing levels that generate the input.[12]

Applied to individual circumstances, such ratios tend to stimulate debates on whether the local conditions are comparable to the survey findings. For instance, I have collected staffing ratios for secretaries and typists as compared to document-origination personnel such as managers, professionals, and administrators. The average is 4.7 secretaries per document-origination person: a very precise number indeed. But in the insurance industry it is only 0.7 because that industry classifies secretaries and document-origination people differently than most other enterprises. In banking the ratio is 2.1; in public administration it is 2.8; in retail trade 6.9; in education 9.0; and in business services 9.8. Within each of these categories there were extreme ratio variations. The point is not whether the numbers themselves are accurate, but whether they can be used to arrive at any relevant conclusions about productivity for different kinds of firms.[13]

Used in conjunction with other methods, staffing ratios can provide a quick synopsis of manpower use. One of the best examples of the use of staffing ratios in conjunction with a whole battery of carefully interrelated variables is the INTROSPECT technique developed by the Consulting Service of the General Electric Corporation. INTROSPECT employs a number of indicators—such as the ratio of managers to operators, the cost of managing each dollar of operations payroll, and managers' time spent in managing people. If the staffing ratios are integrated within a comprehensive planning structure in such a manner—and if they lead to the gathering of comparable data, then they can certainly be useful.

Productivity can be understood best by understanding rare cases of excellence rather than by gathering data about averages or failures.

Staffing ratios can also be applied with profit to exploring the relationship between personnel and results. The public sector is especially attracted to an examination of such ratios. Someone is always ready to criticize either a shortage or an excess. My computer career started in 1953, when I was involved in a consulting assignment for the New Jersey Turnpike Authority. The governor of New Jersey was not pleased when he noticed idle toll collectors on the turnpike. His staff could not reconcile the governor's feelings with the assertions by the Turnpike Authority and by the toll collectors' union that the collectors were overworked. It turned out that both points of view were (partially) right. It all depended on the time of the day and the day of the week when one formed an opinion. All concerned had already decided what they thought to be the right staffing ratio for the turnpike, based on their observations of average traffic. The prevailing assignment of personnel was based on staffing ratios which related the number of toll collectors to the average number of cars passing each toll station. In this case, enormous quantities of punched cards were available, with actual traffic information. A few toll-collection gates showed superior efficiency in their use of people and in minimizing traffic queues. Based on examples of such superior performance, it was possible to simulate the interaction between people and traffic on a card-programmed calculator—which some people called a computer in those days. The outcome was a surprise. There were enough toll collectors on the turnpike. The problem was that they were not at the right gate at the right time. Aggregate employment was not at the heart of the matter. The essence of the problem was an approach to employee scheduling that did not consider the unique characteristics of how automobile traffic varied at different turnpike gates. Furthermore, the scheduling rules did not give adequate consideration to the special, local needs of the toll collectors.

To deal with the New Jersey Turnpike toll-collection issue by means of a revision of average staffing ratios—as was originally suggested—would have been useless. What worked was a simple scheduling formula designed to deal with the real customer problem: how many cars would be allowed to wait in line at any gate during the peak traffic period.

Staffing ratios, when used to represent an approximation of productivity standards, should not be applied unless external measures of quality of service are also involved. My preferred solution is to please customers by unusually efficient use of both people and machines. Standards for judging productivity should be constructed not from averages alone but also from insight into the examples of excellence we have found and studied.

Micromyopia

If overall objectives are not clear, perfection in managing details may provide a specious feeling of satisfaction.

Micromyopia is the most unsatisfactory approach to productivity measurement because it is based on the idea that all office tasks can be rationalized by breaking them down into minute, controllable elements.[14] Once they are reduced to such elements, their efficiency is presumed to be determinable. The key assumption here is that efficient work elements will assure efficient results. Microanalytic techniques are frequently applied to office environments organized and managed along lines similar to a paperwork factory.[15] The purpose of this approach is to control employee motions. The objective is elimination of unnecessary work and detection of unsatisfactory work practices. Industrial-engineering expertise is applied to the design of every individual work step in order to achieve the optimal balance between tasks done by the machine and work performed by an operator. This procedure presumes that all work events can be specified in a precise manner.

Micromeasurement techniques are based on the industrial-age model of how people and machines interact in work. This model assumes that complete determinism rules over office activities. Of course, all work activities are preprogrammed by outside experts, subject to consent by the operators. Microplanning is now seen as the panacea— both for the operator and for the machine. All contingencies are supposedly provided for. Micromyopia in its extreme form can become a kind of totalitarianism: it is easily abused as a method for exercising complete surveillance over work behavior.

There is a crucial relationship between the level of procedural detail and the extent to which employees are distrusted.

I do not know how prevalent the micromyopic approach to office-productivity management is. Consultants offer a wide range of methods which offer varying degrees of microanalysis.[16] These studies are in great demand for business situations calling for independent verification of claims by office workers with regard to their efficiency. There are some situations in which relations between management and office workers are so poor that only outside observation provides a tolerable approach for reaching agreement about expected levels of output. The setting of minutely specified work standards and the ultimate appearance of collective bargaining on the scene seem to go hand-in-hand.

Extreme incidents of micromyopia are rare because they show up only under conditions of extreme waste. However, bad cases of micromyopia are almost always to be found wherever elaborate office procedures have been programmed without significant participation by the personnel who have to live with the system. I often detect micromyopia when I ask to see a schedule of modifications to computer applications. If hardly any changes come from operator suggestions, it is likely that poor employee relations prevail.

Detailed office-productivity standards are used infrequently: it is difficult to get them installed. Even after a great deal of effort has been expended to define standards for every conceivable office event, a thoroughly programmed clerical department will still have a large number of activities inexplicable by formal means.[17] The drive for rationalization of every possible office task is powerful indeed. Once an organization starts on the way towards micromyopia, it finds it hard to stop. If it did, it would find itself staring at productivity indicators showing large amounts of useless office work.[18] Unless an organization attempting total control becomes isolated and fixed in its office work, there will never be enough time available to define everything that is going on. As attractive as micromyopia may be to the orderly, quantitative mind, this technique cannot deliver satisfactory productivity measurements in a changing office environment.[19]

Productivity Indices

If one does not understand a situation, increasing the complexity of calculations may make it appear that formerly hidden information has suddenly been revealed.

Productivity evaluation encounters further difficulties when output- or input data are not reported in identical measurement terms. Such circumstances require the assignment of a measure of relative importance to each component in order to achieve a composite index of efficiency. If the individual measurements are not really comparable, then the comparison is virtually useless.[20]

I distrust the approach described above: it will be misused in due course. If the aggregate index is favorable, the gain is reported as evidence of accomplishment, even if it hides damaging trends. If the aggregate shows losses, the weighting factors are recomputed. The weighting factors are usually assigned through negotiated judgments. Even if they had a satisfactory rationale when originally proposed, they may well lose their validity for showing how the various unit measures relate to the overall business as conditions change.[21]

A more rigorous approach to the computation of productivity indices can be derived from accounting practices. This technique compares
output- and input costs during periods of inflation. This productivity-
indexing method also allows for the adjustment of data to reflect
shifts in product mix or in prices. All quantities expressed in terms
of physical units are converted to common units. For instance, a grocery manufacturer converts cans of coffee, boxes of detergent, and
rolls of paper to equivalent cases of grocery goods. Changes in product
sales—such as an increase in the sale of smaller-size cans in lieu of
large cans—are also adjusted accordingly. This technique involves
elaborate weighting computations to convert all quantities to a common
base. Prices and costs are also adjusted to conform to a common
time period.[22] For instance, all 1984 purchases are translated into
equivalent 1969 prices. Similar techniques are used to represent changes
in the labor and the capital content of a given product. Prices of
1984 cars, for example, would be adjusted for higher electronic and
plastic content as compared with 1969 cars. In all of these instances,
changes in quality are not considered. It is thus difficult to account,
say, for the differences in gasoline consumption between 1984 and
1969 motor vehicles using this method.

Price- and volume-adjusted productivity ratios are sometimes useful in dealing with figures at the level of an entire industry or an
economy. Applied to individual businesses, however, they often lead
to distortions in reported performance: the modern office environment
is subject to too many changes in terms of expected results. As far
as input is concerned, the introduction of information technology, at
reduced unit costs, distorts the adjustment factors one might hope
to apply to capital costs.

**It is not what one *does*, but how one *counts*, that tells management
what it would like to hear.**

A certain amount of gamesmanship is necessary to select adjustment factors which reflect favorably on reported results. My favorite
story in this respect concerns a factory manager in a totalitarian economy who, year after year, earned the top productivity bonus in the
entire industry. His factory produced nails; the production quota was
based on a "total-factor productivity evaluation" set in kilograms of
output adjusted by price of the materials, based on a ten-year old
index. Every year he bought more expensive steel and increasingly

confined his production to making larger nails. When he was finally caught, he was making rarely used, enormous nails—from expensive alloys!

Incomprehensible precision is preferred as a substitute for imprecise understanding of productivity.

Even if the accounting treatment of the detailed data entering into the base-year adjustments is rigorous and the weighting factors are extremely accurate, the typical evaluation exercise drifts into great numerical complexity once it is initiated. I believe that computerized facilities for churning out large arrays of numbers (such as the various "-calc" routines now easily available on microcomputers) have added to the amount of numerical manipulation—thus hiding further what the numbers actually mean. The total-factor adjustment technique thrives on an elaboration of matrix calculations. Any financial analyst sitting alone in his cubicle with a brand-new personal computer will be happy to oblige the inquirer with as many complex cross-multiplications as the machine can perform. The arithmetic capability wins over the ability of people to use such productivity numbers in an intelligent way. There is nothing to be found in the manager's conventional operating report or in daily experience to explain the meaning of the complex productivity indices computed by such elaborate means. Consider, for example, that for a shop-floor interpretation of the total-factor productivity index the manager would need to account for material-based output weighting, for labor-based input weighting, for physical input weighting (such as raw materials and BTUs of energy), for price adjustments, for base-plan adjustment, for inflation, and for changes in capital inputs. Consequently, these techniques are primarily useful for planning purposes.

Revenue-Related Productivity Measurement

Convenience of measurement is not a good enough reason for using the method that offers it.

Management often becomes easily frustrated by the details of various productivity indexing schemes: the methods are either not sufficiently rigorous and are therefore misleading, or they serve no useful purpose. Confronted with this dilemma, a manager looking for an easy way out may reach for another option, namely, calculation of revenue-per-employee. This is a simple computation which seems to satisfy everyone, as evidenced by the fact that it is a most frequently used indicator of productivity. Its easily understandable approach is that revenues which increase faster than the number of employees are always a good indication that people are becoming more efficient.

The computations are unambiguous—except that they disguise more than they reveal.[23] For instance, *Forbes* magazine has been reporting in its annual industry review a ranking of firms according to productivity. From the 1982 *Forbes* report I selected two companies, one at the bottom and one at the top of the scale, ranked according to productivity expressed in sales/employee:

Company	Sales/Employee	Assets/Employee
A.T.&T.	$ 64,000	$ 146,000
First Executive Corporation	$4,590,000	$9,278,000

Does this ranking imply that the First Executive Corporation is seventy-two times more productive than the giant A.T.&T.? Does the fact that the First Executive Corporation uses sixty-four times more assets per employee explain its higher revenues per employee? These questions cannot be answered in the absence of a great deal of additional information. Yet corporations and operating units continue to compare their productivity standings using just the revenue/ employee ratio, simply because it is the most convenient format to use.

The most frequently used methods for evaluating the effects of information technology investments are characterized by the attitude that work does not change. The purpose of an investment is to increase output. As a consequence, a smaller number of workers will be needed to perform existing functions. In addition, the purchase of new machines is justified by the argument that no additional personnel need be hired. Office workers are regarded as operators whose work can be standardized. Industrial-engineering methods, then, are the appropriate solution for estimating productivity gains. From an analytical point of view this reinforces the idea that office automation is not really different from factory automation.

Even though output/input productivity measurements have their place in routine job situations, I see their applicability as being limited to only a small number of situations in the office. This is why I believe that established methods of productivity analysis derived from the factory should be applied only with great caution to knowledge work involving information technology.

7

The Effectiveness Approach to Productivity

Every job contains some discretionary work elements. Every job involves some use of information. The conventional definition of productivity as the ratio of tangible output to tangible input therefore excludes important considerations. The concept of productivity, then, must be modified if it is to apply to information handling. "Information productivity" has at least two aspects. One has to do with the internal efficiency with which office tasks are carried out. The other, far more important aspect, concerns external effectiveness—which determines the quality and the utility of the output.

Efficiency vs. Effectiveness

Driving a car that gets 100 miles per gallon is not *effective* if you are driving around without purpose.

Information productivity must be defined within the proper context. Information, except as an aesthetic experience, is not a consumer good. Information has economic value only when it is used by people

116

to make things or to deliver services. Using information is different from using material objects. For instance, valuable information gains still more in value when it is listened to, exchanged, or distributed. By contrast, the use of everyday objects depreciates their value. Information's raison d'être lies in its dissemination, whereas goods are produced to be possessed. For instance, the more people share information, the more its importance will increase. Information which nobody uses diminishes in value. Objects are consumed until they are useless. Information can easily be shared without being consumed in the process.

Objects and information behave according to different laws. No wonder they require different techniques for measurement and evaluation.

These fundamental differences between goods and information explain why computations of productivity which work for the production of physical goods are misdirected if applied to information.

I have chosen the term "effectiveness" to capture the distinctive attributes of information work. The definitions of "effectiveness" and of "effectiveness-productivity" are essential for judging the value of information technology. Of all of the insights this book attempts to convey, the ability to distinguish effectiveness from efficiency is the most important one. When this difference is not understood, it becomes the source of most of the problems encountered in deciding how to use computers. As the workforce shifts from the production of objects to the production of services based on information, the ability to enhance effectiveness becomes far more important than the question of whether or not one can measure efficiency.

Effectiveness is a social concept: it applies to groups. Efficiency is an individualist concept: it applies to isolated acts.

The sum of many efficient information activities may still not add up to an effective information service. Office technology investment in support of executives, managers, and professionals has no justification without first examining the roles of those individuals.[1] The productivity of a manager, for instance, is an element in the results delivered by the entire organization for which he works. Management effectiveness is a team result. Likewise, the ultimate productivity of a research team can be evaluated only by judging the number of successful innovative products introduced by its company.

Efficiency is desirable, if only as a way of getting something accomplished without physical waste: efficiency is included within the effectiveness point of view. The question of efficiency is just one of many variables to be evaluated when one judges whether an organization is effective. To weigh the effectiveness of information technology demands an understanding of whether, and how, information technology will deliver improved results to the organization in question.

The most useful way of examining effectiveness is from the standpoint of customers. The thrust of effectiveness thinking is toward behavior which will be transmitted throughout an entire organization, whereas efficiency is something more localized within the confines of isolated office functions.

Effectiveness Is Not a Ratio

Effectiveness can be defined as people cooperating to produce a result in which the value produced exceeds production costs, so that the product may be sold for a profit.

The first prerequisite of organizational effectiveness is, of course, survival of the organization. The second prerequisite is growth. The third prerequisite is a combination of the first two: the ability to generate enough surplus for continued investment in self-renewal, and thus in ever-increasing wealth. Whereas efficiency was defined above as a simple *ratio* of output over input, effectiveness is defined in Figure 7.1 as an *inequality,* computed by sequentially subtracting all input costs from revenue.[2]

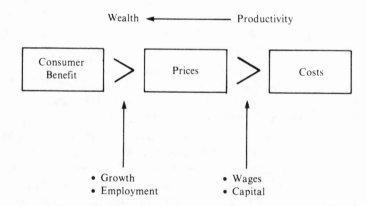

Figure 7.1   Effectiveness-Productivity as an Inequality

According to this simple formula, effectiveness-productivity is present if consumer benefit exceeds the prices which the consumer pays. This creates growth, our second condition of organizational effectiveness. Effectiveness-productivity is also present, as we saw, if sales prices exceed costs of production. This assures survival, our first condition of organizational effectiveness. The distinction from the simple output/input ratio arises from the fact that in the effectiveness formula, we have *two* ratios. They are interlinked by means of a key variable: price.

The concept of effectiveness-productivity depends upon the presence of a pricing mechanism in which the customer has a choice of which output to purchase. The "philosophical" distinction between effectiveness and efficiency has a direct bearing on the question of which social design is chosen to obtain a desired output from any individual, group, or business. Direct feedback between customer and supplier is the essential prerequisite for effectiveness-productivity.

Efficiency is an elitist concept. Effectiveness is more egalitarian: the consumer ultimately votes by paying—or refusing to pay—a stipulated price.

The efficiency ratio presumes that a design choice has already been made by an expert, a manager, or a legislature, defining needs in terms of expected quantity and quality. All efficiency computations imply the existence of a hierarchy which decides what is to be done.

The effectiveness-inequality method suggests that the correct output is known only by the customer: it is determined by the vote with which customers exercise their choice, the decision to buy or not to buy at a given price. Effectiveness measurement is therefore more suitable for judging the productivity of that sort of service in which competition exists. Effectiveness measurement can be applied to information monopolies—such as headquarters staffs—only indirectly, in the context of the entire organization's marketplace performance.

The distinctions between efficiency and effectiveness should not be taken as mutually exclusive. Effectiveness measurement is just an evolutionary step towards handling the increased complexity of new information-based services which the simpler output/input ratios cannot address adequately. Effectiveness is determined by the forces of consumer demand, whereas the efficiency analysis approach had its origins in the need to control supply. The industrial engineer and the systems analyst are the designers of efficiency. When effectiveness is at issue, the user and the consumer call the tune.

Organizational Effectiveness as a Design Objective

An effective organization tends to create increasing amounts of wealth to be divided among workers, management, and society. An efficient organization is comparatively more concerned about its internal functioning than is an effective organization.

Organizational effectiveness is demonstrated by a steady conversion of productivity into new aggregate wealth. It utilizes wages and capital in such a way as to create goods and services commanding favorable prices. Organizational effectiveness generates enough surplus for information workers to acquire the means—such as new skills and computers—to develop their own work roles even further. It creates jobs that did not exist before. It can be viewed as a human invention for reversing the law of thermodynamics which holds that losses will always exceed gains from energy production because of the inherent inefficiency of any conversion process. Put another way, in physics, the sum of any combination of energy resources will always be less than if each individual resource were added separately. Our effectiveness-inequality theory describes precisely the opposite situation: if an organization is effective, the whole will always be greater than the sum of its parts because of gains in productivity. Organizational effectiveness is the engine which drives progress. It is a means by which the ever-present processes of decay and disintegration are reversed in human affairs.

At this stage of historical development, a new tool has been placed at mankind's disposal, a tool which can keep the inequality signs of Figure 7.1 pointed towards continued effectiveness. It is a tool that uses hardly any energy and negligible amounts of material. This tool is the computer, used to manage information—a totally nondepletable resource.

But in what way does this new tool function, exactly? How does the force of organizational productivity influence the relationships among value, price, and cost in an economy dominated by information-handling costs? Information technology is gradually modifying the time-tested, industrial-age forms for achieving success. To provide a perspective on the changes involved, I will explore how the interaction among machines (as physical devices and information-handling tools), man, and work may evolve in the information age.

Information-Age View of Optimizing Organizational Effectiveness: The Role of Man

To develop a useful model for measuring information productivity, we must reexamine some of the prevailing assumptions about the role of man in handling work. Consider the abstract view of effectiveness in the information age, as shown in Figure 7.2.

Understanding the idea of personal effectiveness begins with the realization that in office work, most activities require the human mind's flexibility in order to deal with an enormous variety of both standardized and unprogrammed tasks. The mind's ability to deal with information is the primary economic incentive for office employment, rather than motor skills per se. As most work shifts from the industrial to the service sector, and as computers automate highly structured and standardized work, an increasing share of the remaining information work becomes relatively unpredictable and unstructured. The effectiveness of information labor depends upon a person's ability to make the right choices among a large number of options, most of them only vaguely defined.

In the electronic age, work design is reoriented to emphasize the human faculties of judgment.

The entire focus of the information age is on people rather than on machines. Labor becomes the scarcest and most expensive economic factor in production. If real gains in per capita wealth are occurring, it means that average labor costs are increasing. At the same time, the relative costs of information-technology capital must decrease. If the information age is to improve the standard of living, the differential between rising labor costs and declining capital costs must be offset by the steadily rising productivity of information workers. Increased productivity of information workers means increasing their productivity in the use of accumulated information capital.

The principal mental faculty employed in the industrial age was the worker's procedural memory. In contrast, the information-age em-

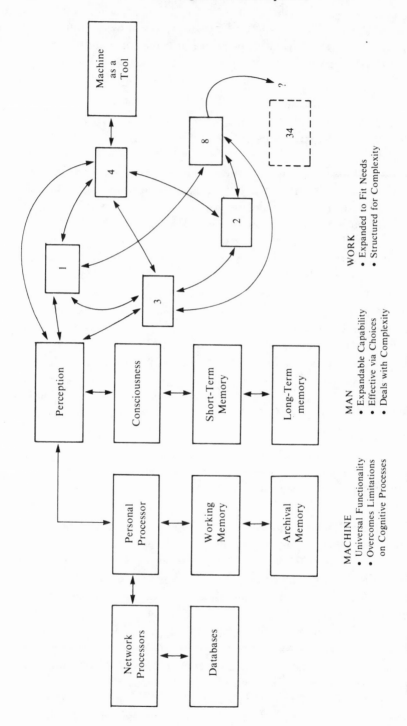

Figure 7.2 Information-Age View of Optimizing Work Effectiveness

ployer does not value this capability so highly because transferring procedural details into computer memory is very easy. What is now of greatest value is man's unique faculty to apply insight, discrimination, and judgment to complex situations—and then make effective choices. Imagination, creativity, understanding, and sympathy are human attributes which are not transferrable to a machine.

Effective management provides workers with incentives to move low-value work to others for whom this work would amount to a high-value task.

If work cannot be reallocated, it should be automated as soon as this is economically feasible. The inequality formula in Figure 7.1 should be the guiding principle for work rearrangement. For the entire management process to succeed in stimulating the growth of effectiveness, it must produce mostly winners and few, if any, losers. Sharing in the gains produced by effective organization should be one of the motivating factors. Without everybody's participation in such gains, work enlargement and work rearrangement will be difficult to agree upon.

Due to the intricacy of information work and the overwhelming interdependence of information workers, there is no way a central authority can mastermind such a delicate reallocation of work roles. This is why a commitment by every participant to ever-changing patterns of activities is an absolute prerequisite for growth without the enormous costs of organizational disruption. In the absence of agreement on a continuous and cooperative process for changing work-roles, the organization will stagnate—except when management direction or outside intervention forces it to change.

If such information-age changes in the role of man prove unachievable, it will probably be due to one or both of the following limitations. First, management may continue its adherence to the industrial-age model of organizational design. Second, there may not be an adequate supply of people able to acquire those skills which have traditionally been viewed as the special preserve of managers and experts. There are indeed many circumstances in which functional illiteracy, hostility between workers and management, or fear of unemployment might foster stagnation. Under such circumstances, work rules would become rigidly fixed. Individual roles would be downgraded by factory-like automation. In such a case, however, we would be dealing with an ineffective organization, one incapable of competing in a world where

organizational effectiveness would give great advantages to more adaptable competitors—to those able and willing to make superior use of
their people.

Information-Age View of Optimizing Organizational Effectiveness: The Role of the Machine

**Computer software, not the computer itself, is the key instrument
of the information age.**

The effectiveness view of the worker's role dictates that he should
decide how to use a computer: the computer's design should not dictate
how the worker should operate. This contrasts with what we find in
the industrial workplace, where the physical characteristics of the machine define the scope of work done by the individual. Appropriate
information technology must have almost unlimited adaptability in
order to cope with radical differences in the ways people work in a
rapidly shifting business environment.

Viewed from the operator's standpoint, the value of the computer
consists in its ability to overcome such physical limitations as the
brain's computational capacity or the narrowly restricted capacity of
the eyes to retrieve information accurately and quickly from a large
file. But the machine must first "understand" what to compute and
what to look for. This calls for a machine with sufficient versatility
to match an individual's level of training and thinking. The machine
must be able to follow changes in the operator's ideas about what
ought to be accomplished. Such a machine should even be able to
adapt to the operator's work habits. Such a machine becomes a *personal*
device: one which fits the operator like a comfortable old garment
rather than like a tight plaster cast. The ideal machine becomes unique
by its acquired responses to the operator's wishes, even though it
may be physically constructed from standard circuits. The vision of
such an ideal machine is no longer mere science fiction. Experts in
the field of artificial intelligence have made enough progress to suggest
that within the next ten years a personal computer possessing acquired
habits is a reasonable prospect.

The general scheme for an information worker's workstation is
outlined in Figure 7.3.

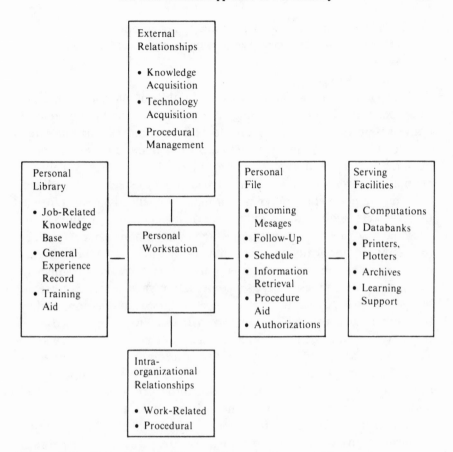

Figure 7.3   Functions of a General-Purpose Personal Workstation

The effective user of this equipment is successful because he has rapid access to whatever information he needs. This is possible because the personal computer is endowed with the full repertoire of a company's business procedures.

Easily-made alterations in the job functions carried out with the assistance of the personal computer are economically valuable because they remove technical obstacles to the gradual transformation of work. The problem with work enlargement is that it must be negotiated carefully and only gradually. It involves the transfer of work previously performed by others. It requires new people to do new jobs. In this respect, the computer should not be seen as just a machine to execute tasks, but also as an ever-present personal tutor. This calls for a machine able to recognize the difference between work and learning.

In the electronic age the effectiveness of organizations depends on technical and political cooperation which permits easy communication.

The effective information worker should not have to remember the procedural details for gaining access to other networks or remote databases or for how to communicate with other individuals: the external electronic environment is subject to too many changes, dictated by its own technical evolution, for this to be possible. A network cannot keep everyone on it fully informed about the technical modifications taking place at every point. For maximum effectiveness, information workers should know only their own personal computers. The personal machine should contain just the right amount of local memory to keep it automatically aware of changes by the operators of external networks. The personal computer must be endowed with sufficient procedural capabilities to act as a combination gatekeeper, interpreter, butler, and private secretary. To support the global interaction of effective individuals, personal computers will have to be equipped with the software equivalents of international courtesy and of knowledge about business practices in culturally and economically diverse locations. For such a scheme to work, both the personal computer and the various network processors must fit into a well-defined, universal network design. Such a development cannot take place in isolation; it requires international coordination, international standards, sharing of business goals among cooperating organizations, and the political good will necessary to keep communication links open.

Agreements are necessary among equipment suppliers, telecommunications carriers, database providers, and international standards organizations to extend effective communication beyond the boundaries of individual organizations. It is gratifying to see industry associations advancing the potential of universal communication. The retail industry, ocean shipping, railroads, trucking, the banking industry, and insurance carriers have taken the lead in demonstrating how a personal computer may extend its role far beyond local purposes. There are already numerous examples of suppliers and customers who routinely communicate by computer to simplify the handling of their business affairs by eliminating intermediaries.

It was the mechanical engine which made it possible in the industrial age to transfer the otherwise dormant power of coal and oil to the service of man: the result was improved efficiency in the production of goods. I see a similar process going on as the personal computer makes it possible to channel almost infinite amounts of information directly into the service of the consumer through information networks. Improved service effectiveness will be the outcome.

Information-Age View of Optimizing Organizational Effectiveness: The Role of Work

Effective work is enlarged in scope, variable in procedure, asynchronous in time, automated in execution, and subject to instant feedback.

The concept of work itself changes in the electronic age. The effectiveness of the office worker originates in his ability to deal with many variables simultaneously, to probe for new answers that were not previously accessible. Such ability is ideally suited to deal with the nonstandard tasks characteristic of managerial, professional, administrative, and service occupations. The new directions in work design harness the latent talent of information workers to accomplish the work necessary to satisfy customer needs. The new work designs also permit a great deal of discretion in bypassing unnecessary work steps, steps which are presently dictated by rigid procedural routines.

Information technology can provide people with more interesting work than they now do. Effective individuals can become involved in activities for which they have not been trained as specialists. Work can be structured so as to bring a person up to the limits of his capabilities, thus maximizing the value of office workers.

Information work in the industrial age is performed synchronously. The poor service so frequently provided by information workers is often due to the mere fact that the workers must be physically present and available before a customer's request can be attended to. Everyone must be in the same room for a meeting. A consultation can take place only when the client can be available at the same time as the professional. Satisfactory service levels from industrial-age information workers require overstaffing to cover peak periods.

Electronic networks function most economically when operated asynchronously. Local memory is inexpensive and can store both requests and answers until people become available. Inexpensive logic can discriminate among requests providing a much more appropriate handling of customer needs. Higher productivity is realized from better time management, both for the requestor and for the service provider.

The effective organization accumulates much of its information capital in the form of systems software. Such software manages the flow of all work—for example the management of energy use in buildings, the scheduling of messages from computer to computer, the assignment of work to various electronic devices, or the recovery of messages when parts of the network fail. If electromechanical machines perform physical work—such as a mail-delivery robot or an optical scanner doing data-entry work—the systems software, not a person, will supervise such operations. The information-age worker modifies the instructions contained in systems software; he directs the computer that, in turn, controls the robot. Effective information workers do not continuously apply their hands to a control panel to manipulate computer devices. Automated work becomes increasingly abstract work: controlling the controllers. What is left is work that takes advantage of the human mind's skill, judgment, and learning ability.

Useful indicators of effective information-work design include the presence of direct feedback signals to the users. Such feedback aids in the recognition of whether the right task is performed, whether the quality of the output is correct, whether responsiveness is balanced with regard to the situation at hand, and whether the quantity of output is the desired one. Computer applications that deliver information about errors or defects too late to make corrections, or which inform only controllers—such designs are inherently defective. I also fault networks that provide services without supplying indications about the costs of services soon enough to allow the user to alter his information consumption patterns quickly, if he desires. The absence of useful feedback about costs necessitates an evaluation that is removed from the workplace. Information technology has the unique attribute that it can easily and inexpensively provide instant feedback about its price. One reason why rapid feedback about the cost of computer services is so rare lies in the industrial-age attitudes of computer-center managers: information about pricing is reserved for management; the users do not really have the opportunity to make many worthwhile choices.

The effective worker can change a work pattern to fit the customer's needs rather than follow a fixed procedural routine. Effective information work is more like discovering the way out of a complex labyrinth than following instructions on how to assemble a toy.

Information-Age View of Optimizing Organizational Effectiveness: The Role of Markets

Information is not a privilege. Its value must be determined by its users.

The transition from the feudal system to the modern industrial state can be attributed to the development of a market economy more than to any other single cause. It was the market economy which generated an allocation of capital responsive to the demand for new products and fostered economic growth based on innovation. The drive for industrial efficiency was propelled by competitive forces.

The principal drawback of advancing industrialization is that increasing portions of labor costs are removed from the direct production of goods and services, where they are subject to the discipline of competition. With industrial progress comes an increased number of information jobs in government, health, education, and corporate administration—areas where competition is only a remote influence. All organizations have a natural tendency to seek a monopoly position in order to maximize their gains. Enough of a competitive market for industrial goods exists to assure that monopoly positions cannot be maintained forever. In the delivery of professional, managerial, and administrative services within large organizations, or in the public sector, the market mechanism hardly enters the picture. Such conditions, perhaps more than any others, explain why the costs of information work escalate, while the effectiveness of large, integrated information organizations keeps declining. My research on organizational productivity has shown that companies purchasing at least half of their information services in the marketplace are significantly more productive than those who maintain their own personnel to perform more than three-quarters of all office tasks.

For benefits to be greater than price—which is a part of our inequality for determining effectiveness—there must be a way customers can exercise meaningful choices in obtaining information service. This rarely happens because most information work allows little or no choice of supplier. There are exceptions, however. For instance, there is a great deal of competition in the travel business, in advertising, in entertainment, in publishing, in stock brokerage, and in consulting. Still, I estimate that less than 50% of all information work in the United States involves any significant user options. The costs of all business management and all information work in the public sector are included in the non-optional category.

As long as customers have no alternatives, it is possible to compute only the *efficiency* of suppliers, not their *effectiveness*. A government agency, whose actions are regulated by law, and whose budget is a share of tax revenues, can improve only its efficiency. However, even in the absence of a market mechanism, it is possible to develop benchmarks to measure *relative* efficiency by comparison with acknowledged examples of excellence. For instance, it is possible to develop multivariate statistical methods for comparing the performance of all fire departments in a state with those few which are most successful. Constructing such benchmarks of excellence requires much more effort and much more data than what a competitive marketplace accomplishes through a small number of customer pricing choices. The special advantage of the market mechanism, then, lies in its low-cost information efficiency in channeling resources to where they are of greatest value.

Using the Information Middleman

To increase the time available to information workers for serving their customers, reduce the time devoted to intraorganizational communications.

Systems which orient their services to customers have low internal communications workloads. Their workers are as close as possible to the customer contacts. This approach makes it necessary to create different links with the central support organizations because it is not possible to break up all resources into customer-sized groupings.

The special link for reorganizing information work in the electronic age is the "information middleman." This person, or small team, can communicate with any of the centers representing shared resources, while simultaneously dealing with customers. The information middleman represents, on a local scale, all of the services available from the entire enterprise. Specialists still have their role in the central units, where they are utilized as tutors, innovators, experts, and developers of new knowledge. The information middleman can thus view the support staff as suppliers of useful know-how rather than as monitors or controllers.[3] Each "middleman" can electronically reach the specialists' accumulated expertise, either by inquiring directly into the specialist's files or by access to programmed expert advice. For in-

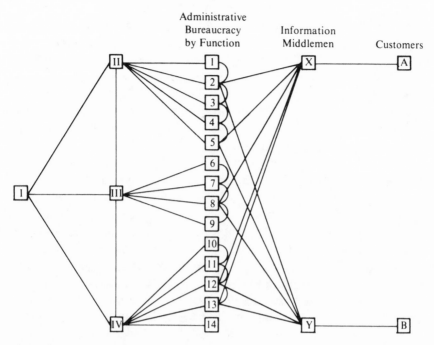

Figure 7.4 The "Information Middleman"

stance, the knowledge of central office specialists in market research, product performance analysis, and technical maintenance can be very useful in assisting with a sales call to a sophisticated customer.

The burden of information coordination within the organizational bureaucracy is eased because responsibility for a customer's needs is fixed at a single point of contact, rather than distributed among many. Such an arrangement allows for the reduction of redundant intracorporate communications as compared with the relationship illustrated in Figure 1-2. The focus can be on how to deliver the right services. Less ambiguous incentives for relating rewards to results can be designed. The relationship between the middleman and central resources such as support specialists can be more direct. Shared resources can be supplied in response to demands from the middleman as a variable cost, rather than applied to the entire organization as a uniform overhead tax. Such an arrangement could open the entire organization to information middlemen, who would be able to choose which central services to use and which to disregard. In this way an organization could begin to create an internal marketplace for support services.

The airline reservations system is a classic example of the development of information middlemen, and of the way computer technology makes this possible. A customer can contact a representative of any airline and complete the entire process of booking and paying for flight reservations, interline connections, and hotel and rental car reservations. From the standpoint of productivity, this system is a marvel of effectiveness. Without this decentralized execution by an information middleman, supported by centralized resources, today's large volume of air traffic would be too costly to manage.

The airline reservations system is simple from the standpoint of the relationship between the airline agent and the customer: yet the airline industry required more than fifteen years to develop the current global reservation networks. The airlines were, however, only the precursors of decentralized job design based on computerized aid from central support. Banking services, insurance-policy placement, grocery-store reordering, packaging design, hotel reservations, entertainment bookings, truck transportation, stamp auctions, tanker-fleet management, and many other new applications are appearing. They replicate the successful airline model, while finding innovative ways to deal with their own unique market situations.

Completing all information transactions at the point of direct contact with a client offers solutions where current administrative methods are powerless. Consider, for instance, the current difficulties in administering social welfare payments. At present, a welfare applicant spends an enormous amount of time approaching various federal, state, and local agencies to establish need and eligibility. This process is incredibly wasteful, expensive, demotivating, and generally counterproductive. The solution is to use social caseworkers as information middlemen. The objective would be to increase the authority of the caseworkers to handle *all* assistance programs—without their needing to be an expert in any particular one of them. The trade-off between the specialized expertise of central bureaucracies that all welfare clients must visit in a prescribed sequence and the generalized ability of the social worker to deal directly with each client favors the middleman approach. The central agencies can audit results by means of computer-to-computer communications.

The Middleman's Workstation

The revolutionary changes of the electronic age are not to be found in computer technology itself, but in the new ways its benefits can be distributed.

The information middleman's special attribute is his ability to manage information when confronted with a customer. Easy access to low-cost technology is needed. This technology must be integrated with the rest of the organization before it can be effective. The personal workstation is the primary support tool for the information middleman's economic existence. It allows him to deal with shared sources of information and with the specialists whose assistance he needs.

Knowledge, today transmitted through informal contacts among knowledge workers, is gradually being transformed into computer programs representing office procedures as well as business customs. Formal policy manuals disappear as they become incarnated, as it were, in the software of each workstation. The automatic routing of messages through the network replaces what we now call "organizational channels." The effective information middleman is, then, freer to respond to customer needs, since he has been relieved of routine procedural details. The workstation is a keeper of the standards set by management, which still remains accountable for maintaining consistent results.

The ultimate goal should be to extend the influence of the information middleman to facilitate interaction with a growing community of specialists. Ultimately the information middlemen are the building blocks from which a worldwide information marketplace can be organized. Information middlemen thus become the personal analogues of the department store or of the mail-order catalogue. They combine a broad range of information services that can be customized, transformed, and packaged into services of direct value to a customer. The merchandise buyers insure competitive pricing in the marketplace. In the same way, the information middlemen can shop on a worldwide scale for the most effective delivery of information services.

As an example, a financial consultant equipped with such a personal workstation can monitor the total insurance, budget, taxation, retirement, and investment needs of a family as the situation of the family changes over time. With such help, the family receives comprehensive insights into its financial condition. By using a broad range of services, a single information middleman can replace many of the existing tax counselling, insurance, legal, and retirement advisory specialists. The middleman, acting as financial consultant, can shop around with as many institutions as needed to make available the best possible combination of resources. The middleman's personal workstation thus becomes the single most important focus of training and experience. If his workstation is augmented by a system providing authorization,

password, security, credit validation, and customer activity-review capabilities, the new financial middleman can deliver comprehensive services which are presently available only through separate distribution
channels, and inconsistently and inefficiently at that.

The Information Economy and the Competitive Marketplace

Behind the idea of the information middleman lies a more fundamental
concept—that information workers can become more effective by moving them from positions within an administrative hierarchy into services which are subject to competition.

The major economic changes brought about through airline reservation systems are not to be found in administrative cost reductions
made possible by electronic terminals. The real revolution has been
in the *convenience* which has made airline travel so easy, and the
confidence customers have as they engage in competitive shopping
for the best flight. Travel agents and even individuals can use an
electronic database to find out directly the best combination of fares
and departure schedules for a trip. The effects of convenient purchasing—raising airline revenues and lowering prices—far exceeds any
possible cost reductions achieved through the more advanced reservation systems themselves.

An economic and social transformation is upon us. It will utilize
the computerized information middleman as one of the agents of progress. This development involves a structural change that makes it
possible to move managerial and administrative work from overhead
jobs in large organizations to market-oriented information services
in smaller organizations. This trend is already visible when one notes
that the 500 largest industrial organizations in the United States have
experienced practically no growth in employment over the last ten
years, whereas their revenues (after inflation adjustment) have risen
by some 11%. Simultaneously, smaller organizations have been adding
employees. The explanation is that large companies have been increasing their revenues by shifting portions of their costs to more efficient
suppliers. By purchasing goods and services in the marketplace, rather
than producing them on their own, they have come to recognize that
competition can improve profits.

The transition from the feudal system to the modern industrial
state was propelled by the transfer of the fastest-growing economic

sectors to the market economy. I see the transition from the postindustrial economy to the information-service economy advancing by a similar process. Our society will move large segments of high-growth information work into the marketplace; the result will be a large gain in effectiveness.

With an adequate understanding of science, it is relatively easy to predict what technology may develop from it. However, it is extremely difficult to anticipate the social and political effects of technology because they are largely the outcome of unexpected secondary influences. Predicting the invention of the automobile was relatively easy. What was difficult was to visualize the suburbs, drive-in movies, regional shopping centers, and traffic congestion which the advent of this new device made possible.

A similar consideration applies to a discussion of information technology. Forecasting the characteristics of computers in the year 2010 is relatively easy. It is the transformation in the way work will be organized which is so hard to visualize. Productivity and organizational effectiveness will be the dominant forces in the coming rearrangement of our society. The influence of the marketplace will be decisive in steering us in that direction.

8

Value-Added Productivity Measurement

Without productivity goals business has no direction. Without productivity measurements business has no control.[1]

Productivity is an index of how successful an organization is in the use of its resources. It measures results from a broad range of activities. As a measure of efficiency, it applies to the production of physical objects. As a measure of organizational effectiveness, it can apply to the performance of management. Understanding managerial productivity and measuring it are prerequisites for analyzing the effects of information technology. Toward that end I will use the concept of "value-added" productivity as a practical method for tracking the elusive evidence as to whether computers contribute to the improvement of organizational performance.

Value-Added Measure of Labor Productivity

I have found that the clearest way to measure management productivity is through the ratio of management's value added divided by the costs of management. A few definitions are necessary to understand the applicability of this approach.

The total value added by a business unit is computed by subtracting from gross revenue all purchases of components, services, raw materials, and energy. It is essential to focus strictly on those portions of the business output which are direct consequences of the managerial actions one wishes to examine. If a management function such as purchasing is especially effective, for example, it will increase the total value added by improving the terms under which the supplies produced by others' labor are acquired. If advertising makes effective choices, not only will the purchase costs for advertising media decline, but value added may grow further as revenues increase.

Total value added can be further subdivided into elements which distinguish the contribution of capital from the contribution of labor. Labor value added can be broken down further into its operating and its management components. The distinction between operations and management is important because these two kinds of labor are handled in different ways.

As the first step toward productivity analysis, the contribution of capital to the total value added must be subtracted.[2] This is the major distinction between the approach suggested here and other productivity measurement techniques based on value added.[3] The contribution of invested capital to value added has such a decisive effect that

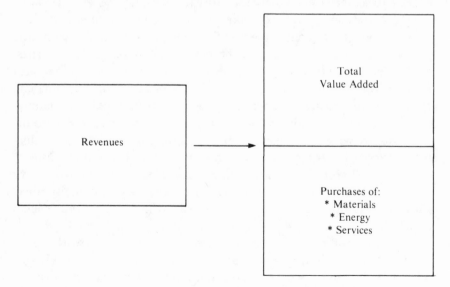

Figure 8.1   How Total Value Added Is Determined

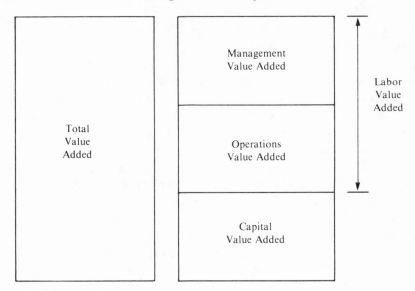

Figure 8.2   Components of Total Value Added

unless it is accounted for separately and explicitly, the contribution of labor to productivity will be always overstated.

The separation of the capital from the labor contributions is also critical when examining the payoff from computers. Usually, analysts fail to distinguish between labor and capital effects. It is common practice to assign all productivity gains to operating personnel. Only rarely is an attempt made to make the necessary adjustments for increased productivity contributed by the deployment of added capital.[4]

The next step is to separate the contributions of operations and management, the two major classes of labor value added. For our purposes, operations will be defined as work done by people designated by such names as direct labor, "blue-collar," goods-production labor, operatives, clerks directly serving customers, and billable professionals. The costs of personnel engaged in operations may be evaluated by straightforward methods for measurement of physical output. Many "white-collar" employees may be also classified in operations if they are a direct, variable cost of an enterprise's output. Incidentally, this is why the traditional distinctions between "white-collar" and "blue-collar" labor have ceased to be useful for productivity evaluation.

The labor value added by management includes the work done by all people classified as overhead personnel: organizers, knowledge workers, information workers, executives, managers, and administrators. The productivity of these people is a reflection of their effectiveness, which can be determined by an examination of what remains after the value-added contributions from all other sources have been accounted for.

Having made these distinctions, one can proceed to compute total labor productivity. The entire computation can be shown in the classic form of productivity = output/input—except that in this method output is defined with the aid of a variable determined by the marketplace, that is, by revenue.[5]

For instance, in analyzing the labor productivity of several oil refining companies with different degrees of integration (from exploration through refining and distribution), subtracting the cost of purchased oil and the value of mineral assets makes it possible to compare labor productivity on a more realistic basis. Similarly, if a company purchases all of its telecommunications services from a telecommunications carrier, the costs of these services should not be included in value added because they represent labor and capital costs incurred by others.[6] On the other hand, if telecommunications facilities are operated internally, labor costs, capital investment costs, and depreciation should be included in the value added because this technology is made productive through the effectiveness of management.

A similar calculation of labor productivity can be obtained by adding up all of the cost elements under the direct organizational control of management. Either method allows one to make period-to-period comparisons which show either productivity gains or losses.[7]

Value-Added Measure of Management Productivity

The economic value of management can be measured by finding out what is left after everyone else has been paid.

After all purchases are subtracted, after the cost of capital has been accounted for, and after payment of wages and benefits to operating labor, what remains is management value added. It includes all profits and taxes plus whatever difference remains from revenue.[8] Management productivity is then computed by dividing management's value added by the cost of management.

The key factor in arriving at this management productivity ratio is the definition of management cost: it includes wages, salaries, bonuses, and benefits as well as directly related expenses such as office space and the perquisites accorded management personnel. It also includes depreciation, long-term lease payments, and royalties and fees for all technology involved in support of management. It *excludes* product-related information-technology expenses if the firm is in the business of selling information. For example, the cost of computerized phototypesetting technology in a publishing firm would be a part of the direct cost of goods. Similarly, in an engineering consulting firm, where the cost of a drawing would be estimated as a direct cost, the expense for computer-aided drafting would be included among product-related information expenses.

Our purpose here is to focus sharply on those managerial activities which involve passing, analyzing, storing, and assembling information so that others, directly engaged in activities related to products, can function more effectively. Given this focus, changes in the management productivity ratio will indicate how personnel engaged in organizing have improved performance of the enterprise as a whole.[9]

Value-Added Measure of Information Technology

The technique I have chosen for analyzing the effectiveness of information technology assumes that the value added attributable to information technology is an incremental change within an already established level of management productivity. Information-technology productivity, then, indicates whether increments in the productivity of management are growing faster than the costs of providing information technology.[10]

There is a limit to the amount of information one may extract from any productivity ratio, however. That is why I have found productivity indexes, used alone, so unsatisfactory. The strategic aspects of information technology are best explained in terms of their influence on business results, such as changes in market share, improved product quality, increased market penetration, higher profit margins, and enhanced customer service.[11]

To gain strategic insights about information-technology investments, one must apply the techniques derived from strategic analysis of business units.[12] This is why the entire value-added approach finally ended up as a part of the multifactor PIMS (Product Impact of Marketing Strategies) database rather than as an outgrowth of financial or econometric methods.

Strategic Analysis of Information Technology

To deal with the complex issues of evaluating information worker productivity—which I defined in a much broader sense as management productivity—a new research program was started in 1983 as part of the PIMS database. The PIMS organization was chosen because it has accumulated, over more than fifteen years, perhaps the world's largest experimental collection of financial and nonfinancial data about more than 2,000 businesses. The uniqueness of this database lies in the multiplicity of pertinent variables available for evaluations. It is designed to permit multifactor correlation studies on the effects of revenue, competitive position, capital investment, research and development, labor costs, and more than 200 other variables relevant to generally accepted measures of financial performance. The objective of this program is to gather and analyze actual business data. Businesses enter their own information into the PIMS database and receive evaluations of their financial and competitive position. The data covers at least four years of history for each variable and includes not only financial history, but marketing information, competitive data, cost profiles, industry information, and indicators describing the structure of the business.

The PIMS database has evolved from what was originally a strong manufacturing orientation. A new program, known as "The PIMS Program on Management Productivity and Information Technology" calls for businesses to provide supplemental data involving over forty new items. The principal innovation of this approach is the split of all labor and capital into operations and management categories. The new approach also includes a thorough analysis of information-technology purchases and expenses.

The objective of the program is to allow participants to assess the contributions of information technology to management value added, while simultaneously keeping all of the other strategic variables linked to changes in management productivity. The entire scheme is neither a financial nor an econometric model. It can be best characterized as a collection of historical profiles of actual business experiences which makes it possible to distinguish patterns of failure from patterns of success. When a new company's data is entered, its patterns are matched against successful and unsuccessful look-alikes in the database. The PIMS technique uses the accumulated experience of many firms to pinpoint whether applications of information technology can be reasonably expected to succeed or fail.

Perhaps the best way of understanding the PIMS methodology is to compare it with the protocol followed when making a medical diagnosis. In medical practice, information obtained from a new patient is matched against known signs of health and sickness. Diagnosis then follows from a systematic evaluation of such indicators. The physician may not only cure the patient but also, in the process, expand his or her understanding about sickness and health.

The PIMS methodology is designed to permit analysis of the value contributed by subdivisions of a firm. Since the total value added must be made up by summing the contributions of individual operating units, there is an upper limit which productivity claims may not exceed. The observation that the total cannot exceed the sum of the parts is trivial—unless one has attended budget meetings where claims to the contrary are made.

The PIMS program uses management value added as a means of tying overhead costs to business performance. The PIMS database is also used to augment the existing methodology for creating target productivity estimates, and for assessing reasonably achievable levels of improvement. The probability of realizing unusual promised gains will be compared with actual profiles of achievement already in the database. Underachievers may be evaluated as to their progress. This approach then permits the computation of reasonable targets, also known as "par" values.

The greatest advantage to use of the existing PIMS database lies in its ability to relate other strategic variables, such as market share, vertical integration, and product quality to management productivity. The correlation between frequently used operational measures, such as return on sales, return on investment, market share, and management productivity, is very high.

Application to Studies of Specific Companies

Detailed information about management costs, purchases, and information technology is not always adequate at the business unit level to make computation of productivity ratios possible. There are situations in which one needs to get a quick insight into a company's overall productivity performance before being able to diagnose what strategic or tactical moves would be advisable. A number of corporations publish financial information that allows the computation of labor productivity indices based on value-added analysis, provided that total payroll information is also available.[13] I am encouraged by the discovery that labor productivity indices are comparable not only within a specific industry, but also across several industries, once the effects of different levels of investment, payroll, and vertical integration are accounted for. Labor productivity information compiled in this form seems much more understandable and easier to apply than other techniques.

Such an analysis can be used to examine the ramifications of a proposed information-technology investment program. For instance, if a company shows labor productivity below the trend line, it may more seriously consider information-technology investments that reduce labor costs. If a company's labor productivity is above the trend line, consideration should be given to capital conservation and to market development improvements with the aid of information-technology investments.

Productivity Analysis at the Departmental Level

For a departmental example, I selected data from the 1981 National Retail Merchants Association's financial data book. My objective was

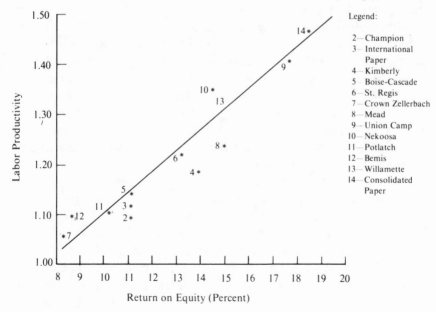

Figure 8.3 Labor Productivity (Ratio) vs. ROE (1980) for Paper Manufacturers

to focus on the results and the ratios for twenty-seven U.S. department stores with sales in excess of $100 million a year.

In the period from 1977 through 1980, pre-tax earnings, expressed as a fraction of sales, declined from 7.47% to 5.50%. In the same period, information-technology costs increased from 9.54% to 10.23% of sales. The net effect of these opposing trends was a large increase in the ratio of information-technology costs to pre-tax earnings—a 56% increase. The question, couched entirely in conventional financial terms, was as follows: Are the department stores spending too much money for computers?

To gain a better insight into the situation, I examined all of the information-handling costs of department stores. As a first step, I isolated those store functions that were dedicated to the processing of information. All categories engaged directly in the handling of merchandise were excluded, that is, all operations activities such as sales- or warehouse labor. Next, I decided to examine only those information functions which were heavily automated, such as invoicing, accounting, and credit. The heavily automated functions showed a modest cost decline of 1.3% per year, largely attributable to improvements in the credit department. The improvements in the labor costs of automated departments were offset, however, by an almost equal increase in the costs of the data-processing department.

After four years of computer automation, there was little to show in terms of improved overall cost performance by labor-intensive departments handling routine paperwork. In heavily automated departments, productivity declined by 0.17%, while in the data-processing department it increased by 0.07%. I considered this to be a questionable trade-off. It was an unsatisfactory performance because information technology should deliver substantial gains in performing traditional paperwork functions: it is one of the few sources of realizable productivity improvement in this area.

Next, I sorted out information functions that were not influenced in any significant way by computers. The labor costs in these departments were four times greater than in highly automated departments. The labor cost increases in the departments not subject to automation were substantial and accounted for about half of the deterioration in the overall profit performance for the department stores. Executive office management and personnel administration accounted for most of the cost increases. This indicated that some other developments—unrelated in any way to information technology—were taking place.

Here we see a classic case of what happens when management

concentrates entirely on automating routine administrative tasks: in the department stores this amounted to less than one quarter of all information work. My conclusion about this situation was that even though data-processing results were disappointing, there were other developments, related to unusually high cost increases in the staffing of headquarters, that needed examination before any cuts in information-technology expenses could be made with confidence.

This highly condensed version of a department-level analysis illustrates how the value-added approach to labor costs and to information technology simplifies a diagnostic overview of otherwise complex trends. The value-added measure of productivity sets up ratios that do not need to be adjusted for rapidly rising labor costs, for changed patterns of purchasing, or for the changing prices of information technology. The value-added ratios also make comparisons possible across a group of stores with completely different employment patterns.

Sensitivity Analysis

Executives responsible for investments in information technology are coming to realize how closely they must relate such investments with overall strategic planning for those investments to make sense. As long as computer technology was used merely to reduce operating or overhead expenses, the relationship between technology investments and business strategy was more remote and indirect. This is why expenditures for computers over the last twenty-five years concentrated almost exclusively on eliminating growth in clerical and secretarial jobs.

One of the interesting by-products of value-added analysis is sensitivity analysis: the ability to predict how improvements in any part of the business will affect total value added. For instance, in a material resources company, I isolated the effectiveness of the purchasing function as the most rewarding opportunity for information technology. Previously, the organization was concentrating almost exclusively on a companywide office automation program for secretaries and typists. Sensitivity analysis revealed that the most optimistic productivity projections for all of the 150 secretaries and typists would be infinitesimal when compared with even modest gains within the purchasing department.

It is possible that none of the high-leverage parts of an organization can usefully absorb information technology. In that case, all that remains is the relatively easy target of text-processing automation, with its easily verifiable productivity results from reduction of secretarial and clerical labor needs. One should not, however, pursue even the easier opportunities unless one has tested whether they are worth it.

A major advantage of the value-added approach to investment analysis is its strategic overview of all potential investment areas. It provides a framework for examining the entire range of options before embarking on a particular project. This technique permits management to ask questions about the proper allocation of information-technology investments to various activities. It militates against the possibility that only projects with well-organized proponents will be considered. One should not look for opportunity only where the situation is well illuminated. Opportunities for really great gains frequently lie where nobody has looked before.

Auditing and Benchmarking

One should not be too critical about the absence of credible economic analysis of information-technology expenditures. There are very few organizations which can perform the kind of audits needed. Nevertheless, the track record of information technology can and should be established by using benchmarking tools and by means of historical reviews of actually realized information-technology gains.

To illustrate this point, there is the case of an organization that has been highly visible in advertising its prowess and its avant-garde applications of information technology. I still remember the two-page advertisements in the *Wall Street Journal,* where the company's president pointed out wage increases and technology-cost decreases as the rationale for rapid computerization. The advertising then proceeded to outline a massive investment program to reduce labor costs by investment in technology. An examination of the firm's record indicated what appeared to be a real winner. Revenue had almost doubled while information costs were up only about 35%. Unit labor costs were up by nearly 20%. The technology/labor ratio had increased by only 3.8 percentage points. A fantastic success story? Not by value-added standards. Information productivity, as measured in terms of the enterprise's total value added divided by total information costs, had in fact declined by 17%. I believe that a productivity-based auditing and tracking report would have alerted management much sooner to a situation in which the information technology investment rate had outrun value-added improvements.

The Limits of Value-Added Analysis

Management productivity is an outcome rather than a cause.

To understand the productivity of those who manage organizations, we should first agree on how to measure their performance. There are a number of points to be made about the limitations of the value-added approach in measuring managerial productivity.

First, value-added productivity should not be viewed as a result of individual's activities. Accomplishments are only discernible for an organization as a whole. In other words, the excellent executive cannot be considered to be productive if the rest of the organization cannot translate his intentions into results. Consequently, the productivity of management must be measured by its performance as a team, rather than by summing up individual efficiencies. Unlike the case of operational results, the productivity of management is not calculated by aggregating the productivity of each manager—even if it were possible to track each manager's work. Due to the large amount of shared resources represented in managerial overhead, unbiased measurement of productivity through the summation of parts is not a practical idea anyway. The efficiency of overhead expenses is not definable in itself. This is why the only realistic method for justifying information-technology investments for managers and professionals is to regard such investments as an aggregate in relation to the operation of the entire business. The justification of equipment as a timesaving device is valid only for people in operations. Management should acquire information technology as a way of improving the effectiveness of the entire management process, such as by making it possible to change organizational design. Information technology itself may not save any time: it may actually require *more* time to arrive at a small number of really important decisions. What counts, of course, is whether the decisions reached are the right ones.

Second, management productivity must be verifiable by existing reporting methods. Productivity results based on value added must tie in with published measures of financial performance— the external yardsticks by which others judge results. Firms spend large amounts of their overhead to maintain their accounting and financial control systems. Planning, budgeting, and reward schemes for all corporations are built upon the foundation of these generally accepted systems. It would be highly impractical to consider erecting a management productivity measurement system that would be independent of a base that is already so pervasive. Insofar as the current methods of financial reporting may be distorted for accounting, tax, or regulatory reasons, adjustments to the published data must be made. For example, adjustments for proper valuation of assets will be necessary to reflect actual profits. This limits the applicability of value-added computations to operating units which have a profit-and-loss statement and a balance sheet. Public sector organizations may apply value-added evaluations in the absence of market prices and profits provided that an independent benchmark for the value of their services can be established.

Third, it should be recognized that to measure management performance using value added based only on current profits is too limited an approach. A broader measure of management performance, reflecting a firm's ability to grow and to increase its value to shareholders is desirable. Some of this can be done by adjusting current expenses for research and development, or for training, to include only those expenses which can be expected to have long-term payoffs. This is why a truly comprehensive evaluation of the value added by management must also tie in such strategic factors as investments in gaining market share, in expansion of the product line, in growth of shareholders' equity, and in increasing the skills of employees.

Fourth, the use of office automation technology in support of management personnel recognizes that we may displace labor cost, improve revenue, increase prices, add to capital expenses, improve quality, and gain in market share—or do any of the above in some combination. The value-added method for analyzing productivity improvements concisely expresses a large number of these variables as an aggregate, but it becomes useful only when it is included as a part of a much broader, multivariate analysis of strategic performance.

Fifth, the key measure that we have defined as management value added is based on the premise that those who plan, direct and control bear full responsibility and accountability for the results. They should also receive the full credit (or discredit) for the way the organization performs. Suppliers, government, financial institutions, and operating personnel all can make a contribution to the value generated by the enterprise only if management successfully integrates them into the organization's functioning. It follows that the value added of everyone other than management is determined by actual cost. For instance, the value added by factory labor would be set at its labor cost. If there is any sharing of value-added gains in the form of incentives, these are considered to be added expenses rather than an indication of effectiveness. If management had previously agreed to be excessive wage demands, this would be reflected in our computations by a reduction in the management value added as well as in reduced growth, as the organization became less competitive. Similarly, if management had increased its debt by investing in unsuccessful ventures, there would be a reduction in the management's value added. Poor management will yield negative management value added. In other words, management would be paid in excess of its contributions. Under such circumstances, productivity measurement based on value added will not be a very popular index—at least not in management circles. If, however, management is successful, there will be many claimants to share the newly recognized source of wealth. In this case, the simple method for computing value added could become subject to intense attempts at manipulation. The acceptability of value added will be limited by its unforgiving (i.e., objective) characteristics.

Sixth, underlying our approach is the assumption that it is possible to estimate how management actions will affect costs, purchases, market share, pricing, competitive advantage, product quality, and revenue growth. This presumes that a marketplace exists which will respond to management's actions and will act as an arbiter of management's value. In cases where management is a multilayered bureaucracy, with more than six levels of management between management decisions and the marketplace, it is unlikely that information-technology investments in support of management can be clearly related to identifiable gains in management productivity. Based on early indications, it appears that the proposed methodology has a bias in favor of smaller strategic business units, enterprises which have a strong profit orientation, and organizations which have a relatively simple structure. In cases where most of the market share-, pricing, and strategic growth decisions are fixed by regulation, political decision making, or cartel agreements, it is unlikely that management value added would be a useful concept. It is, therefore, important to realize that a large portion of knowledge labor will not be amenable to the value-added approach, and that benchmarking comparisons will have to apply to such forms of information work.

To make computations of management productivity possible, a technique based on value added rather than on output/input is proposed. Illustrative examples show how this technique can capture a much broader spectrum of influences affecting managerial investment decisions than is the case with simple efficiency-based ratios. A major research program to test these concepts is currently under way. A great deal of work needs to be done in applying value-added methods before all the advantages and disadvantages will be known. However, as the focus of computer technology and of office automation shifts from simple clerical automation to more strategic uses, it can be expected that the value-added technique will gain in its applicability to investment decisions.

9

Investment Profitability

Investment in information technology is a business strategy designed to substitute information-technology capital for information-handling labor. Improved effectiveness may be realized through better quality, cost reduction, decreased uses of resources, enhanced use of employee talents, or improved customer service.

The future of information technology will be shaped by the user's abilities to extract favorable returns on information-technology investments. The ratio of capital to output can increase only if there are attractive new profit opportunities to support further capital formation. The current business scene is characterized by a euphoric belief that innovations in information technology will sustain the present rate of expansion in the demand for computers. I am convinced that the potential productivity gains from computers are much greater than what industry is actually reaping. Yet there is insufficient evidence that current investment returns from computers will support the market forecasts which forsee an indefinite continuation of the current growth rates.

Preference for High Tech

Computers have captured the imagination of the country as the spearhead of economic progress.

It is clear that United States capital investment is increasingly turning towards high-technology industries. How rapidly this shift is taking place can be understood best when one examines not only annual investment rates per worker but also the absolute levels achieved as the result of cumulative expenditures.[1]

At the current rate of investment, the high-tech industries have already overtaken basic industry. It will require another five years, at present rates of growth, for high-tech investments to equal basic industrial capital stock, per worker. Of the increases in total capital stock, by far the fastest growth has been in the computer sector.[2]

In 1982 the computer and office-automation industry had overall revenues of $114 billion, with total industry employment of about half a million. In addition, users employed another 1.5 million full-time workers, such as programmers, systems analysts, and equipment operators, to support the information technology products. Altogether this represented 2.0% of the total workforce.[3]

The conventional wisdom is that investments in electronic support to information workers have been inadequate and, therefore, incremental returns on capital should be high.[4] The fact is that in 1982, 33.4% of all producer's durable equipment investments were for computer equipment, while conclusive evidence proving that these investments are highly profitable remains to be shown.[5] The belief that computer investment is inherently profitable sustains an extraordinarily strong level of expenditure on the automation of the information workforce.

The computer industry's rapid growth is particularly noticeable in end-user expenditures. End-user technology expense budgets are estimated to be about 50% of total direct costs for supporting all of the installed information technology. The balance of the expense represents the users' internal expenses for the costs associated with workforce automation.[6] Based on these projections, one can anticipate a yearly $600 to $650 billion information-systems budget supporting management by 1990. This would represent perhaps as much as 10% of the GNP. Such an enormous use of scarce resources, under conditions of increasingly costly capital, warrants a close examination as to the payoff obtained.

The United States is not the only country to expand investments in information technology. For instance, in the area of office-information technology alone, the actual U.S. share of total worldwide expenditures is declining. Similar patterns can be seen in the tele-communications and home computer investment sectors on a global scale. Virtually every country is racing to acquire information technology.[7]

The implications are clear. One of the most explosive investment booms in history is under way. It is fueled by an enormously favorable reception to everything connected with information technology. Are these growth rates sustainable—and if so, for how long?

The current expansionary cycle promises to follow a long-established pattern, in which falling profit margins place limits on the growth of further investment. The falling profit margin of the suppliers is not, however, the most important concern. Instead, the most important determinants will be the result of market forces and of demand saturation among customers. What really matters is whether the customers' own profit returns from information technology will be high enough to sustain their increasing demand for computer products. The levelling-off of the computer boom will result from the inability of user-managers to justify further investments.

What Drives Demand for Computer Technology?

The dampening in demand for information technology will not come from decreasing opportunities to improve the productivity of information workers. Considering the size of the information workforce and its growth over the last few decades, it is unlikely to have reached such high peaks of effectiveness that it will soon run into diminishing returns from a lack of opportunity. Besides, the penetration of personal workstations is still less than 10% for professionals and managers even in the United States, and certainly less elsewhere. Potential demand to support even the most optimistic information-industry forecasts is certainly present.

The question is not one of potential demand but of realizeable demand. Will the total of $600 billion of end-user expenditures be economically affordable? Will it be profitable? Will it be manageable as the emphasis shifts from investments that improve efficiency to investments that increase organizational effectiveness?

Proving Whether Computer Investments Are Profitable

Examining the record of past gains is always a good way to begin an estimate of what the future may bring. Unfortunately, well-documented evidence about the contributions of information capital to improved productivity of the economy is difficult to find. Jonscher's Ph.D. thesis on "Models of Economic Organizations" represents perhaps the one exception. Considering the amount of investment that has been chanelled into this segment of the economy, such neglect is noteworthy, to say the least. There is still no theoretical framework that describes how to gather data on actual information-technology investments and how to assess the results.

There does exist a large collection of anecdotal case studies, obtained largely from the experience of individual firms. These studies tell about inventory cost reductions, about manufacturing-management improvements, about simpler warehousing, and about more efficient dispatching, among other things. There is also a large accumulation of findings from case studies such as those surveyed in Chapter 2. There are hundreds of well-documented descriptions of how gains were realized in individual projects. All of these studies portray how the efficiency or even the effectiveness of particular people or groups of people was improved by means of computer technology. The implied message in each of these cases is that if all of the individual gains are summed up, the firm as a whole will also show improved performance. This is not necessarily true. The sum of small efficiency improvements does not always add up to an aggregate effectiveness gain.

The problem with the anecdotal approach is the high degree of selectivity involved in collecting the evidence. The literature contains only success stories: a scientist would have to reject most of the cases as part of a biased sample. To prove whether information technology is indeed profitable requires a large number of independent observations. Patterns of success as well as of failure would have to be analyzed under conditions in which both good and bad experiences are compared. In terms of acceptable scientific discipline, this calls for a sample of companies using or not using computers, under comparable circumstances. Proof of the superiority of information technology would be then found if one could identify superior profitability with computer users and inferior profitability with nonusers. This assumes, of course, that the effects of computers alone could be isolated from all other effects. Another proof of the positive contribution of computer technology would rely on industry-wide studies showing that segments enjoying a high rate of investment in computer technology demonstrated consistently higher productivity and profitability than segments which had not made such investments.

Ostensibly, such studies are so scarce due to the difficulties in collecting data and then devising a method to filter out influences unrelated to computerization. I do not agree that methodological and statistical obstacles explain the dearth of factual studies. Medicine uses medical epidemiological studies to isolate much more complex physiological variables pertaining to lung cancer, diabetes, pesticides, and the effects of food additives. From a purely analytical standpoint, there are no significant differences in the statistical methods needed to test a new cancer drug or to demonstrate the effects of computers on organizations. There has simply been insufficient attention devoted to the question of why some companies use computers very effectively and others do not.

Until recently, the technical problems involved in getting computers to do what they were supposed to do at a reasonable cost—the supply side of the computer revolution—have overshadowed the question of whether computers were economically viable. I sense that a major alteration in emphasis is about to take place. It will be a matter of only a few years before the demand side of the computer revolution will take precedence. Information technology will become so plentiful and so easily installed that management will be able to pay attention to economic objectives rather than concerning itself primarily with the means of getting the jobs done. As this refocusing gradually takes place, the issues of investment levels, payoffs, efficiency, and, especially, organizational effectiveness, will become paramount.

Computerization and Performance: The Wholesaler Case

So far, I have been able to find only one statistically valid case study about the economic effects of computers at the level of individual firms. In this case 138 wholesalers were examined.[8] The wholesalers all had total sales in the range of $1 to $10 million per year and had comparable profiles in the way they conducted business. There is no reason to believe that any bias was involved in selecting the businesses or in the way the findings were classified. The firms owning computers and making extensive use of them included both high- and low-level performers, as measured in terms of ROA (return on assets). Similarly, firms not using computers had both high and low

ROAs. Here we have a controlled sample of sufficient size and variety
to provide an adequate test of whether using computers makes any
economic difference.

The entire study consisted of classifying the firms into approxi-
mately comparable groups (as defined by the range of applications):
firms with "no usage" of computers, firms with "medium usage,"
and firms having "heavy usage" of computers. In each situation the
criterion of performance selected was the commonly used ratio reflecting the profit performance of the firm in terms of average return on
assets. The research findings were as follows:

	Average Return on Assets
No computer	11.3%
Medium usage of computers	9.8%
Heavy usage of computers	8.8%

The average return on assets for the nonusers was significantly higher
than the average return on assets for the heavy users, with the medium-
level users falling almost exactly in between. The data supporting
the study show a very interesting profile in the way ROA quartiles
were distributed in each group to make up its average. Only 11% of
the companies with no computer use were in the lowest quartile. Medium users had 30% of their sample in the lowest quartile. Heavy
users had a sizeable 43% of their sample in the lowest quartile. In
fact, the averages alone are not adequate indicators of the true situation.

My conclusion about the distribution of the sample is that the
risk profile of companies which used computers heavily was much
greater than that of companies without computers. To quote the re-
searchers in the case: "The low-performing firms tended to be rather
small firms with above-average operating expenses. Computers may
significantly increase the total operating expenses. . . ." [9]

Another way of looking at the sample is to notice that among
the heavy users 30% were successful companies who used the computers well. The average for heavy users was so low because 43% of
the sample, in the lowest quartile, depressed the average. Whether
the laggards were in trouble for other business reasons anyway, and
the cost of computers simply added further to their woes, is not clear
from the data supplied. Most likely the answer would be the same
as that indicated by other studies of the general effects of capital
investments on business profitability. [10] A high level of capital invest-

ment relative to value added makes good firms better and bad firms worse. Firms that do not have their communications in good order prior to attempting automation will only compound their difficulties by further investments in information-handling technology. The following rule is, therefore, suggested:

Install automated office systems only after improving business communications as far as possible by other means.

In the wholesalers' case outlined above, the rule sheds light on the diversity of results. The poor performers that invested heavily in computers were most likely trying to solve their other problems by means of a technological panacea.

The suggested rule may also explain why wholesalers without computers had superior average ROAs: they had fewer losers than the group which used computers heavily. Also, their costs would not have been influenced adversely by the turmoil which the introduction of information technology always creates, at least initially. Without computers, the chances are that much greater reliance would be placed on people with individual initiative rather than on employees following highly structured systems and procedures. But one cannot be sure, because too many other variables become involved when making the apparently simple correlation between computer usage and return on assets.

Even though the wholesaler study is unusual in its scope and quality, it leaves more questions unanswered than it resolves. Not enough data from the individual companies were published to allow satisfactory explanations for the observed differences. Attributes other than computer usage, such as market share, wage levels, employee morale, overhead costs, debt–equity ratios, management structure, management style, and marketing effectiveness could help to distinguish why the high-performing heavy users differed from the high-performing nonusers.

Management Productivity and Information Technology

Gathering a wide array of variables and generating comparisons between patterns of success and failure is an ideal technique for finding out which conditions make investments in computer technology profitable. The approach is to collect large amounts of detailed data from each firm and then to subject these data to what is technically called "multivariate cross-sectional correlation analysis." Comparisons are made not only for the current situation, but also over a period of several years to show how new trends may develop.

Multivariate analysis is an essential tool for analyzing complex interactions. For instance, let us assume that we want to know how medical expenditures improve life expectancy. This is not just a theoretical exercise. The effectiveness of expensive new treatments must be validated before they are approved for general use. A new pharmaceutical may cure one disease but simultaneously cause regrettable side effects. Merely comparing life-expectancy figures with levels of medical expenditures will not give us very useful results. Some people with very low medical expenses will have both very high, as well as very low, life-expectancy; similarly, people incurring very high medical expenses may be at either extreme of the "healthiness" scale.

The practice of medicine requires experimental isolation of subtle relationships, as was the case in establishing the link between smoking and various maladies, or in proving that excess cholesterol is associated with heart disease. Statistical studies of both health and disease are necessary to set medical insurance rates and to determine life insurance premiums. Medical research employs multivariate analysis of experimental data to separate predictable consequences from unprovable assumptions. Drugs are tested not only to substantiate the manufacturer's claims, but also to reveal how they should be used as a part of an overall medical treatment.

Relating information-technology expenditures to productivity results is comparable in difficulty to establishing the relationship between medical costs and health. We must be able to demonstrate, from valid data, which business environments are detrimental to productivity. We must be able to test hypotheses about why certain organizations enjoy unusually favorable results from information technology, while others are actually damaged by it. We must be able to identify the effects of nontechnological influences along with the gains from the use of computers. We must be able to find which combination of technology, people, and investments will deliver the best results. We cannot declare a firm's information system to be successful if the business continues to deteriorate.

The long-term value of research in this area lies in its ability to aid in establishing the influences associated with the incidence of low productivity. When sufficient numbers of high-performance as well as low-performance companies are included in the research database, it will be possible to calculate what levels of management productivity can be expected compared with a firm's competitors. It is conceivable that a low performer may be above the productivity benchmark, thus indicating good management; it is also possible that a higher performer is below the productivity benchmark, thus indicating the feasibility of further productivity improvements.

Based on an admittedly small sample of businesses, there are already good reasons to conclude that there is no direct and simple correlation between management productivity and information technology. They may in fact be unrelated. The preliminary findings of my research raises doubts about the assumptions which managements in the businesses I have sampled so far must have made when they increased their computer-technology budgets in pursuit of improved productivity:

1. Computers will not make a bad business good.
2. Automation is a great cure, but it is not a panacea.
3. A bad strategic situation cannot be corrected by automating it.
4. Automate success, not failure.

This testing of the concept of management productivity based on value added was completed late in 1983. Forty businesses signed up for the pilot program. They provided detailed data covering the period from 1978 through 1982. Altogether, 200 measurements—each supplemented by information on more than 100 variables describing the businesses—were entered into a research database maintained by the Strategic Planning Institute. Elaborate security precautions were in place, audited by a major accounting firm, to make sure that the identity of a participating business could not be traced. This was the only way to obtain revealing financial and marketing data about each business. As in the case of a medical research project, individual names are less relevant than the physical and mental condition of those under scrutiny. The primary purpose of the pilot program was to validate the value-added concepts and to test the analytical techniques that link management productivity to information technology. The secondary purpose of the research was to explore whether and how information technology was affected by the strategic position of the businesses.

The research findings apply only to the forty companies' experiences over the five years under study. The pilot program had only limited data, even though the sample is large enough to be representative of what one may expect in further study. The results are adequate for validation of methodology, but certainly not sufficient to establish definitive rules. At this moment, an effort is under way to enlarge the database by at least 150 more businesses so that it will be possible to arrive at more widely valid conclusions in the future.

In the absence of any comparable research, the pilot study results are, nevertheless, indicative of a number of significant trends:

1. *When confronted with the need to reduce overall employment, the ratio of operating personnel to managers remains constant.* During the five-year period in question the total employment of firms participating in the study declined by 30%. Management employment, as a percent of total employment, remained at the same level (16.5%) in 1982 as in 1978.

2. *Management got no closer to either customers or to operations.* Closeness to customers and to operations was reported in terms of the number of organizational layers intervening between the chief executive officer and the immediate customers, or between the chief executive officer and the first level of supervision. On the average, the chief executive officer was three organizational layers removed from customers and four organizational layers removed from first-line supervision. Despite a 30% reduction in the total number of personnel, the hierarchy remained the same over a five-year period.

3. *Management costs as a percentage of revenue continued to rise.* It seems that overhead costs were managed by controlling the numbers rather than the costs of management employees. The more costly executive, professional, and managerial personnel increased as a percentage of total employment from 44% to 47%, while the number of lower-paid support personnel decreased. This explains why the cost of management as a percentage of revenue rose steadily from 21% to 24%.

4. *Payroll costs are only about half of total management costs.* This finding was one of the most surprising and may be distorted by the presence of a number of companies with large advertising costs classified as externally purchased management expense. At any rate, the management payroll accounted for only 55% of management costs. Purchased services and capital investments made up the balance. In view of the magnitude of such purchases, I am convinced that insufficient attention is given to them when considering information-technology investments. Attention to information-technology projects is currently focused almost entirely on displacement of labor.

5. *There is a strong relationship between the extent of vertical integration of management and management productivity.* Vertical integration is defined as the fraction of total management costs supplied by

the business unit. If external purchases or centrally provided services are increased, vertical integration decreases. Moderate levels of vertical integration were found to be most productive. Businesses with vertical integration below 50% exhibited moderately declining management productivity. Businesses with vertical integration in excess of 75% showed rapidly declining management productivity.

These findings seem to support my belief that organizations which attempt to be excessively self-sufficient build up large fixed administrative costs and remove too many people from any external test of viability. If this is confirmed by data from many more cases, it will justify a policy of using purchased services rather than hiring new staff when high levels of vertical integration are reached.

6. *Information technology, as a percentage of management costs, continues to rise.* The median information-technology expenditure, as a percentage of total management costs, was found to be 8%. However, total management costs also include external purchases. Therefore, the more meaningful comparison relates information technology expenses to management wages and salaries. The ratio of information-technology related costs (which includes computers, telephone services, programming, and similar services) rose from 21.5% of management labor costs to 28.2% over a five-year period for the users in the top quartile. In such firms information technology became a major share of the administrative cost of conducting business. Such high levels of expense were totally unexpected.

7. *In more than 40% of these companies, management costs exceeded value added by management.* A large fraction of the companies showed productivity below 1.0: that is, input exceeded output costs. Large costs for capital were the principal source of diminished value added. There were also good performers. More than half of the companies had productivity in excess of 1.0, and 16% of them delivered management productivity in excess of 3.0. High-performance management showed that it could deliver three dollars of value added for every dollar they received in salary and benefits.

8. *Information-technology costs showed no correlation with management productivity.* A large number of companies spent less than 10% of management costs on information technology, while delivering 2.0 or better productivity results. There was an equivalent number of companies that spent between 22% and 41% of management costs on information technology while experiencing poor productivity. Then there were companies that spent well over 50% of management costs on information technology. They had, on the average, high productiv-

ity—but one could also find instances of very high-, as well as below-average productivity in the sample.

9. *Year-to-year increases in information technology expenditures showed improved management productivity if the companies' strategic positions were superior to begin with.* In businesses with an already well-established strategic potential, measured in such terms as market share, product quality, or utilization of assets, information technology investments paid off nicely. Year-to-year increases in information technology expenditures were correlated with year-to-year increases in management productivity. Under-performers either did not show improvements or actually deteriorated.[11] Companies with an inferior strategic position showed declining management productivity even with increasing levels of information-technology costs.

Does Capital Investment Increase Productivity?

The idea that trading capital for labor is always "a good thing" is perhaps behind much of the current thinking when information-technology investments are authorized. I thought it might be worthwhile to search for evidence whether such a substitution is indeed rewarding. In preparation for the White House Conference on Productivity in 1983, the Bureau of Labor Statistics compiled many findings to document historical trends in productivity.[12] Behind the much-lamented drop of U.S. productivity to a mere 0.4% per annum growth over the last decade lies the strongly depressive effect of diminishing capital productivity: −2.6% per annum. It follows that capital investments were made in unnecessary, ineffective, or poorly utilized assets, thus lowering overall productivity gains.

Labor output per hour also declined in the 1973–81 period, but the net productivity growth rate of only 0.4% was caused more by a reversal in the role of capital than by the declining contribution from labor. The warning is clear: overinvestment is likely unless capital investment decisions are prudent.[13]

The Case of Missing Productivity Gains

There is a worthwhile study which examines the comparative changes in labor and capital that have taken place in the banking and insurance industry.[14] The results do not support the idea that high levels of investment in computers necessarily yield improved overall productivity. In the banking and insurance industry, the rapid rise in the capital-to-labor ratio is almost certainly influenced by large increases in computer automation. In ten years this ratio almost doubled, from 0.64 in 1970 to 1.125 in 1980. At the same time, capital productivity declined from 1.508 to 0.856. This could perhaps be explained by the principle of diminishing returns on capital, except that labor productivity did not change during this period. It remained at 0.964 of output, practically the same as in 1970.

These econometric analyses of productivity are by no means the full story of what happened to the banking and insurance industry during the 1970s. The effectiveness of the entire financial services system and what has happened to the quality of financial services enjoyed by U.S. consumers are dimensions which have not been captured in any of the index numbers. The stagnant labor-productivity numbers simply show that even in America's two most automated service industries, there is no discernible effect on labor productivity as result of extensive investments in computers.

Another Case of Missing Productivity

The Bureau of Labor Statistics has kept a detailed record of productivity in the banking industry, one of the most highly computerized sectors in the economy.[15] One would assume that with large increases in capital equipment, the number of people employed in banking should grow more slowly than output. That is not the case.[16] Even though output-per-hour grew somewhat, the index of total output for the banking industry now stands at 106.1%, whereas employment stands at 115.7%. So much for the allegation that computers cause overall unemployment.

Capital investment cycles typically follow a pattern that leads from an exuberant initial growth to a sustainable economic level when maturity is finally balanced with fundamental demand. Investments in information technology are not exempt from this life cycle, except that the transition from the euphoric to the subdued stage may occur more rapidly than previous investment cycles might lead us to expect.[17] This by no means reverses my assessment of the exceptional promise of information technology, which remains an enormously potent force for achieving productivity gains.

My emphasis is on the need for a more sober approach to insure that investments in information technology will pay off; as a consequence, new surplus can be generated, which in turn can be used for further investments. Disappointed customers will not long remain customers. New techniques of investment analysis based on organizational effectiveness should be adopted by management to make sure that information-technology investments deliver the results they promise.[18]

10

The Paperless Office

It is scarcely possible to engage in business conversation these days without encountering the topic of computers and office automation. Normally conservative business journals compete to establish their high-tech image by publishing high-tech feature stories dealing with computer technology. Newspaper and magazine articles about the coming computer revolution are exceedingly popular. Computer buzzwords and jargon have permeated the English language.

One bit of jargon that has attained exceptional popularity amid the speculation about what the office-of-the-future may look like is particularly interesting. "The paperless office," however, is a misleading term.

The prevailing views about computers are technologically based and therefore simplistic. They miss the subtlety of the new information tools. For instance, the fact that information can now be conveyed electronically to a display tube and then electronically manipulated with great ease leads many to the conclusion that there will not be any further need for paper in offices. If the office-of-the-future will be paperless, as alleged, then it may be financially foolish to invest in new plants that make paper, especially if it takes well over twenty-five years to amortize such an investment. It may be also imprudent to invest in research and development of new ways to print more economically.

This chapter illustrates how such cursory observations can be misleading and can lead to fallacious conclusions, especially if based only on technological considerations. The "paperless office" is just one of many misnomers in the general area of information technology. Others deserve similar scrutiny.

Toward Paperless Information Systems

The rapidity and ease with which text can be moved electronically and then displayed on a Visual Display Unit (VDU) has led to the unwarranted conclusion that the "paperless office" is one of the primary characteristics of office automation.

The frequently quoted book *Toward Paperless Information Systems* is just one indication of the tremendous interest in developing computer systems that would do without paper.[1] Getting rid of paper is an easily articulated objective. Many leading executives take this objective quite seriously as a simple way of expressing what they are trying to accomplish by computer investments. In January of 1982, I heard the chairman of one of the largest United States insurance companies make the pronouncement that by the end of 1983 his company would be free of paper. Although the insurance company did eliminate huge numbers of unnecessary forms and install new computing equipment, there was no noticeable difference in the total amount of paper used in its offices by December of 1983.

I think that the chairman was simply appalled by his excessive administrative costs. He should have realized that paper is actually quite cheap, and that the truly excessive costs are caused by unnecessary labor expenses. The chairman should have motivated his organization to remedy that problem if he wanted lower administrative costs. By going after pages of paper instead, he pursued a merely symbolic goal. Zealous pursuit of such displaced, instant remedies can actually cause an increase in costs; the effort expended in chasing after pieces of paper may divert attention from the real problems of unresponsive customer service and ineffective organizational design.

The Federal Paperwork Reduction Act of 1980 actually legislated the elaborate annual counting and reporting of pieces of paper eliminated from government transactions. Counting pages of paper while overall costs are escalating and the scope of the government's activities is changing may be of some use. But it avoids dealing with the more fundamental questions of evaluating the actual results delivered by a government agency. I have examined the annual paperwork reduction reports and found them inconclusive, to say the least.

In an effort to clarify what is fact and what is fiction about the paperless office, I will examine both the economic and the human factors involved.

The Economics of Paper

There is a relationship between the method of office communications and the use of paper. The economics of paper consumption changes with electronic printing.

Office paper usage, per information worker, has been growing steadily since 1946 at a rate about double that of the growth in the GNP. My projected paper-consumption estimate, per information worker, for 1992 is 24,600 pages per year. It is a conservative estimate because occupational shifts continue to favor those personnel who use a lot of office paper. For instance, operations labor—which uses only small amounts of office paper—continues to decline, whereas professional and technical manpower (notorious gluttons for paper, at rates of more than 300% of the average)—continues to increase.

We can feel safe about our forecasts of increased paper consumption in the office because of the proliferation of the means to make copies. The number of data-processing–high-volume printers will most likely increase from the current 250,000 to more than 420,000 by the end of the 1980s. A substantial growth in office printers is also anticipated: from 2.1 million in 1982 to at least 11 million in 1988. I view electronic printers as highly efficient engines for low-cost printing on paper. More printers certainly generate more paper copies. Moreover, the rapid introduction of VDUs actually promotes the making of copies because VDUs are a very effective means of generating originals. Inexpensive originals breed conveniently produced and inexpensive copies. Copies require paper.

In 1983 I appeared before the American Paper Institute at a meeting devoted to exploring the future impact of electronics on the paper industry. Preceding me on the platform was a consultant with a well-established reputation as an expert on the office-of-the-future. The expert's conclusion was that the VDU screen is so efficient as a means of manipulating text and graphics that people will make much less use of the printed medium in the future. His presentation included about sixty transparencies which he himself produced on his personal graphic computer. To illustrate his point, he noted that at least 240 sheets of paper were saved in the process of preparing his presentation as compared with his prior approach, in which he had to employ a graphic artist to prepare the visual aids. I noted that an unusually large number of transparencies were used during the presentation. The expert agreed: there were so many because they were so easy to produce, he said. This brought the net savings, based on comparison with old methods, down to only 60 sheets of paper. However, the presentation was executed with such skill that all of the 180 attendees wanted copies of each chart. There was thus a net increase in paper consumption of more than 8,000 sheets of paper due to creative use of the electronic medium!

Another way to check on our projected growth rates is to look at the fastest-growing part of the office business: computer paper shipments per billion dollars of GNP. Such shipments increase at an 8% compound growth rate. Electronic printing has generated an enormous capacity for printing information at a materially reduced unit cost.

It is not paper that is expensive. It is the labor cost that surrounds its use that costs the big money.

To understand what the trends in paper consumption mean, we need to go back to economic fundamentals. Starting with the economics of an office copier is as good a way of understanding the issues as any. In today's office a very efficient copying and duplicating technology is surrounded by very inefficient and expensive office labor. When we come to text creation, we observe that it takes anywhere from $10 to $100 to create an original page. Then we put this original through a copier at $.025 to $.06 per page. Then we use up another $1 to $5 per page to deliver the text to the ultimate users and store it there. There are practical limits to how much one can improve upon the copying of printed originals. There are, however, virtually no limits to the cost-reduction opportunities in the labor that precedes and follows copying.

Incidentally, the economic successes of xerography was one of

the major marketing surprises of the 1960s. Using purely engineering-
and cost-displacement analysis, it was not possible to predict the extraordinary rate of acceptance and use of this technology. As a matter
of fact, the rejection of Chester Carlson's invention by leading United
States corporations and the initially low market forecasts by the Haloid
Company remain as classic examples of a technologically biased
myopia.[2] However, if we examine what has happened on a global
scale with the growth of complex bureaucracies starting in the late
1950s, we will discover that the office copier is the ideal machine
for maintaining low-cost lateral communications in increasingly lay-
ered and structured organizations. The office copier fulfilled a need
that could have been anticipated only through socioeconomic analysis.
The ubiquitous office copier had an immense potential demand awaiting
its invention because it was needed to facilitate the operation of large
organizations. Whether multinational corporations form the building
blocks of a future global commercial society, or whether the decentralized, entrepreneurial organization becomes the preferred way to structure business is likely to have a much greater influence on the future
use of paper than any merely technological development I can think
of. The large, vertically integrated organizations have a greater propensity to rely on written information in order to keep their various functions integrated. They will produce office text in large quantities
because when text is circulated it is not the cost of paper, but the
cost of coordinating communications that can be reduced.

What electronics and computers *can* do for the customer is to
reduce costs in offices where large amounts of labor are consumed
in handling text. With today's technologies the potential reductions
are very large. By replacing a metal filing cabinet with an electronic
one, the labor cost of handling information drops by 60%. By replacing
a mail basket with electronic mail, the labor cost of handling information drops by a further 40%. These cost reductions reflect the ability
of text to travel under computer control. Even so, this technology
still costs too much. At present it takes $.90 to send a page of text
electronically. The total estimated annual volume of electronic text
transmission remains a relatively insignificant 2 billion pages. The
projected 1995 costs for transmitting a page of text within the United
States is about $.08. At this price, it is estimated that the equivalent
of 250 billion pages of text may be entrusted to the electronic transmission medium each year. Even this would amount to only about 15%
of the total volume of office paper finally· generated by office printers
and copiers. Fascination with purely technological solutions results

in the premature conclusion that the office-of-the-future must be fully electronic and without paper.

What is not generally understood is that the major portions of projected savings do not come just from installing electronics, but from the means which people acquire to handle their business differently. The flow of information can be made much simpler when handled electronically. In an electronic environment, the jobs people do must be changed in order to achieve the full savings potential.

Human Factors

Once an economically feasible and technologicaly efficient electronic system is installed in the workplace, there still remains the question: Will people use it? Whether the office-of-the-future is to be paperless will not be revealed by searching the technical literature for clues about what is likely to happen. The right questions must deal with probable changes in the behavior of individuals, such as: Will people still read in the future, or will they just talk and look at pictures? If people continue to read, will they do it from some sort of a direct electronic display or will they continue to prefer the printed page?

I believe that a more complex, high-technology society will demand increased, not decreased, reading. Reading is still the most efficient method for communicating words. Literate people can read text two- to five times faster than they can hear it read by someone else.

The raw speed of receiving input is not the only factor to be considered. The eye can "backspace" its scan of a sentence in order to improve its comprehension of the message. The ear cannot backspace. If the spoken word is to be clarified, at least a minimal dialogue is necessary.

Speaking and hearing are necessarily synchronous, even in video teleconferencing. That is, everyone concerned must be present for communication to take place. Reading is asynchronous, that is, the author and the receipient can be separated by time and space without essentially disrupting communications. As a broad generalization we can say that all synchronous communications are rapidly growing in cost because they require idle labor to wait until useful communication can take place, whereas asynchronous communications are rapidly declining in cost because messages can be received on demand. Synchronous communications continue to be favored for unstructured conversations because they are highly adaptive to complex interaction among individuals, whereas asynchronous messages are preferred for situations in which the structure and the form of the communication can be defined in advance.

Our society is very complex now, and will require even more intricate coordination in the future. People, therefore, will have to read more—unless or until some radical new technologies of communication become practical. In a multicultural, global business environment, the asynchronous aspects of reading translated text are particularly attractive. Reading will continue to have a 10:1 to 30:1 advantage over hearing in business communications, especially for understanding of new ideas and for learning about new experiences. In global business and scientific communications, text will clearly dominate over the verbal medium as the means of minimizing language barriers.

The future of reading is well assured in the conduct of business. With innovations in the techniques for creating, distributing, and printing text, the importance of the written medium relative to the spoken medium is likely to increase.

If we can accept the idea that reading will not disappear in favor of more staff meetings or television broadcasts from the head office, the remaining question should deal with the medium through which reading will be done. Will it be paper or the VDU?

I have tried to identify the critical factors that may have a bearing on either choice. In conjunction with each of these factors, it is possible to utilize the following six-point checklist, which contrasts the characteristics of reading from paper as compared with reading from a VDU:

1. The human nervous system has a special control mechanism for coordination of the hand with the focusing muscles of the eye. Among the first things a baby learns is to focus on objects in its hands. The nerves and muscles that control focusing connect the hand and the eye directly.[3] Therefore, it will always be much easier to read something that is held in the hand than something that just sits on a table.

2. The coordination of hand and eye also allows very rapid scanning of paper text and paper files. Even if the computing power to process ten million instructions per second were inexpensively available in a VDU, the machine would still not be able to keep up with the intuitive way in which people leaf through a book or browse through a folder.

3. There are some major problems involving the contrast between

a terminal that generates internal light and a piece of paper that reflects light from the environment. Our minds and eyes are much better equipped to deal with reflected light.

4. For the eyes to relax, they must be allowed a focus to infinity at frequent intervals. The fixed positioning of the VDU in the office environment, usually against a wall or an item of furniture, may create problems for relaxation. A person must use body movements to permit the eye to sight a more distant object.

5. The adaptability of the eye to a great range of illumination makes it much more compatible to the changes which take place in the environment when information is reflected from paper than when displayed on a VDU. When illumination levels in the office are set at high levels, as is customary for correspondence and drawings, this will clash with the optimal environment for VDUs, whose light is not reflected but comes from within. For best viewing of VDUs, a fairly dim environment is preferable. It will be visually uncomfortable if an engineer uses a dark green-on-black VDU in a brightly lit drafting room while making frequent references to handwritten computations. Not only will the VDU screen mirror reflected lights from the overhead fixtures, but the eye will have difficulty adjusting between the bright light that is optimum for paper and the lower levels of light that favor the VDU.

6. Paper is much more adaptable than electronic information equipment. Until VDU technology makes great improvements—developing totally portable and book-like VDUs, for example—it will have many disadvantages with regard to location and position for use. The need for a power supply, the need to hold the body in a rigid position for focusing, and the potential for all sorts of mechanical and electrical inconvenience are just a few of the inherent disadvantages in the use of VDUs.

Readers may be interested in some comments taken from the critique of a computer conference—organized through an adaptation of an electronic mail network—for forty-five top executives: "Printers are essential. No conference should be initiated without them." "A printer would have helped. . . ." "Printers are essential to an interactive discussion." "My staff indicates that the computer conferencing procedures were fairly easy to use, aside from the lack of a printer." "We just received the printer and expect this will improve the final discussion. . . ." "I feel sure that had we had a printer available, there would have been considerably more activity." [4] Complaints about the difficulty of reading lengthy text from VDUs were the single most frequently mentioned technical criticism of the computer conference.

There are, however, important advantages which favor VDUs over paper. These advantages will ultimately increase the number of equivalent "pages" read electronically over those read on paper. VDUs win over paper in the following areas:

1. It is easier to use VDUs for rapid receipt of brief messages.
2. They are superior when immediate action must be taken.
3. They can be used in interactive situations.
4. VDUs can perform complex data- and text-retrieval tasks.

VDU growth will come almost entirely from new applications, rather than through elimination or substitution for old uses.

Messages received over VDUs will be a different kind of reading material from what is read today on paper. VDU text will be used in addition to, not as a substitute for, existing habits and practices. VDUs also have attributes which paper lacks. Psychologically, they have a much more immediate relationship to a human than paper, since the screen can be made to respond, whereas paper cannot. After all, maybe the right way to examine the human factors question is not in terms of paper vs. VDUs. I think that the only valid debates are those aimed at finding out the best combination of *both* media to improve the quality of human understanding.

Reading vs. Comprehending Information

It must be clear by now that the new electronic era can easily drown us with the information it can generate. How can all this information be absorbed by the human mind? How can we distinguish between the efficiency afforded by being able to read all of the text that is generated and the effectiveness involved in comprehending it as useful information?

We cannot trust projections based only on current technology to anticipate the evolution of electronic printing. Probing into the origins of printing may give us some better clues, because this may reveal to us some of the underlying forces that have shaped its evolution so far. The whole idea of Gutenberg's invention was based on standardized text, mass-produced for mass distribution. In fact, book printing— using uniform, precast metal letters produced by means of a standard-

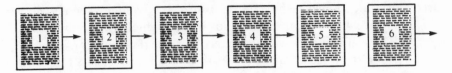

- Mass Production

- Standardized Contents, Sequentially Organized

- Original Expensive, Copy Expensive

- Text Stored

Figure 10.1   Gutenberg Text

ized manufacturing process—can be seen as the earliest example of industrialized mass production.

The VDU should not be viewed as a total opposite of paper, a medium that will eventually replace it, but as a complement that will help us to obtain the benefits of both media. We should use the flexibility of the VDU and the visual qualities of printing in combination as a new communication medium. Interactive text is based on the principle of generating printed information only in response to human wishes, as conveyed by electronic means. Figure 10.2 outlines the process by which text can be assembled by electronic means from a collection of various sources. It represents human knowledge as an exploratory structure that the individual mind searches by means of computer-aided displays. Recorded knowledge is then retrieved by means of computer-aided choices as a unique collection of text pages. The retrieval is accomplished as a one-of-a-kind operation in meeting specific user needs.

The basic concept behind interactively composed text is precisely opposite to that of the Gutenberg text. Each selection of a block of information is a unique combination of ideas, produced in a customized form for individual needs. It does not cater to the needs of standardized mass markets. It is the ultimate in adaptation. The concept of a personalized document is well suited to the need of individuals to explore, to learn, and to provide customized services themselves. It is the textual form for the narrowcasting of reading and learning material in the same way as the printed book represented the first industrial-age example of broadcasting. Its business uses will be determined by changes in the patterns in which future enterprises may choose to function. For instance, the "information middleman" would be a consumer only

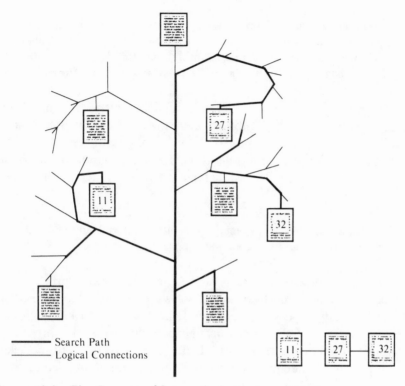

Figure 10.2   The Concept of Interactively Composed Text

for interactively composed text, since his needs would remain unique in each instance.

An interactively composed textbook would be assembled by an individual searching through various databases and files for information and combining only those specific paragraphs or sections of interest. He would use a VDU that does not just imitate a page of text, but creates a display that opens several simultaneous views into logically related topics. Such a multiple perspective is possible only by electronic means because it creates a multidimensional view of information, combining the flexibility of text and graphics with the analytic properties of the computer. What you see on such a screen are "windows" which show the relationships among various pieces of information stored electronically, either within the workstation or elsewhere within the network. "Intelligent" software makes it possible to combine information in one of the windows with that in another. If changes are made in one source of information, the internal logic of the computer will make corresponding adjustments in related information.

Interactively composed text is the next great breakthrough for communications because it will change the dimensions of human capabilities—perhaps even more than printing changed the dissemination of knowledge when it introduced the mass distribution of text.

The new approaches to creating, composing, retrieving, and distributing text will make it possible to break the tradition of specialization that has characterized our industrial culture; they will permit individuals to become multipurpose generalists. The many windows into information will help make it possible for individuals to deal with a much more complex world.

The future text is an assembly of printed material edited by the reader, rather than by the author.

The real innovations in the future use of electronic printing will not be so much in hardware as in software. The electronic printers of the future will possess enormous logical powers to keep up with the explorations of the mind through complex networks, producing interactive documents as a by-product. The key to the future of electronic printing is "demand publishing" of information collected from databases all over the world.

The Future of Paper

There will be a lot of paper in use in the year 2000. There will be more of it, per capita, than at present because there will be so many more originals from which copies can be made. The information workforce will be more than twice the present size. The price of delivering text from electronic originals will be significantly lower than is currently the case—perhaps 90% less. The quality of electronic printing—incorporating color, graphic designs, and pictures—will make this means of communication attractive to use. The "intelligence" of printing and composing machines will be of a sufficiently high order to cope with the enormous variety of electronic forms in which originals will be represented. All of this assumes that the present sociopolitical hurdles preventing the exchange of electronically communicated text will be resolved through international standards. In this area we should expect to see the same progress as that achieved in international telephony, which now permits home-to-home dialing around the globe.

Paper will not be used for archival storage of routine business records. Optical recording by means of lasers provides a much better means for the filing of information. Paper will be used for reading, due to its greater human compatibility. Ink will be applied to it by direct electronic means. This also implies the need for a very efficient paper recycling industry, since office paper will be used mostly as a relatively short-term working surface rather than as an archival medium.

VDUs will not replace reading. They will deal with the logic of information search, with composition of text, and with terse, highly structured messages. Electronic printing will be the technique for generating an increasing variety of books, magazines and documents. Electronic printing will be especially important for generating large graphic pages, usually in color. Electronic displays will be closely connected with the process of making individual choices for printing. The future of electronic printing will be assured by the accessibility of electronic text through worldwide communications networks.

Ineffective use of labor, rather than the cost of paper itself, is the reason for high office-document expenses. Large cost reductions are feasible by means of electronic communication. But human factors favor the use of the printed page for any extended reading. As VDUs are accepted as the means to create and search for information, selective printing of personalized text will become a highly attractive means for improving learning and understanding. The "paperless office" will not be one of the outcomes of office automation. Large amounts of paper will continue to be used, even though paper's archival role will diminish.

PART III

THE
SOCIETAL
PERSPECTIVE

════ 11 ════

Technology, Structure, and Strategy

Information technology can shape how people are employed in organizations. Industrial structure, customer service, and competitive survival all enter into the picture when the effects of information technology are assessed. The purpose of this chapter is to show how our understanding of the composition and effectiveness of information work in changing.

The Big-Organization Theory About Growth of Office Work

Large organizations are not growing. Nor do they employ ever-increasing numbers of office workers.

One of the theories frequently offered to explain the steady growth in the number of office workers is based on the idea that larger organizations require increasing amounts of information to achieve improved coordination. If this assumption is correct, one should find an increasing proportion of employees engaged in information occupations as the size of organizations increases. A recent study of this relationship revealed that the fraction of information workers declines as organizational size increases. Similarly, the fraction of managers declines as organizations increase in size from less than 20 employees to more than 1,000 employees.[1]

The trend is unmistakable: larger establishments employ relatively fewer information workers than smaller establishments. Very small establishments also classify twice as many of their employees as managers as compared with large organizations. One way of interpreting this data is to assert that larger organizations are more efficient. Another way of looking at the same statistics is to argue that in smaller organizations more people can make important decisions. Still another explanation is that smaller organizations are more frequently found in the service sector of the economy, where more managers are required to get the work done. Conclusive answers are hard to come by, even though it has been shown that midsize organizations score much better than giant corporations in terms of growth in sales, income, assets, and employment.[2]

The question of bigness as an indicator of profitability also arises when we examine the profitability of organizations in small markets vs. those in big markets. Again, small is better.[3] The data run counter to the popular idea that efficiency is gained by having the smallest possible number of managers control the largest possible number of employees.

All of these facts appear to contradict each other. This is because they describe only the surface of much deeper changes in employment patterns and in economic performance. Our economy is passing through a transformation. Simple generalizations based on previous trends do not serve us well. As patterns of employment become more dependent upon what happens in the national and global economy, one needs to dig deeper in order to find out what is really going on. With the rise of the service sector and the corresponding decline in the industrial sector, giant organizations have gradually become less important in the economy.[4] Also, the profitability of concentrated industrial businesses is generally in decline, whereas the profit in relatively small service businesses remains high.

One key to understanding the divergent trends in information employment, in organizational size, and in profitability is to observe how, as they grow, organizations employ information workers.[5] In small service establishments, for example, most employees are information workers. As service establishments grow, however, they reduce their information-worker employment even more rapidly than manufacturing establishments do. Consequently, the growth in the number of information workers could not have come about through the needs of large corporations. The opposite seems to apply. The growth in the number of small service firms has been the principal stimulus to the creation of new jobs for information workers. We employ more information workers because the economy has favored smaller organizations as well as information-worker intensive sectors such as consumer services, government, health, and education at the expense of concentrated industries.[6]

With most of current economic growth taking place in the service sector, which presently accounts for 71% of total employment and for 66% of the GNP, the increased demand for information workers and for management personnel is assured.[7]

An increasing proportion of costs for items provided by the goods-producing sector (such as agriculture and manufacturing) is attributable to service intermediaries. When one examines a $2.00 packaged food item in the supermarket, perhaps as little as $.20 of its price is directly assignable to the "goods-producing" activities in which farmers, food-processing workers, and transportation workers are directly engaged. Administrative (i.e., information-processing costs) are tagged on to the price as the product moves from the field to the refrigerator. Produce brokers, produce shippers, receiving and inspection clerks, quality-control inspectors, accountants, auditors, factory managers, warehouse managers, warehouse clerks, packaging-materials designers, brand-advertising agents, shipping dispatchers, supermarket managers, supermarket checkout clerks, and advertising by the store itself—all add their costs to the item before it reaches the consumer.

As another example, manufacturing (with only 20% of its workforce in information-worker categories) increasingly employs wholesalers (with 33% information-worker employment), transportation companies (with 30% information-worker employment), and finance intermediaries (with 65% information-worker employment) to handle product distribution.

Product Costs, Information Costs, and Organization

In the service economy, distribution logistics rather than production costs determine how much information expense is tagged on to the final price of a product.

The full cost of the office work contained in any consumer product cannot be discerned just by examining employment data or by studying the occupational profiles of a particular industry. It is very simple to shift office work from one middleman in the distributive chain to another. To arrive at the total cost of office work contained in a product's price, one must trace the product from initial production to final consumption. The total cost of information then involves tallying up a chain of information-handling transactions. Whether there are too many or too few information workers in the chain is more a function of the effectiveness with which the entire chain is organized than of how efficient the workers are at any one place in the sequence. If the channels of distribution are changed, even firms with high internal efficiency may be bypassed.

Only if real prices are reduced through simplification of the entire distribution chain does one have an indication that information workers are deployed effectively. With easy transmission of information about customer needs from the retail level directly to the place where the goods originate, the general tendency of information technology will be to diminish the number of intermediaries in the distribution process. This will happen provided that the products and the distribution system are designed so that customers will be able to use information technology to make their purchasing decisions. The primary effect of information technology on organizational structure would then be found in changed external relationships among different participants in the distributive chain, rather than within any particular organization.

One of the most frequently mentioned ideas about the promise of information technology is that organizational layers within a single company could be substantially reduced. I think that greater attention should be given to the prospect of eliminating costly intermediaries in the delivery of products for an entire market. Ultimately, information technology permits a rearrangement of how goods are distributed on a global scale. Unless a link in the chain of trade and services adds significant value, information technology will make it possible to bypass it altogether.

Information technology simplifies not only how a single organization operates internally. It makes possible the reorganization of an entire industry to deliver improved value to customers.

The full effects of information technology cannot be evaluated just by observing what happens within the confines of a single enterprise.

It is possible to cut services by eliminating information workers, thereby increasing short-term profits. It is equally possible to add new services by adding information workers and thus decreasing short-term profits. Which option is the right one cannot be answered except by examining the effects that either move will have on the value of the product as seen by the customers.

To understand the shifts in employment patterns it is necessary not only to track occupational data, but also to explore the changing structure of the channels of distribution. The exorbitant cost of replacement parts in the construction industry is largely a reflection of an ineffective distribution system. The steady decline in the real costs of electronic components is largely achieved by designing high-quality standardized products so that they may be distributed through streamlined, global channels. Information-technology investments should be increasingly directed to areas where they can influence the way in which products are marketed. This is why the most far-reaching effects of information technology on the future structure of the economy will depend on how that technology is used in distribution. The use of information technology in production will be shaped by the needs of the marketplace for products that can be configured, priced, and selected through electronic shopping channels. We are moving from a supply-driven economy to a demand-driven economy. The design of information systems will have to conform to this reorientation.

The information worker in the large, supply-oriented organization will be a specialist.

In the future all products will contain a large share of information value added in their price. High information contents will be included either directly—as in semiconductor components or in prepackaged training—or indirectly through information costs incorporated in the cost of the item, as with advertising and research. All standard products will tend to become competitively priced global commodities. Where there are large opportunities for standardization and for streamlined distribution, as in the case of consumer electronics, appliances, pharmaceuticals, automobiles, office equipment, and entertainment products, strong forces will favor global consolidation, specialization, and concentration of production in a few enterprises. Information employment in the large central organizations will be quite small, prices will decline, and management productivity will increase as essential conditions for sustaining international competitiveness.

The information worker in the small, demand-oriented, specialized organization will be a generalist.

In the case of products or services requiring a great deal of customizing or expertise, such as in the case of medical services, government services, and education, a strong bias will favor small organizations able to deliver directly to the customer a high proportion of the total value added. To survive, these small organizations will have to maintain easy access to the large supply sources without incurring the costs of passing through too many intermediate layers.

For nonstandard products and services, the largest contribution to the value added will always be closer to the consumer's end of the product pipeline. The closer one gets to the ultimate consumer, the greater the advantages will be for smaller enterprises. This change in the organization of distribution of goods and services will have a decisive effect on the way information work will be done in the future. Information resources will have to support the needs of generalists rather than of specialists.

Information technology will be the principal influence on the way service organizations will operate. In the case of the small, generalist-based service organizations, information technology will become the means for defining the market segments such organizations can serve profitably. Internally, information technology will become the means for deploying individuals in their new role as generalists—people who can integrate a variety of products and services so as to add value in meeting a customer's unique needs.

The role of information technology, then, will be critical externally in setting marketing strategy, and internally in defining organizational design. The chief executive will find a new role as the firm's chief information strategist.

Macroeconomic Analysis

Whether a society is productive or not can ultimately be determined only by consumers.

I regret the lack of adequate economic and demographic data for understanding the information sector of our economy. It is very difficult to project the future of an economy based on information work without data that would track its changing patterns. The government

continues gathering statistics according to Standard Industrial Classification (SIC) codes that break down the total output of manufacturing
industries in great detail. The service side of the economy is described
only in summary. For instance, in the 1972 input/output tables of
the U.S. economy, 4.5% of the line items report on the service sector,
which generates 40% of the GNP. The same kind of detail is devoted
to iron mining, wood containers, leather products, synthetic rubber,
and chemical mining—which account for only 0.15% of the GNP.

Existing employment statistics make very little distinction between industrial employment, which includes both information and
noninformation labor, and service employment, which includes both
knowledge-producing labor as well as personal services such as those
provided by barbers, waiters, and supermarket checkout clerks. Much
of the current rhetoric about declining industrialization is based on
government data that does not provide useful insights into the changing
roles of information-handling workers. For instance, the statistics
which show reduced industrial employment (as defined by SIC categories) do not reveal that many of the distribution functions traditionally
performed by concentrated industrial companies have now migrated
to trade, which is classified in the service sector.

The defects in the data about information workers explains why
the current debate about declining U.S. productivity does not come
to grips with the single most important issue: how to make our workforce more productive if 67% of the wages it receives is paid for
handling information rather than for production of tangible goods.
Because of their fixation on SIC-based government statistics the current
discussions are still restricted by a vocabulary which defines work
strictly in terms of physical output, such as tons of steel, numbers
of automobiles, tons of paper, or railcar shipments. The current talk
about deindustrialization is not very useful in light of the fact that
for more than forty years, over half of the GNP has been generated
not in industry but in services. We lack indicators that would more
reliably illuminate the two key economic issues for the 1990s: how
to improve international competitiveness and how to promote the economic growth of a society in which two-thirds of the value of labor
is devoted to communication.

Occupational data such as classification of personnel into job categories is more meaningful than SIC statistics because the former reflects
what people are actually doing, regardless of what business they may
be employed in. The most useful research on the structure of the
U.S. economy is based on occupational information which classifies

the workforce as either information-handling or as goods-handling. Such research provides us with an understanding of value added within each of the two sectors.[8]

The information sector creates a net $525 billion of value added. Sixty-five billion dollars is purchased from the production sector for capital equipment such as computers. Information-service firms sell each other $128 billion worth of information handling. This would include accounting and auditing services to corporate customers, for example. Some $84 billion worth of books, entertainment, educational services, etc., is sold directly to the final customer. The largest single amount, $506 billion, is charged to the production sector, either as corporate overhead or as purchased services such as advertising. This amount is the critical element affecting the prices that consumers finally pay for goods they purchase. No information is available as to what fraction of the $506 billion is billed at competitive prices and what portion is imposed as an overhead charge to pay for the costs of management. Based on the size of the information services industry in 1972, I estimate that not more than 15% of the $506 billion is subject to competition. The rest of the information sector's costs are tagged on to customers' purchase costs by budgeting decisions internal to each organization. As noted in Chapters 6 and 7, such indirect means of establishing prices do not readily lend themselves to an analysis of productivity gained through the employment of information technology.

Information is primarily a means of production rather than an item of consumption. Calling the postindustrial economy an information society is a misnomer.

The econometric analysis by Jonscher explains how value added is divided between the production and information sectors.[9] Of the $1,087 billion paid by consumers for physical goods, about half was spent on services of the information-handling sector. When futurists talk about the coming of the information society, one should not yet conjure up the image of people purchasing information services as their principal item of consumption. Direct purchase of services from the information sector represents only 8% of the consumers' budgets. Our society does "consume" enormous amounts of information, but only indirectly—as a part of purchases from the production sector. Many U.S. goods are not competitive due to unusually high costs transferred from the information sector to the production sector.

The whole question of how to improve productivity, then, resolves itself into two issues:

1. Can the information sector reduce its charges to the production sector by investing in capital that will increase its own productivity?
2. Can the production sector reduce its operating costs through superior management aided by information technology?

Jonscher's analysis gives us an indication of what the answers may be. The first step is to examine the growth rates for each sector for the period from 1947 through 1972. The key growth figure, which relates to the issue of capital investment vs. output, is the 433% increase in shipments from the production sector to the information sector. The net cost gain of the information sector was 370%, while its costs to the production sector were up by 383%. When compared with a mere 259% increase in purchases by consumers, these extraordinary increases in expenditures by the information sector should be viewed with alarm. The faster growth in the costs of the information sector relative to the production sector means that the former suffered a steep decline in its productivity, despite these large infusions of capital.

The figures on productivity in the production sector are more encouraging. Production-sector costs increased only by 213%, while direct sales to consumers went up by 259%. This is an indication that the production sector was gaining in relative productivity. Whatever its gains, however, they were cancelled by the large increases in costs transferred to it by the information sector.

The Jonscher model does not have enough detail to prove conclusively that poor performance within the information sector is the overwhelming cause of declining productivity. However, it does imply the following conclusions:

1. When the information sector sells its services in a competitive marketplace (that is, directly to consumers or from one firm in the information sector to another), its charges will be lower than when its charges are allocated through corporate overhead, taxation, or other noncompetitive channels.
2. Benefits from the large increases in capital investments within the information sector are not reflected in decreased costs of output.
3. Production-sector productivity improves; lowered costs are not passed on to consumers, though, because production absorbs

the large growth in overhead transferred to it from the information sector.

These conclusions do not leave us with a favorable impression of the promise which lies in an information economy, even though the analysis is admittedly not based on up-to-date data. More current information is needed to tell us what the huge growth in information-sector employment and in information-sector capital consumption have done for economic productivity. I suspect that any 1972–84 analysis will reveal a continuation of the unfavorable trends of 1947–72.

If my assessment is correct, a consideration of how to remedy the adverse trends is in order. Accelerating information-capital investments to increase the output of existing information-sector activities will not improve the current situation. The easy solution—adding cheaper computers in the hope of reducing overhead expenses—will neither improve international competitiveness nor promote long-term economic growth.[10]

Information, Structure, and Strategy

Business strategy should dictate the choice of information technology. Organizational structure will follow.

Until recently, information-system design issues did not require the attention of top management. Management had always been able to assume that a production process determined the configuration of information-management tasks. Information jobs were not subject to much change: they were the by-product of simple relationships with operating personnel and with customers. Only flows that concerned products or services warranted any sort of formal design. Some workers were aided by machines and some were not. Who got such equipment was easily determined by economic analysis on a case-by-case basis.

The economic performance of the enterprise then, was determined by three factors:

1. The kind of business to be conducted
2. The original design of the product flows
3. The availability of people able and willing to carry out assigned tasks rapidly and reliably

If information questions figured at all in this design, they related to questions of control, auditing, and managerial prerogatives. The command structure remained simple. Efficiency was achieved through disciplined execution of operating functions. Information about the firm's environment, customers, suppliers, or competitors was gathered by the marketing and purchasing divisions—and then left to be evaluated by central management, which alone interpreted what information was provided. Management thus reinforced its role as the source of all important decisions.

This model is still found today in most goods-intensive operations; it reflects the tradition of how an efficient firm should function. Once a business strategy is chosen, the organizational structure follows; that structure in turn leaves open few questions about how to design the firm's information system.

As firms evolve in complexity and the business environment becomes more uncertain, the hierarchical organization of the firm adds new managerial functions. In keeping with the concepts of individual efficiency so deeply rooted in the thought patterns of industrial-age management, new staffs are added in narrow areas of specialization. Information design continues to follow the approaches that have always been used to manage products.

There are many firms where these practices are efficient, especially if the products or services are mass-produced goods with little variety. But there comes a time when complexity of coordination, size of management staffs, and operational inflexibility become so overwhelming that hierarchical transmission of all information ceases to be of value. When a firm reaches its limit of coordinative capability, its performance will drop, its profits will decline, and its competitive position will suffer. One way to diagnose the approach of this condition is by comparing a firm's "management value added"/"operations value added" ratio to that of its three best competitors. If a competitor is able to deliver equivalent products while operating with much lower information costs, a dangerous condition is indicated. At this point, information systems design becomes a strategic factor demanding direct involvement by top management, for survival of the firm itself may be at stake. How information should flow ceases to be a secondary outcome of other choices and becomes a primary matter of explicit design.

Firms such as service industries, where the physical cost of goods is a relatively small portion of total expenses, can choose from a broad range of organizational options. Such enterprises are characterized by uncertainty and a continuous need for innovation. They also require a high degree of internal adaptability to changing conditions. Hierar-

chical organizations, whose computerized administrative systems in-
carnate the separation of managers from operators, cannot adjust very
effectively to changing conditions in the marketplace because they
require a great deal of coordination to make any decision at all. Adaptable enterprises now have the option of designing their internal information-handling structure so that it integrates both managing and
operating tasks for maximum flexibility of response to the environment.

The design principle illustrated in Figure 11.1 calls for a halt in
the segregation, along strict occupational lines, of operations from
management. In this scheme, some managers perform operating tasks
and some operators perform managerial tasks by receiving and generating information. The organization as a whole can be stimulated to
broaden the roles of each worker through teamwork. The key features
that make this possible are the robot, for assistance in the handling
of physical workflows, and the personal information workstation, for
assistance in the handling of information flows. Figure 11.2 illustrates
how these productive factors are interrelated.

A person's capacity to master management roles is supplemented
by the procedural memory of his information workstation, which also
includes access to expert know-how. The workstation provides the
necessary tutorial support for on-the-job training. It also makes it
possible for a person to deal with mechanical robots, which in turn
take care of physical tasks.

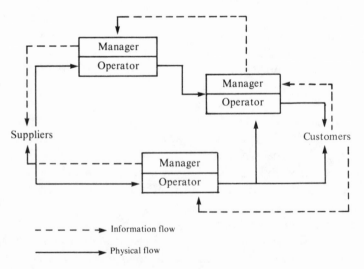

Figure 11.1   Integration of Management and Operations

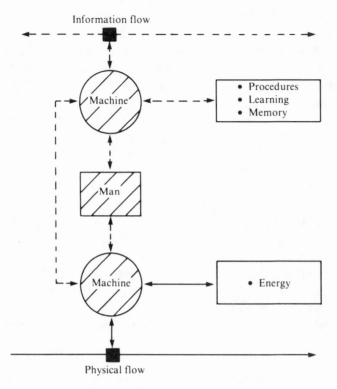

Figure 11.2   Man–Machine Relationships for Work Enlargement

Designing Organizations

Information technology requires that organizations be deliberately designed rather than allowed to evolve spontaneously.

For an enterprise to be made up of autonomous work groups, its internal relationships must be articulated in a way understandable to all employees. For instance, if several autonomous units have conflicting demands on shared resources, settlement of the dispute should be built right into the organizational culture of conflict resolution, rather than require a judicial decision from a higher authority in every case. This calls for the deliberate insertion, at a higher level of an enterprise, of management systems which will preserve local autonomy without fostering decentralized anarchy. Computer networks are well suited to moderating conflict by means of instantaneous evaluations of complicated alternatives. For instance, an organization may experience contention between different channels of distribution attempting to accomplish the identical marketing mission. Rather than install rigid rules which cannot adequately discriminate among unique cases, all parties can simultaneously view the short- as well as long-term consequences of proposed alternatives.

To design job relationships which do not discriminate between management and operating tasks, information technology should be available to everyone. There will have to be an easy relationship between man and machine, so that choices about the characteristics of each personal machine can be made by the individuals concerned from modules that can be arranged to suit their needs. If this is the case, individuals performing both management and operations tasks can deal with a diversity of customers by mixing and matching what is needed for their own personal workstations from a supply of readily available software. Such workers do not require a high degree of technical expertise to make the necessary choices. They are able to assemble and try out a variety of software from a central library of standard procedures representing the accumulated knowledge capital of the entire organization.

The modules representing central know-how, shared databases, and shared techniques fit together only if there is a common architecture allowing people, machines, and standard software to work together without large added costs for integration. Even though the term "information architecture" is ordinarily applied in an exclusively technical sense to describe how terminals and computers transmit messages back and forth, I am using this term in a much broader sense. From the standpoint of organizational design, "information architecture" is really the plan an organization chooses to give its members access to data, to enlarge the scope of an individual's responsibilities by means of acquired software, and to determine who can access another's electronic files and under what terms. The plan also provides guidance on how to insert safeguards against erroneous electronic transactions, how to assure a consistently high quality of work without electronic surveillance, how to test systems modifications without damaging the network, and how to stimulate the exercise of personal initiative in an environment which is abstract and machinelike. Information architecture in this sense also involves the design of a system which can monitor an individual's work electronically to create personal incentives or to attribute productivity gains. Whereas electronic "surveillance" can be viewed as a repugnant and undesirable feature of electronic networks, we should also recognize that a computer is ideally suited for a person to keep score of his own accomplishments (or errors) so that he can channel his efforts in the most constructive directions. "Architecture," then, includes rules about appropriate behavior in an electronic environment.

A deliberate system design pays due regard to how people and machines interact. For instance, it defines what patterns of behavior should be cultivated so that the computer workstation is not viewed as an omnipresent time–motion-study engineer—or perhaps even as a policeman. It specifies how electronic communications with customers should be organized so that an individual aided by a workstation can act autonomously and make legally binding agreements. The ultimate objective of an effective service business should be to make each employee a self-sufficient agent capable of taking care of all customer requests. Competitive advantage in the service sector will then depend on its people's superior information-handling capabilities in satisfying customer needs. To this end, system design must focus on helping people to apply their fullest skills rather than on optimizing the computer system's own technical performance. Such design stimulates the personal initiatives of its operators by means of rapid feedback. For example, this kind of system provides rapid (less than one second) access not only to local databases, but simultaneously to remote computers and multiple telephone contacts as well. The design informs the operator whether he is delivering an improved service to the customer. An indication as to payoff is included along with every customer transaction.

The effectiveness of information workers improves if they are rewarded for delivering valuable services. Their effectiveness declines if they merely get paid for holding a job.

The idea of pricing an individual's information transactions within a network as a way of avoiding central overhead and as a means for promoting innovation is not new.[11] Lawyers, consultants, and physicians in private practice have always been in a position to command superior income because of their direct relationship with their clients.

Organizational design which integrates management and operating functions makes it possible to offer a similarly direct client relationship even in large enterprises. For instance, I think that most corporate staff and public functionaries should earn their keep by means of usage fees rather than through budget appropriations. The electronic environment makes possible client transactions which use totally automatic network accounting to generate revenues that enable individuals to act as professionals rather than as retained servants.

Changing Work Roles

Future organizations will need more, not fewer, managers.

Information technology is supposed to dispense with much of the need for middle management. Mechanization of engineering work is supposed to decrease the numbers of engineers needed. Prognosis after prognosis reiterates the simple formula: if a computer can do what X does, then X will not be needed any more. Such simplification is based on a static view of business and on limited perceptions about the roles of people in the economic environment of the future. I am convinced that with growing use of robotics in factories, the fraction of information workers will increase from the present 56% to over 70% by the year 2000. The U.S. workforce can also be expected to grow to more than 140 million by that date. Simple arithmetic shows that at least some information-worker occupations will have to expand enormously.

Current trends do not support forecasts that the numbers of managers will diminish. On the contrary, all detailed observations suggest that management positions increase with office automation.[12] What adds to the confusion is that as old management jobs are eliminated, the dynamics of the process that creates new management jobs are not as yet well understood.

Information technology will ultimately result in a complete overhaul in present management roles. Along the way it will create a large array of vastly more productive jobs. In this process of creative destruction, the weak link is the middle manager, about whose fate everyone is so worried. Indeed, concern about the continued viability of the manager as a coordinator of specialists is justified. Over two-thirds of the contemporary manager's time is expended in passing intraorganizational information to others. We know that most of these tasks can be performed much better through computer networks. The role of the manager as a coordinator and as an information intermediary will largely disappear: in its place we will see the manager assuming an important role as an investor.

With the advent of the information middleman, enormous operational efficiencies in the handling of information work will be realized. However, rising costs of labor will make it necessary to devote an increasing share of a firm's revenue to investments in the future, rather than just to cover current expenses. This capital expenditure will not apply to information technology alone, but even more to investment in human capital. A great deal of management time is needed to provide proper guidance for such activities as training for quality, growth, and work enlargement, building up an individual's experience on the job, and reducing employee turnover through leadership-inspired motivation. None of this can be done by means of a computer program. The manager of the future will have more work to do than anyone dreams of today. The ranks of management will expand, not shrink, although the manager of the future will have to possess distinctly different skills from those presently required.

The manager of the future, in his role of investor, will take over many of the responsibilities presently cloistered in the executive suite. As long as investment decisions were essentially of a financial nature, it was possible to restrict them to top executives. Managing investments made in *people* can be done only where those people are. With most of the investment decisions out of the hands of top executives, they will finally have time for their truly essential role: to be the planners, strategists, and creators of a unifying vision of the enterprise and articulators of a shared language that binds the parts into an integrated whole. The top executive can then also concentrate on his or her role as the innovator and entrepreneur. With a large increase in the number of small- to medium-size enterprises in the future, I anticipate an expansion in the demand for people who can fill executive and management jobs. The fraction of the total workforce in executive and managerial jobs can be expected to increase from the present 11% to perhaps as much as 17% of a workforce larger by some 40% just twenty to thirty years from now.

The greatest changes in work patterns will be found among professional and technical personnel; they presently account for 16% of the total workforce and can be expected to rise to 24% in the next two to three decades. They will be the largest occupational group, delivering most of the information services which our high-tech society will require in such large quantities. The rise in average compensation levels for this group will lead the average increase of per capita income for the entire society. In contrast to current fears that a high-tech society may become a "two-tier" society, the professional and technical group will create the conditions for a large concentration of highly paid wage earners at the middle of the income distribution curves.[13]

Professional and technical people will change their current roles as specialists, controlled in every respect by their coordinators–managers, to become generalists who include many traditional managerial functions in their everyday work. They will provide full service to customers, rather than just working on small fragments of it. They will be the equivalents of the factory of the past—except that now they will be delivering both producer *and* consumer services, rather than producer *or* consumer services. Their jobs will expand in complexity. Due to the fast pace of technological change, their know-how will be subject to rapid obsolescence. Consequently, this group will become large consumers of training and education. A significant portion of their time, perhaps as much as one-fourth, will be devoted to improving their work skills.

The low-paid and personally unfulfilling support tasks currently performed by clerical and secretarial personnel will be largely automated. This will open career-advancement opportunities for over 16 million employees, mostly female, now in such positions. Twenty to thirty years from now they will still represent about 15% of the workforce, which means that there will be more than 20 million jobs in clerical categories. But these jobs will be totally different from what we understand as "clerical" today. Instead of performing support functions, with scantly discernible economic value added, these jobs will include many of the specialist tasks now performed by professional and technical workers. We already have sufficient experience to know that clerical personnel can deliver superb results in such positions, provided that their organizations make the necessary investments to make such work possible. Huge expenditures will be necessary to move the mass of clerical jobs from traditional work circumstances into a totally new environment. The expenditures, however, will not only pay off in the long run: they will be essential to continued economic success as qualified personnel becomes increasingly scarce.

Sales occupations will change from being the tail end of the distribution chain to become the leading force of their organization's responses to the intensely competitive marketplace. Sales occupations will grow from the current 11% to at least 15% of the workforce within thirty years. The role of salespeople will be enlarged from being distributors to becoming general managers of that market segment within which they compete. With high-tech products, what is done *after* the sale is the key to profitability and to maintaining an ongoing franchise for supplying a customer. One of the important new missions of the salesperson of the future will be to train and educate customers. Training of sales personnel will require a lot of time, since teachers have to be better educated than their students if they are to be successful.

Designing organizations of the future cannot proceed on the assumption that this merely involves rearrangement of existing occupations and skills. Organizational design must recognize that information technology will totally transform traditional roles. Executives will be upgraded from investors to planners. Managers will be upgraded from coordinators to investors. Professional and technical personnel will be upgraded from specialists to generalists engaged in organizing the delivery of services to customers. Clerical personnel will be upgraded from support-staff members to specialists in the delivery of information services. Sales personnel will be upgraded from distributors of information to general managers of customer care and retention. Only such upgrading can create organizations that will deliver increased value for everyone—lower prices for customers and higher income for the workforce.

Macromyopia

The history of information technology can be characterized as the overestimation of what can be accomplished immediately and the underestimation of long-term consequences.

The attitudes of information-technology managers are a curious mix of overoptimistic faith in the power of the latest technology, blended with a totally conventional view of what the ultimate results will be. I call this peculiar syndrome technological macromyopia. The costs of the next technology project will always be underestimated. The implementation lead time for the latest product will always be much longer than expected. On the other hand, hardly any systems people could have visualized in 1974 how rapidly personal computers would spread through their organizations by 1984. If we look back to the scenarios for computer applications proposed by systems people in the 1970s, their projections were nothing more than extrapolations of the accepted practice at that time.

What are the reasons for an attitude that lacks both short- and long-term realism? It is true that managements look for quick remedies to redeem exaggerated promises. It is also true that there is a strong institutional bias against disturbing established relationships. This dis-

courages unconventional thought about the long-term effects of information technology. Contemplation of the extraordinary is frowned
upon, since it may reveal risks that inhibit funding of new projects.
All of these influences are found among the motivations which favor
technological macromyopia.

Disregard for past experience is another reason for the prevalence
of technological macromyopia. The nontechnological aspects of information technology installations are not well understood. Proposals
for new information systems usually dwell only on factual, technical
matters—which automatically limits their scope to a small fraction
of what needs to be known. The greatest share of ultimate project
costs is mostly to be found in uncertain long-term outcomes: as in
retraining and in the redirection of established organizational patterns,
for example. These topics are difficult; experience in dealing with them
is limited. It so happens that in information technology projects, the
costs of technology can always be contained, whereas the uncertain
costs are practically unbounded. No wonder that even if individual
tasks match short-term budget plans, overall project costs escalate
when all project expenses are added up, since new tasks have to be
added in order to get the entire job completed.

How about the wildly inaccurate estimates of what the long-term
effects will be, long after the budget and schedule overruns are forgotten? These too are caused by disregarding people's tremendous reser-
voirs of initiative and adaptive capacity to use improved tools. After
many misses an individual will find a few adaptations of computer
technology that make the entire experience worthwhile—practically
indispensable, in fact. A few successes will always exceed initial expectations, but only after long searches for the right match between user
needs and technology.

The behavioral origins of technological macromyopia suggest how
it may be cured. Since factors of organization, learning, and implementation really shape what is achievable, managers should orient their
planning around these factors when contemplating information-technology projects. Organizational design, coordination with business
strategy, and training to accept new approaches should have the highest
priority. This approach contrasts with prevailing practices, which plan
for the placement of technology first and only afterwards for organizational adaptation. The most fashionable of the current theories regarding the introduction of technology into the workplace are based on
the concept of "phases" of growth. Evolution is seen as a gradual
progression towards increased technological sophistication. Adherence

to this model is prima facie evidence that technological macromyopia prevails. It is the "fire, aim, ready" school of systems planning.

Instead of growth through a progression of technological phases, I recommend an approach which explicitly completes planning of the organization's evolution in know-how and business strategy. Technology choices will follow as logical choices. A wholesaler might plan an acquisition of information technology by identifying the causes of some of his business disadvantages relative to competitors. The causes could include costly inventory, limited distribution, an excessive product line, problems with product delivery, or simply a lack of purchasing effectiveness. It certainly would not follow that the generally accepted patterns of progression should begin with mechanization of the payroll and with introduction of word-processing systems for secretaries. Next, the wholesaler in question ought to assess the existing staff's skills and capabilities to absorb a strategically important new computer system. For instance, if it is desirable to overhaul the purchasing function and information technology makes that possible, then the entire design process should begin with retraining the purchasing people. Effective education will explain to them how to make a successful transition to their new roles, which may include participation in system development. The choice of technology may thus be almost the last matter to be decided.

This critical point can be illustrated by the following case. A few years ago a government agency built a model computer system to solve its severe administrative problems. As time passed, the people operating the system became mere appendages of the computer, since all available investments were absorbed by the drive to achieve maximum automation of even the most trivial clerical tasks. The technology's design dictated that operations personnel should perform increasingly narrow and mindless tasks. The cumulative investment in the software and in the computer equipment was compounded over a long period of time. When external changes imposed new demands, they could be dealt with only by squeezing new requirements into the old procedures.

After a few years, obsolescent technology and rigid organization finally caught up with the system. Employee dissatisfaction rose. Failure- and error-rates reached scandalous levels. At this point, both the system and the people operating it lost all adaptability to evolutionary change because their energies were fully taxed just keeping the indispensable system from falling apart. Consultants recommended that a brand-new system be built at another site to replace the existing technology as well as the existing organization. Those running the current system had to be motivated, however, until the new replacements were ready. The cost of creating a duplicate environment was enormous—and the human costs associated with job displacement were astronomical. Needless to say, the entire project collapsed when those operating the old system found it easy to make the new system fail. The government agency in question has not yet recovered from the ravages of this experience.

The lesson to be drawn from this story is simple: Do not let technological priorities get ahead of organizational consequences. In any information system, the value of the people operating it will always be worth much more than the accumulated hardware and software—unless a deliberate decision is made to reduce the people to mere appendages of the computer. If most maintenance expenses are allocated to the advancement of technology rather than to the development of people, someday the penalty will have to be paid. Obsolescence is a term applicable not only to technology. People and organizations also age. A computer system never becomes obsolete because electronic circuits cease to work, but because people cannot use it effectively anymore. Sometimes this is due to changes in the external environment. In my experience, it happens primarily from internal causes. When external failure is finally analyzed, it comes as a revelation that the system had been rotting from within for a long time. Rigidly organized applications, administered by organizations which do not develop their personnel to meet new challenges, add up to a sure prescription for disaster.

———————

Managers who want to learn more about making investments in computer technology usually sign up for studies in computer literacy. This endeavor may enhance their general education, but it will waste their time in other respects. The proper way to learn how to manage computers is not to study technology per se. It is more important to learn how information technology can be shaped to meet the needs of organizations. The sequence, evolution, and application of information technology must be secondary to the pursuit of managerial objectives. Knowing something about "bits and bytes" is not a bad idea— unless it leaves the manager with a case of technological macromyopia. The role of good managers is to integrate diverse demands for internal resources so that the entire organization succeeds in using information technology to improve its competitive position: Always subordinate technology to business strategy.

═══ Chapter 12 ═══

Information and Societal Productivity

Understanding the patterns of the past is essential for interpreting where we are at present and where we will go in the future. This chapter develops an evolutionary perspective. We can view each major stage of historical development in terms of the methods it used to manage its principal source of wealth. Mankind has always used tools to aid in its managerial endeavors; information technology is simply the most recent of them. If we are to understand its far-reaching consequences, we must take a broad view of our progress.

A Four-Stage Historical Perspective

The organizing principle of a hunting society is tribal. Its primary resource is nature.

When a society is based on hunting, it is primarily concerned with extracting food, clothing, and shelter from the natural environment. Unceasing labor is necessary because little accumulation is possible to carry a tribe through a period of adversity. All social institutions

are shaped by the need to exploit nature. The tribal form of organization is universally found to be the most stable one for managing a
group of hunters. In real consumption, a hunting society cannot expect
to generate annual wealth (in terms of today's equivalent costs) in
excess of $25 per capita. If a hunting society is successful, its population
increases beyond the resouces of its food supply, leading it to extermi-
nate the animals it depends on and despoil its trees and other inanimate
sources of wealth. Any remaining surplus is consumed in warfare
with neighboring tribes for larger hunting territories. If a successful
hunting society pushes beyond the limits of its organizing capability,
its prosperity declines.

To overcome constraints on further growth, a successful hunting
society may shift its economic base to exploit a new source of wealth:
land.

**The organizing principle of an agricultural society is feudal. Its pri-
mary resource is land.**

A society based on agriculture is primarily concerned with extracting wealth from the land. Unceasing labor is necessary because only
modest accumulations of wealth are possible. Its institutions are shaped
by concerns about land tenure and the privileges associated with it.
Feudal organization is one of the most stable forms for governing
and controlling land. Law, religion, social class, and politics are understandable only if one bears in mind questions dealing with the management of land. An agricultural society cannot generate income in excess
of $250 per capita, in today's equivalent terms. If an agricultural society
is successful, its population increases beyond its supply of food; it
devastates the land by overgrazing and overplanting, and creates an
unproductive, costly nobility which consumes most surplus in warfare
to gain more land. If a successful feudal society pushes beyond the
limits of its management's productive capabilities, its prosperity declines.

To overcome inherent constraints on further growth, an agricultural society may shift its economic base. It can restructure its institutions to employ a new source of wealth: machines that can create
wealth from capital accumulation.

**The organizing principle of an industrial society is nationalism. Its
primary resource is capital.**

A society based on industry is primarily concerned with extracting wealth from its capital assets. An adequate supply of low-cost agricultural products is already secure. Agricultural employment declines rapidly. Unceasing labor is necessary to create a growing surplus—the means for creating additional capital. The total wealth is now sufficient to sustain a nation without complete devastation even during periods of economic adversity. The institutions of the industrial state are shaped by concerns about the ownership and control of capital investment and claims on the division of surplus. The corporate form of organization, chartered by the nation-state, seems to be the most stable for managing industry. Law, government, economic power, distribution of income, social class, and politics—all of these are understandable only in the context of industrial management. Based on current income statistics for developed countries—whose real per capita income has stagnated for more than a decade—industrial societies do not seem to be able to generate real incomes (in 1979 terms) in excess of $6,000 to $10,000 per capita.

Even a successful industrial society misallocates its capital in unproductive ventures, ineffectively employs the human resources of its workforce, acquires a large and unproductive managerial overhead, creates costly state machinery to correct various malfunctions, encourages the use of political power to secure a lopsided distribution of wealth, and consumes much of the remaining surplus in diverse military expenditures by the state. When the successful industrial state ceases to be efficient, it will resort to central economic planning, to price controls, and to regulation of manpower as a means of preserving the status quo. The managerial elite will protect its interests in the industrial order; it will subvert continued growth by favoring taxation of the high value-added growth opportunities in order to subsidize the declining industrial sector. The political imperative of maintaining established interests will be masked by nationalist appeals, by arguments in favor of preserving employment, or by agitation against intrusions of foreign culture. Consumer needs for long-term economic growth, as the only means of securing a better standard of life, will be compromised as the resources required for productive investments are appropriated by the state for other purposes. If a successful industrial society pushes its development beyond the limits of productivity and further evolution set by its institutions, its prosperity declines.

The only way for an industrial society to progress beyond its built-in limits to further growth is by shifting its economic base. It can restructure its institutions in order to exploit a new resource: the latent talents of its entire population to create wealth from an accumulation of knowledge.

The organizing principle of a service society is global cooperation. Its primary resource is knowledge.

A society based on services is primarily concerned with the extraction of wealth from the capabilities of its people. The role of information technology is totally subordinated to this objective.

An abundant supply of low-cost agricultural and industrial products is already secure. Agricultural and industrial employment declines rapidly because of the high levels of efficiency attained in those sectors. The service society is characterized by incessant investigation of how to create new and superior services. Wealth is extracted from high value-added benefits in the delivery of high-quality services on a global scale. The accumulated wealth should now be sufficient to secure for everyone a decent standard of life. There should be no economic adversity. The only threat to survival might come from political breakdowns.

All of the institutions of a service society are shaped by questions of the ownership and control of knowledge and by the attempt to share equitably the opportunities such knowledge provides. Individual enterprises attain their position by superior competitive performance in serving customer needs and not by government franchise. The autonomous, market-driven, service-oriented form of an enterprise is the most stable organizational structure for managing knowledge workers. Individuals are members of enterprises in which they have a direct gain-sharing interest. Education, research, patents, copyright, software, access to media, law, government, economic power, social class, and politics in such a society are understandable only in terms of access to the new knowledge requisite for entry into competitive markets for services. A service society may generate real annual income of $40,000 to $100,000 per capita because limitations on the physical consumption of scarce resources have largely been removed. The amount of knowledge that can be created and the services are, for all practical purposes, infinite.[1]

Lest one conclude that I view the service society as the ultimate stage of social perfection, I want to note that it is already possible to speculate about the outlines of a social order to follow once the service society reaches its own limits of development.

If a service society is successful, it may overinvest in supporting unproductive individuals for political purposes, it may misdirect its educational system to increase the power of the state over mental development of individuals, it may misapply the talents of its workforce to destructive forms of enjoyment, it may create costly totalitarian institutions to compensate for societal malfunctions, and it may consume any remaining surplus in the attempt to preclude further evolutionary changes through further development of knowledge. If a successful service society pushes its development beyond the productive limits of its managerial capabilities, its prosperity will decline.

What may happen when a successful service civilization starts its decline is anybody's guess. This possibility is many decades away, not just a few years, as futurists have suggested. Orwell's 1984 was, after all, too early a date for the creation of a society completely monitored and directed by a computer-aided dictatorship. Information technology, and especially telecommunications systems, are still too expensive, technologically cumbersome and operationally incompetent to make an Orwellian surveillance system workable much before the year 2000.

The entire evolutionary progression can be summed up in the form of a diagram, as shown in Figure 12.1. Society becomes more productive by deploying increasing amounts of new resources. Productiv-

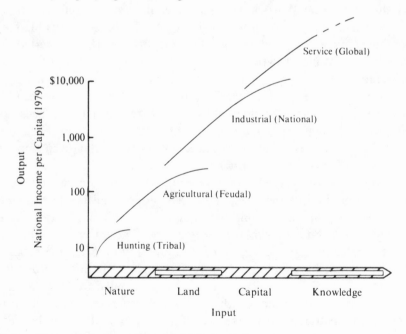

Figure 12.1 Evolution of Societal Productivity

ity is extracted from the introduction of new economic means into the marketplace, gathered over a larger geographic area. Productivity grows when new forms of capital, such as land, machines, energy, and ultimately knowledge, can be accumulated and invested to overcome the natural limits of mankind.

This model of societal growth suggests why countries at the forefront of our industrial civilization are now stagnant. They have stopped growing because they have been successful in reaching the limits of industrial production. Productive capacity now vastly exceeds the capacity of markets to absorb industrial output. Advanced industrial countries have installed elaborate institutions for redistribution of income to solve problems of the past rather than to invest effectively in growth opportunities of the future. Productive capacity is not used because the political emphasis is on allocating supply, not on growing demand.

Information technology cannot be used to solve societal problems. Only social solutions can accomplish that.

Half of mankind is still emerging from the agricultural stage of development. Another quarter is progressing through the early stages of industrialization. A worldwide service civilization, therefore, cannot be realized in the near future. It cannot even become a plausible scenario as long as most of the world's surplus wealth is diverted to arresting economic growth rather than promoting it. Computers and information technology provide the practical means by which a global service-based society can be made to function. But for many decades to come computer technology may receive misplaced emphasis, as technocrats attempt to solve deeply rooted institutional problems by technological means. That simply will not work: it may even impede society's ability to progress further.

National service-based economies will continue to be constructed on the foundation of the older industrial order. That is the meaning of the lessening intensity in industrial production which is taking place in the United States and in Western Europe. These trends, then, can be interpreted as just the beginning of a much more extended process that will result in a global economy and a global political order. In this process it is a mistake to associate the ability to manufacture computers or to make semiconductors as an assurance that the transition from industrial society has successfully begun. Unless people make effective use of computers to increase the overall productivity of a society, making devices like the semiconductor will just add to an already poorly utilized inventory of capital assets.

Productivity gains in a successful service society are realized by people engaged in lifelong learning. The transition from an industrial economy to one based on services is, then, primarily a transformation in the way a society uses its human capital. The highest investment priority for a society contemplating the transition to the electronic future should lie in education and in motivating its population to take advantage of new opportunities. Creating one's own computer industry should be seen more as an indirect means to further progress, rather than as the primary objective.

Differences in the Sociology of Work

There is a diametrical contrast in the work attitudes characteristic of an industrial culture and those of a culture based on service. Values which are a prescription for success under one system lead to failure under the other. To better understand what transformations are needed in the workplace to increase the acceptance of information technology, I shall consider several areas in which attitudes will have to undergo complete reversal.

Simple jobs based on common skills will be replaced by jobs demanding individual competence.

As pointed out before in this book, industrialization requires interchangeable parts. People must also fit this pattern, because total predictability is a prerequisite for running a clerical operation which processes standard tasks. Interchangeability of human operators in handling data-processing equipment is achieved by making each job simple and replicable, and by requiring only skills that represent the lowest common denominator in knowledge. One ends up demanding hardly any skills at all. Discretion and quality control are programmed right into the central computer. Enormous amounts of highly paid programming labor are devoted to coding even the smallest exceptions directly into the logic of the machine, since the human operators are instructed that unprogrammed situations must be referred to management. One invests systems analysts and programmers with knowledge about the business rather than upgrading the skills of those who are supposed to do the job.

The essence of the service economy, however, lies in customized responses and in adaptive handling of a client's wishes. A broad range of adaptive behavior thus becomes a prerequisite for delivering services without referring every new question to another specialist. By supporting each person with a general-purpose information workstation and by asking people to upgrade their skills continually, one enables them to provide a greater variety of valuable services. The result is a well-motivated and highly knowledgeable workforce with a great deal of understanding about the business. The exercise of discretion and judgment becomes the responsibility of the individual employee because no computer program can be written to cope with all of the conditions that may occur. Highly paid programming labor will be devoted to innovation and to the design of new means by which the organization may serve new client needs. The technologists will also become more productive, since the users of workstations will be qualified to make informed requests for new features with which to endow their personal equipment.

Standardized jobs will be replaced by jobs with variety.

Industrial-age organizations define information jobs in terms of the procedures which are followed. Jobs are identified by means of standard grades into which all behavior must fit. People are assigned to minutely subdivided occupational and wage classifications. Employment analysts, personnel administrators and collective bargaining agents alike reinforce the view that work is best controlled (or protected) by fitting people into tightly systematized, well-specified boundaries. Administrative operations characterized by such an environment use computers as the equivalents of physical conveyor belts to carry work from one rigidly circumscribed jobholder to another.

Service-age organizations, however, define information jobs in terms of the employee's relationship to clients. They assign few general occupational- and wage-classification titles. Organizational decentralization and market segmentation further strengthen the view that work is best accomplished by assigning people to jobs designed around customers, within flexible boundaries, defined by market needs rather than by the administrative processes. Administrative operations characterized by such an environment need computers only as an aid in piecing together appropriate responses to customers' requests. Variety on the job comes from the fact that an administrator will hardly ever encounter precisely the same situation twice. This flexibility in response is precisely why the customer will always view the service-oriented information worker as someone who adds high value to the business relationship, rather than serving merely as a bureaucratic impediment.

Isolated tasks will be replaced by jobs with a sense of task completion.

Industrial-age organizations design jobs in terms of discrete clerical procedures. The flow of work tends to be routed to specialists. There are "dedicated" computers and specially assigned peripheral devices that process the workload in standardized batches. This leads to an isolation of tasks and a loss of sensitivity to the individual customer's identity in the process of handling transactions. For example, a change in a person's salary grade might be referred to headquarters in Atlanta, while vacation pay may require authorization from central payroll authorities in Cleveland. If these events happen to coincide, the changes are that the person's actual payroll check at the plant in Peoria will not be issued on time. If any elements are missing, batch processing stops. The approach of isolating and standardizing individual business transactions is prevalent in the current use of computers. It works extremely well when all goes according to the prescribed routine. When too many exceptions occur, the operators of the system find it very difficult to keep up, and the processing sequence malfunctions. Since correcting an error most likely involves a long, complicated, and carefully prescribed process, the individual affected will observe a deterioration in the quality of service.

Service-age organizations, however, are designed to assure high-quality completion of a client's administrative work, even under adverse conditions. The flow of work is channelled to people who understand both how the client operates and how the internal organization can respond. There are specialized computers designed to handle each subset of the administrative workload. Even more important, there are computers that integrate all of the part into a meaningful whole. This leads to the visibility of all work done by an employee for a particular client. It stimulates a high sense of identification by service people with their customers. For instance, a change in the grade of a person still could be referred to headquarters in Atlanta, while vacation may still require authorization from central payroll in Cleveland. However, the people responsible for paying workers in Peoria will be in a position to prevent delays in the regular paycheck. This integrative approach to processing business transactions works well if organizations have been designed according to the principles of decentralization. It is the approach to be preferred when changes are frequent and when rapid adaptations to local conditions are essential for serving the customer well.

Immutable jobs with a finite scope will be replaced by jobs with opportunity for learning and change.

Industrial-age organizations define jobs in terms of the factory process. Inflexibility in industrial design is applied to the way in which jobs are assigned to people. There is no way of changing the scope of a person's activity except by physically moving him to another assignment.

The design of computerized jobs has largely followed the patterns learned from factories. Data-processing operations were initially organized around a disciplined, sequential, and totally predetermined handling of punched cards. As data-processing operations grew in scope, their managers drew rigid lines between the roles of data preparation, equipment operations, programming, systems analysis, and administration. The same attitudes spread to wherever remote computer terminals were installed. If any learning took place, it was accomplished by sending personnel to formal courses where they acquired specific qualifications so they could leave one position and assume another. According to industrial-age principles, even training was treated as a predetermined factory process in which people without knowledge were fed in at the start of the course and qualified employees came out at the end.

Thus the social structure of a computerized operation came to be patterned on industrial principles. Such operations also acquired many of the counterproductive patterns of industrial factories—including the workers' inclination to consider unionization their only recourse from an unpleasant and restrictive workplace. Seniority issues, wage compensation disputes, and conflict about work quotas appeared even in those high-tech enclaves previously deemed immune to such confrontations between management and labor. The origins of these conflicts can be attributed to work designs that are too rigid and confining.

Service-age organizations, however, design jobs so that people do not need to be reclassified or physically moved if they wish to upgrade their roles or their earning capacity. Work is viewed much more as a cooperative team effort, where the entire team progresses by expanding its influence in a constantly changing and evolving competitive environment. Immutability is out of the question because the dynamic behavior of the marketplace is simply too unpredictable to construct organizations, organize information flows, and write computer programs that could even come near to dealing successfully with what is happening. The workplace, rather than the classroom, becomes the primary location where learning and individual development takes place. Jobs are designed to encompass the widest possible spectrum of activities. Personal growth takes place as people learn to deal with all of the pieces that fail to fit preprogrammed computerized routines.

Jobs with entirely predetermined options will be replaced by jobs with autonomy for discretionary decisions.

Industrial-age organizations thrive on standard procedure manuals, printed forms, and elaborate systems to assure that several approval signatures are secured before any important action is taken. The desire to achieve perfection propels efforts to predefine and predetermine all eventualities. When the motivations of a compulsive programmer are combined with the fixations of an accountant in search of absolute certainty, their efforts will give birth to a computer program which a robot can be taught to operate and an intelligent person will find dull. However, by no means can all external realities be captured by coded routines. If the program is imperfect (and all computer programs are) the employee will often be caught in conflicts. A significant part of available time will be devoted to finding ways of circumventing the computer—thus giving rise to a destructively ambivalent relationship to a technology that is supposed to assist, not impede, the workers who use it.

Service-age organizations, however, will thrive on worker initiatives. They too will have standard procedure manuals, printed forms, and elaborate security systems for quality control. They will focus on serving customers and on obtaining the highest possible commitment from their people in support of their enterprise's objectives. Standards of performance will be defined externally, as seen from the standpoint of the customer, rather than internally, in terms of some expert's opinion what expected behavior is. Good systems design originates from the operating people's motivation to make their jobs more productive and more satisfying. Due to constantly evolving conditions, the information systems will never be seen as approaching certainty or completeness. Rather, they will be conceived as communication links that can be used to speed up an individual's capacity to make discretionary decisions. Systems design will include easy communication with customers and with support experts. Any mismatch between the logic programmed into the network and what happens in everyday operations will receive immediate attention, because it is here that the organization finds out how it can improve. Employees in a successful service organization will devote much of their time to improving the computer system, thus establishing a relationship that increases their sense of personal accomplishment.

Socially unrelated jobs will be replaced by jobs where social support comes from fellow-workers.

Industrial-age organizations isolate workers by means of job design. Only experts, whether they are industrial engineers or systems analysts, have sufficient knowledge about the entire operation to define a worker's relationship with others. A worker has little to say to his associates about the content of work, except perhaps to complain about it. In a computerized operation, the large size of the accumulated error list is an indication that individuals are doing a job according to procedure—but not cooperating to get work completed. Even if operators wish to make corrections, they may not be able to do so because their experience does not provide the needed skills. Specialists such as quality control experts, maintenance programmers, and expediters view the fixing of errors as their prerogative. This is why individuals will not display much work-related enthusiasm. Their attitudes will be more like those of riders on a bus who have simply boarded it for a trip.

Service-age organizations, however, emphasize worker teams as the nucleus of job design. Groups are assigned well-defined missions and are left to allocate work among their members. The objective of each team is to achieve as much self-sufficiency in coping with information technology as resources permit. Therefore, experts such as systems analysts, programmers, or communications specialists are brought in as consultants and teachers rather than as decision-makers. A great deal of social interaction is necessary among team members because each individual must be flexible enough to cover another person's learning time. People become much more dependent, not only on each other, but also on external assistance. There is no place where a team can deposit its errors or its "suspended transactions" (a datacenter euphemism for not having the slightest idea what to do next). If the computer system does not respond, the team can always resort to manual means, or to some improvised solution for making the corrections necessary to get the job done. The team possesses enough skills to accomplish that. Specialists are engaged only to make corrections requiring unique know-how. In this way, any organization that immerses itself in the values of a services-oriented culture will display the spirit of a winning sports team. Work attitudes will reflect the "team members'" dependence on each other for success.

Employment in the Service Society

The economic role of the customized electronic message is to make possible the expansion of producer and consumer services as the primary occupation of the workforce. With mechanization, agriculture can operate with less than 3% of the workforce. With robots, factories can operate with less than 15% of the workforce. Economic growth is fueled by an enormous expansion of employment in the service sector. For the service sector to be productive, for its real prices to fall, and for its "product" to be in demand in the marketplace, it must continue delivering productivity gains. With the elimination of layers of overhead and with work enlargement, the information elements of the service industries should set their productivity target at a minimum of 5% compound gain per annum.

If productivity gains displace labor, where will all of the new jobs come from? What will people actually do in the new service jobs? How can full employment be assured?

Since full employment is presently the most persistent social concern, let us begin with the prospects for technological unemployment caused by the computerization of society. Herbert Simon put the issue very well when he pointed out that full employment is always possible.[2] It can be forced by government action. For instance, there was an enormous labor shortage in ancient Egypt when the pyramids were built. There are also planned economies that define unemployment out of existence by the way employment statistics are kept.

Ultimately, what really matters is the increase in aggregate net productive output of a society, because if there is no growth, there is nothing additional to distribute, and no way of gainfully employing a growing workforce. This is why I prefer to talk about productivity growth and how it relates to increased output.

Employment levels are an outcome. For instance, employment levels may increase because productivity has declined: It now takes a larger number of people to do the same job. Do we wish to use this means to foster full employment? That is easily accomplished. Government could distribute work coupons entitling people to work inefficiently and for only a limited time period. Government could create an even greater amount of unnecessary work than is presently the case, thus increasing employment further. Subsistence work could be forced on every unemployed person and thus, through reclassification, eliminate the problem altogether.

Obviously, none of these is a desirable solution. Increasing the value added per capita is essential to the production of more wealth for more people. If robots can perform $20 per hour tasks for $1 per hour, the society does not benefit from protecting such jobs against displacement by automation. A society whose average wage rate is close to $10 per hour does not gain by diverting scarce resources to protect jobs worth $1 per hour. At a recent congressional hearing on the potential effects of computers on employment, a great deal of concern was expressed about the fact that a large keypunching job was contracted for completion in a foreign country. I explained that the work was exported because the fully allocated cost of keypunching in the United States is close to $20 per hour. The equivalent cost of doing the same work in very low-wage countries is about $3 per hour. But it costs even less—the equivalent of $1 per hour—to perform the same kind of keypunching in the United States by means of a Kurzweil omnifont scanner. There is no reason why costly government subsidies should be expended to retain overpriced manual keypunching work in the United States. Investments are needed to create jobs that increase the average wage rate in society through high value-added work, and not to hold onto activities that are competitively not viable.

This is why I see education, especially in the form of on-the-job training, as the single largest occupational activity in the service economy. The dynamics of the future economy require restructuring the scope of most jobs at least once every seven years. Setting up 10% of information workers' labor time as a training budget to prevent obsolescence is a reasonable estimate of what it will take for organizations to remain competitive. There will still remain another 10% allowance to be made for the rapid depreciation of the information workers' skills. It is reasonable to ask workers to make an investment of their own time in furthering their own development. If 20% of the information workforce's time in the year 2000 is consumed in training and in education, that is equivalent to 15 million person-years. There will be zero growth in new entrants into the workforce after 1985. If output per capita is to increase, even with high productivity we can expect shortages in labor supply, rather than unemployment, from the effects of education and training alone.

The prescription for economic growth, then, encompasses all of the following: increased productivity in the production sector; new international markets; decreased overhead costs; increased effectiveness of capital investments; new domestic markets for services. The role of information technology investments in achieving each of the above objectives is decisive.

Human Capital

The next long-term cyclical upswing in the economy will be propelled by an investment boom in support of the service sector of the economy. The problem with the information sector of the economy does not lie in the fact that it may not be receiving a sufficient amount of producer's durable capital.[3] As a matter of fact, there are indications that this sector is receiving more capital than it can profitably use. In the information sector of the economy the decisive capital is not that embodied in computers but that invested in the appreciation of human capital.

Enhancing human capital is essential for future economic growth. It translates directly into prospects for increased employment opportunities. Human capital appreciates not only through education, training, and software development. It is also compounded through collective experiences accumulated by organizations that have successfully developed new businesses. It is indicated by the premium price the stock market is willing to pay for expected future earning capacity. Human capital is destroyed not only by a lack of investment in research and development, which currently enjoys a great deal of attention, but also by a demoralized workforce, a high rate of employee turnover, frequent reorganizations, and by temporary subsidies that disguise a firm's fundamental inability to remain competitive.

A productive service society advances primarily by finding new ways to improve its returns from investments in human capital. If that is done, service sector output will increase, prices will decline, demand will go up, average wage rates will gain, and employment will increase, because an expansionary investment boom generates new jobs in excess of needs to support current consumption levels. The following strategies are likely to pay off:

1. Reduce the costs of bureaucracies by divesting them of most overhead functions. Have their functions performed, at competitive market prices, by service establishments. Management services, office services, training, vocational support, facility management, real estate administration, municipal services, preventive medicine, and so forth, are already the fastest-growing parts of the economy. The business service industry is investing heavily, not only in fixed capital, but also in trained teams that can deliver services with much greater effectiveness than insiders. The growth rate of professional service firms exceeds the growth rate of computer businesses. Telecommunications networks make divestitures of in-house specialist functions not only technically feasible but also highly effective.

2. Revise present accounting practices and taxation laws which recognize only traditional economic goods—land, buildings, and machines—as assets. Accounting practices do not recognize that human assets are the most important possession of any organization. In my view the value of the human capital of an organization is approximated by what is left after the "shareholder equity" reported on the balance sheet is adjusted for expected shareholder returns on capital.

For instance, the conventional financial statement may dwell at great length on a firm's equipment depreciation practices without recognizing that people also depreciate unless their work is replenished through continuous training, team work, motivation, and a strong sense of belonging. The conventional corporate financial statement treats buildings as an asset and people as an expense. The opposite should apply. People are the only real asset and the building in which they work is nothing but an expense.

Current taxation laws view investment in human capital as if through the wrong end of a telescope. The entire scheme is designed to subsidize consumption of housing, of medical services, and the standard of living of selected groups. One can depreciate a rental property. One can deduct for theft, dentists, political contributions, oil wells, and business-related entertainment. The tax system does not recognize that the most important asset of an individual is his education, training, and know-how. It is the ultimate basis of his future earning (and taxable income) capacity. It is also the principal resource on which our advanced society depends for its international competitiveness. Yet there is no depletion allowance for obsolescent skills. No depreciation is permitted for losses of occupational skills in a society whose pace of change in technology is accelerating. There is no investment tax credit for education.

The current debate about economic policy and competitiveness reveals a strong bias in favor of public incentives for technology capital in preference to investments in human capital. Industrial training expenses are only one-tenth of capital expenditures. With 26% of United States adults considered to be functionally too illiterate to carry out even the simplest operating instructions, and with annual employee turnover rates approaching 30% in service occupations, we are in danger of diverting our investments from the needs which are critical to make a service society more productive.[4]

In order to progress toward a prosperous service society, changes in accounting and in taxation will have to take place. One cannot construct a building if the measurements are defined in terms of weight rather than in terms of length. One cannot build a service society if the measurement system is defined in terms of returns on invested capital rather than returns on invested labor.

3. Transform the workplace to enhance the role of generalists. Our educational system, unions, employment classification system, and even our management training are rooted in the industrial-age belief that specialization is the direction into which to channel all talents. One of the causes of our chronic unemployment is that people cannot easily adapt to new work habits. People should be helped in acquiring skills for work enlargement, for cross-training, and for computer-assisted work so that they may become more flexible rather than narrowly confined to specialized jobs.

Casting information technology applications in the mold of industrial-age concepts inhibits their acceptance. Development of people must dominate acquisition of technology. Emphasis on learning how to make effective investments in human capital rather than in computers is one of the central imperatives for creating a service society.

13

Information and the Media

The service-based society is dependent on electronic media. The extent to which the electronic message replaces other forms of communications is presently subject to wide-ranging speculation. It is proposed here that changes will not be dramatic and that current media will continue to perform the missions they were designed for.

Speech as the Medium of a Hunting Society

Speech still provides the best method for short, transient, person-to-person communication.

Most hunting societies remain geographically confined. A tribe requires only a limited amount of communication to engage in hunting and in warfare. The social role of speech is in the creation of signals understood by all tribal members. There is no need to retain any of the messages except in the form of stories which recall past exploits.

The conversation of such hunters is distinguished by brevity, discontinuity, and a strong preference toward acting out ideas. The subjects covered in speech move from issue to issue, seemingly at random. The topics are chosen by reacting to others. Most conversation is conducted in the present tense. Gossip and hearsay, tradition and taboo shape opinions. Personalized gestures, subtle shifts in body posture, grunting, snorting, nonverbal sounds signifying a pause or a change in the topic; hand and finger indications, facial expressions, eye movements, and other subtle physical signals are important to convey the real intent of words. Different expressions are used when speaking to outsiders and insiders. Only insiders can really understand what an individual means by certain expressions.

Not a single sentence in the preceding paragraph was quoted from books describing speech patterns of primitive tribes, even through it is compatible with what anthropologists have reported. The descriptions were in fact taken from contemporary studies reporting on management communications.[1]

Hunting and warfare are functions that can be found—in a more civilized form—in modern business, and speech will always remain the preferred means for dealing with such activities. When analyzing office communications to find out what activities may be displaced by electronic means one should remember that there will always be verbal contacts which have their origins in early forms of mankind's behavior. Such exchanges will not be converted to the electronic medium until and unless they can be technically improved to convey the many nonverbal attributes of conversation.

Writing as the Medium of an Agricultural Society

Writing combines the recording of information with the means of maintaining authority. It has performed these tasks for over 6,000 years and will continue doing so in the future.

Agricultural society is largely confined to tending its land. Such a society requires a means for recording evidence about land ownership and about rights to its proceeds, such as taxes, tolls, or tribute. The written word is thus associated with the preservation of the sociopolitical establishment in such a society. "Official" text originates with a special class which can be trusted to uphold the continuity of existing relationships. Thus originates the concept of keeper of the secrets— the secretary; or, as keeper of the administrative process—the administrator. The secretary-scribe and the administrative manager are dependent servants; but they are servants who are in constant demand because their rulers have neither the time nor the skill to create new documents. This symbiosis is further reinforced because the secretary-scribe or the administrator has the latitude to modify the written document in ways that can be correctly interpreted only by other secretary-scribes or administrators with similar backgrounds. I find legal documents, the text of government regulations, corporate procedure manuals, and product announcements from the computer industry to be contemporary manifestations of the craft of the scribes and notaries in agricultural society.

The form of a written message is at least as important as its contents. Observing how the written message is used to conduct official business, one might characterize the text by its formal character and by its exclusion of anything that does not fit into a preestablished order. A memorandum informing the commanding officer of the imminent attack on a city is handled with the same formality as a notice about a delinquent food shipment. The objective of such behavior is to disassociate process from substance and to adhere to correct procedure rather than to convey meaning. The purpose of the stylized format is also to keep outsiders from participating in the process of communication, because only trusted functionaries are considered qualified to deal with the intricacies of an official document.

The descriptions in the paragraph above do not deal with document-handling practices in, say, the fourteenth century, even though they are consonant with what a historian might report. They apply to contemporary bureaucratic methods in government and in business for handling official records. Writing is still used in this way to legitimize the roles of functionaries in the modern office.

When analyzing office communication patterns to discover what activities may be displaced by electronic means, it should be recalled that the presence of many formal documents in contemporary businesses can be traced to procedural relationships between superiors and subordinates which are rooted in feudal origins. The same needs which created the earlier forms promote the current ones. Successful conversion to a more efficient electronic medium can take place only after the underlying institutional structure is fully understood and modified where necessary. Purely technological arguments, which may convincingly demonstrate the abstract superiority of new electronic methods, will fail in practice without such structural overhaul. The nation-state, the tax authority, the trade cartel, or any other administrative bureaucracy will find the conversion of documents from paper to electronic form a traumatic process. An affidavit, an application form, an insurance policy, or even a cancelled check convey much more than just what is printed on the surface of the paper. There are signatures, seals, stamps, attachments, cancellation marks, embossing, specialized forms, receipts, and proprietary documentation which assure not only authenticity but also compliance with a control process which serves as a safeguard that the proper authorities have handled the information. Official paper documents will survive the onslaught of electronic handling as long as institutions deeply rooted in these vestiges of agricultural society continue to operate.

Printing as the Medium of an Industrial Society

Printing provides the basis for mass marketing of ideas. It will continue to be the best means of reaching the largest audience needing standard text for repeated reference.

The scope of an industrial society is defined by the markets it serves. It requires inexpensive means to distribute information about its products. Since only mass production is economically feasible, such information must be atuned to mass audiences. Industrial-age messages must reach as many potential customers as possible, stimulating them to the purchase of mass-produced goods and services.

This generalization applies not only to the merchandising of products but also to the promotion of ideas. What is called "promotion" for the sale of goods may be also labelled "propaganda" for conditioning opinions. News, advertising, entertainment, and mass education stimulate increased consumption of goods or increased penetration of political ideas. The low-cost dissemination of mass-produced messages becomes the primary objective of printed text.

It is a curious coincidence that Gutenburg's invention was the first practical application of industrial methods to low-cost mass production of perfectly interchangeable parts. Gutenburg's invention was not the printing press, as popularly believed, but the handmold for easy, low-cost replication of identical letters cast from a master impression. Here we have an epochal invention in which the means of creating the printed message itself embodies the historical essence of that medium. This event took place 350 years before it was understood as a general concept applicable to all industrial production rather than as an isolated technological accomplishment applicable to printing only.

At first, printing posed a threat to authorities enjoying a monopoly on reading and writing. Yet autocracies quickly adopted this medium as their preferred method of communication because it lent itself to easy control of the dissemination of ideas. Widespread literacy became a tool in the hands of the nation-state, serving to establish and preserve national identity through use of a standard language. The printed word became associated with mass distribution, popular appeal, and manipulation of opinion in national markets.

Advances in machine tools make it possible to disseminate widely the technical means for publishing. Unit costs of printed matter decline rapidly as the length of a production run increases. Gradual innovation reduces the initially high setup cost of the Gutenburg process so that the marginal cost of an additional print approaches the average cost. This is why the xerography process can be classified as the perfection of Gutenbergian concepts and its final evolutionary stage rather than as belonging to some other developmental phase. Even though xerography involves electrostatically formed characters, its economics, not its technology, dictates its place in the evolutionary sequence.

Printing is valuable for business because it spreads ideas that help create a homogeneous market for industrial goods. Commercial printing is characterized by standardization not only in form but also in substance. It shows a strong affinity for information that can be presented in a formalized sequence. Words are edited for consumption by an audience which is reasonably uniform in its tastes and homogeneous in its ability to comprehend the text. A textbook on economics or instructions on how to assemble a lawnmower will each be written in its own standard fashion regardless of the reader's education, technical skill, or prior experience. The purpose of the publishing process is to reach the largest audiences capable of absorbing the messages directed at them. The objective of commercial printed communications is appropriately described as: "Get all the readers that are fit to read."

In analyzing office communication patterns to learn what activities may be displaced by new electronic means such as the visual display unit, videotape, or video conferencing, one should remember that standard printed text can be converted to a visual electronic medium only if it can be re-created in a format as easily handled as that offered by the printed medium. The purchaser of a complicated product, the casual reader, the traveller requiring easily portable text, or the individual seeking fixed reference information will prefer to seek out the printed format for convenience and for ease in retrieval. Instruction manuals, fiction, textbooks, and encyclopedia reference sources will survive the advent of the visual electronic medium, as demonstrated by the very modest success of various schemes to distribute text to the home by means of television screen displays. Information forms related to the mass consumption of standard products or standard ideas will continue to be with us in the future. People who must solve problems of the industrial age—such as locating a standard consumer product—will continue to rely on the printed medium for their information needs.

The Electronic Message as the Medium of a Service Society

The electronic message provides the means for integrating disparate sources of information so as to give a prompt, individualized response.

The scope of a service society depends on its ability to find new means for satisfying individual needs. A desirable form of communication includes inexpensive and highly responsive ways to diagnose client preferences. Such a means of communication also involves access to a logistic system sufficiently responsive to handle not only physical goods, but also to provide ongoing attention to client needs. Delivery systems in a service-oriented society are characterized by closely coupled feedback relationships. This means that information may flow back and forth several times before any action is taken. Instead of making a purchasing decision based on a standard list of requirements, a very large variety of options is available. A service is purchased only after full understanding has been reached about the best combination to serve a client's needs. A service society is designed to minimize the assets tied up in the production and distribution processes. Robot factories produce even at night, on weekends, during holidays. All scrap and rejects are eliminated. No obsolete equipment is produced since all output is generated in direct response to demand. There is hardly any inventory lying around. Besides, services themselves cannot be stocked anyway, since they are consumed as they are produced.

A service-based society uses electronic networks to initiate automated production and to arrange for semiautomatic delivery, so that all output appears to be customized and always brand-new. Customized production is not only technically feasible but is also the lowest-cost alternative. All means of communications are deployed to give customers exactly what they want. Electronic messages handle not only the initial request for service, but also all of the subsequent messages that advise the secondary, tertiary, and other tiers of supply what is necessary to complete a smoothly coordinated sequence of tightly coupled actions. For instance, it is quite conceivable that a request for a genetically modified organ transplant may require thousands of messages and several millions of computations before it is delivered.

The electronic medium can achieve universality without the need to impose uniformity.

The service-age message must be delivered instantly, at extremely low cost, to any location on earth, precisely and unambiguously. This is necessary because the response to it, in most cases, must be totally automated if the cost of the entire sequence of transactions is to remain affordable.

Neither phone calls, nor visits, nor memoranda, nor business forms are practical business solutions if complex and rapid communications must take place before any action is possible. Electronics not only conveys information rapidly; it assures that messages can be made universally understandable. Communicating by speech, writing, or the printed page is associated with too many cultural conventions which render efforts to achieve global standardization hopeless for all practical purposes. In the past, global standardization has been only possible in isolated cases, in which business actions had already been forced into a uniform mold. A standard international airline ticket is a good example of such an isolated case.

Because speech, the written message, and printing are already deeply entrenched in their environment, the universal standardization of these media cannot be expected. I do not believe that Esperanto or its equivalent will prevail. I also doubt that the same size of letter paper or even the same size envelope will be accepted by all postal authorities. Neither books, newspapers, nor invoices can be expected to conform to a globally mandated form.

The inherent universality of the electronic message is hidden in the power of local communication control devices that allow each individual user to connect their workstation with a worldwide network. Such a control device can be programmed to take a message in the locally acceptable format "A" and convert it to a universal standard "B," as well as the other way around. Clients may deal with any supplier by means of the electronic network without having to subject themselves to a totally homogenizing process. The communication controller than serves the role of an ever-present interpreter that translates local language and local forms into universally understandable terms. Voice input into a computer that directly converts the spoken word into text is technically feasible. When the language-and-voice-and-context translation controller becomes universally available as an attachment to every workstation, the electronic network will become a means to the creation of a global marketplace of services, products, and ideas.

Individuality, rather than mass standardization, applies not only to the merchandizing of products and services but also to the distribution of ideas. What was called "customization" to explain how the distribution of goods might take place has its equivalent in "tutoring," used as a term to explain how knowledge can be distributed. Computer-aided instruction, programmable education and training, software-supported simulation exercises, training games, and workstation-prompted coaching become the means to convey expert knowledge to clients so that they can make competent choices from an increasingly diverse array of services. These aids can also stimulate growth in the demand for added services.

Low-cost and rapid response to a client's questions and needs becomes the purpose of the electronic medium. Mass broadcasting declines. Focused narrowcasting increases. It is noteworthy that the telegraph and the telephone, which I consider the precursors of the electronic communication networks, were also the first practical, systematized electronic means for the delivery of point-to-point messages. Here we have two inventions which embody the essence of the electronic medium. The first application of the telegraph and the telephone took place more than a hundred years before the ultimate role of the electronic message in the transformation of society began to become apparent.

The electronic message is associated with the concepts of customized distribution, personal appeal, and individual accountability. There is freedom for everyone, not only to originate ideas but also to publish and distribute them. Public networks are easily adapted to serve as private networks. There is no limit on the subdivision of the communications functions because there are no economies of scale, as seen from a user's standpoint. Even a family may operate its own electronic bulletin board, its own electronic newspaper, and its own electronic post office. To permit easy interconnection among the various elec-

tronic communities, the electronic message promotes the use of English
as the standard international technical and commercial language,
which serves as the lingua franca for other automated language transla-
tions.

The electronic medium also fosters a common professional courtesy
that all participants share. It is amazing to observe the lack of friction,
the prevalence of goodwill, and the cooperation generated by electronic
mail traffic on international networks. These new channels make it
possible to form intellectual communities in large numbers even if
the members are separated by great distances.[2] The universal electronic
message, which ties together autonomous service organizations and
interest groups, becomes a potential antidote against the totalitarian
state, which can tolerate only uniformity and centrally controlled,
standardized media. From the standpoint of control over information,
the state monopoly over media and over their contents is based upon
industrial-age concepts about how to organize a modern society. Any
society that wishes to advance beyond the limits of industrialization
will have to open the channels of communications to allow the creation
and distribution of electronic messages on a decentralized and customized basis. Thus, effective electronic communication can diminish the
power base of centrally controlled institutions. This is why the free
flow of information on an international scale is so widely opposed
by those who have good reason to fear loss of absolute control.

There is a much more threatening scenario, which suggests that
the totalitarian state will deliberately stimulate the expansion of electronic messages precisely because they are so amenable to efficient
police surveillance of every transaction. A massive central computer
can be imagined that would screen everyone's electronic traffic. This
image of the future is very popular with thinkers who accept, without
questioning, a narrow and technical view of what electronic messages
are all about. For a totalitarian state to monitor all transactions, it
would first have to create networks to which there were widely distributed access for most of the information workforce. The technical
evolution of such networks is extremely difficult to control. During
the transition stage from an industrial-age form of communications
to the universal electronic message, conditions are simply too chaotic
to be subject to complete central direction. This is a risk that a totalitarian state would not be willing to take, since it would transform the
way in which power is distributed. So far, the evidence shows that
increasing access to autonomous computing power on a broadly distributed basis promotes the democratization of institutions. The acqui-

sition of microcomputers by office workers and small businesses, for example, has proven to be a corrosive influence on the power of central data-processing organizations to exercise a monopoly over the use of information technology. Whether this pattern will reverse itself as networks embrace the entire spectrum of economic activity should be a source of lively debate for years to come.

Advances in wideband communications networks make the technical means for transmitting electronic messages in color available; ultimately, images will be transmitted in three dimensions. Unit costs for transmitting and storing information decline rapidly as demand for the new services increases. Fixed costs dwindle when a large share of the information-processing load is shifted from a big, expensive central communication utility to individual workstations. There will be an enormous increase in the capacity of the telecommunications transmission channels. The cost of each additional electronic message will essentially be only the labor cost involved in creating and understanding it, because the marginal costs of capital tied up in technology will be practically zero.

There is a fundamental difference between electronic telecommunications and radio and television broadcasts. Whereas the former is an outgrowth of the flexible and personalized services of the telephone, the latter are the final stages of centralized control.

Radio and television transmit standardized messages to mass audiences at high fixed costs and at marginal costs which fluctuate widely. Cable television and new, small radio stations are an attempt to overcome these limitations—but they remain dependent on large numbers of listeners and viewers. Even though radio and television involve electronically transmitted speech and images, it is not the technology but its economic and social effects that dictate its place in the evolutionary sequence. Radio and television are the terminal forms of an evolution that began with printing.

The electronic medium favors services that can be tailored to fit individual needs with a minimum waste of resources. In its verbal form it is citizen-band radio. In its written form it is electronic mail and electronic conferencing. In its visual form it is videoconferencing.

In actual use, an electronic message expresses a great deal about the character, the idiosyncracies, and the interests of the person who generated it. It is a delight to see how messages convey a person's involvement in his work, and how bored handlers of office routines suddenly blossom forth to become motivated contributors. The electronic medium thrives on ideas and suggestions about how to improve the quality of services. It works best for information presented in a flexible format. The surest way to achieve this is to make communications with computers as natural as possible. The proliferation of menus, icons, soft keys, touch-sensitive screens, graphic pads, and the "mouse" attest to the lively interest in this area. Very soon, text processors will be able to interpret spoken language. This will further enhance the capabilities of the electronic medium to serve global communication needs because networks will then lend themselves to much easier automatic language translation.

As the means of communication improve, individuals will not only have greater access to information sources, but will also have greater flexibility in their relations with other people. For instance, an electronically supported class on economics would not depend upon a rigid, prescribed text. Students would first engage in tutoring exercises that would brief them on the prerequisites of the course. Depending upon their observed qualifications, the students would then embark on a series of lessons about the substance of economic knowledge. The real learning would take place when each student explored events influenced by economics from the standpoint of his own interests, using an "intelligent tutor" program. In situations when even this program could not cope with the student's unique queries, the computer might refer the matter to the course author's workstation or connect the student directly to the course instructor for further prompting.

To take another case, operating instructions about how to add a lawnmower capability to the existing household robot would have to be designed to apply only to this situation, since the size and shape of the property as well as mowing requirements would be unique. Depending upon the model of the robot and the extent of reprogramming necessary, the entire process would resemble a learning exercise for the robot as well as for the owner rather than a step-by-step assembly sequence.

Electronic messages augment and diversify individual capabilities by presenting information that already contains a great deal of expert understanding of the recipient's needs. The purpose of the electronic message is to reach every possible client in the most effective, specific way possible. The appropriate description of the electronic message's objective is: "Get all the clients that can be served."

Customized distribution of information is essential for the growth of national and worldwide services. The need for personal contact in the delivery of services will not be eliminated and will always remain the preferred method for providing emotional support to a client. When analyzing service activities to find out which activities may be displaceable by electronic means, one should remember that a personal interview may be converted to the electronic medium only if it can be recreated in a form that resembles already accepted norms of behavior. This is why the videotape of a formal address from an aloof and distant chairman can be used to inform large audiences in remote offices and plants, whereas a videoconference organized for the purposes of building morale of thousands of employees will not accomplish much. The electronic message should be used primarily as a means of introducing completely new services. It should not be promoted as a substitute that will reduce the costs of existing communications methods while tending to impoverish the richness of personal interaction.

The individual, person-to-person or point-to-point electronic message embodies the essence of the service-oriented society. Speech, writing, printing, and even broadcasting will continue performing their unique roles, each of which is deeply rooted in mankind's historical progression from the hunting stage onward. The electronic message should be understood as providing opportunities to deliver completely new services rather than as a direct substitute for already existing communication forms.

PART IV

THE
EXECUTIVE'S
PERSPECTIVE

14

Guidelines for Information-Technology Investments

The foregoing chapters have clear implications for the manner in which the executives in charge decide whether, when, and how to go about making investments in information technology. In order to assure maximum payoff, the following guidelines seem appropriate.

Link Technology Investments to Strategic Goals

Before making any investments in information technology, a thorough and uncompromising assessment of an organization's needs should be completed. Is sluggish product development the principal bottleneck? Does the sales force need support to increase its productivity? Are the customers' perceptions of quality affected by the need to improve administrative performance?

Directions for information technology investment should never be formulated in terms of methods. Going from "batch processing" to "on-line databases" is an implementation tactic rather than a business strategy. Objectives should not be to "introduce personal computers" or to "install decision-support systems." These technologies are

235

not an end in themselves. Rather, they will help to redirect the way management operates if the course of action is already plotted out. For instance, if a firm contemplates a massive decentralization move in order to resegment its markets, electronic mail and electronic conferencing could be introduced as an effective method that will aid in the new operating environment. The procurement of personal computers and of "expert" software would then be subordinate to carrying out a well-defined business mission rather than just innovation for its own sake.

Do Not Look for Specific Justification of Computer Hardware Purchases

Reduce the emphasis on justification for isolated information technology purchases. Information technology should be an integral part of overall business proposals designed to deliver a strategic, marketing, product-development, or manufacturing advantage. Insofar as it is feasible, information technology costs should always be incurred as a variable expense associated with the accomplishment of a specific business mission rather than as a long-term capital cost. If long-term investments are necessary, initial cash expense should be recovered by means of competitively priced user charges. This is why all information technology costs should be planned and authorized along with other expenses, rather than as special cases. One should resist the temptation to buy a computer because it is fashionable, or because someone else has one. One should deny requests for computer equipment when they are made case-by-case on technical grounds. However, one should be willing to fund a profitable business improvement which requires the application of information technology. A computer is like gravy. It is not itself the main course, but with the right menu it surely improves the meal.

Apply Information Technology to Innovation

Link the introduction of information technology with overcoming some of the limits placed on existing relationships. How about providing overnight responses to customer requests for price quotations? How about giving the sales force the means to complete on-site designs?

How about improving the effectiveness of a factory incentive compensation plan by providing shop-floor people with a direct means to see the consequences of their actions? How about gaining a competitive edge by giving service people access to sophisticated diagnostic tools? How about reducing absenteeism by providing portable workstations for work at home?

There is no end of innovative opportunities which form a sound basis for introducing computers into the workplace. Automating existing procedures will, in most cases, deliver only a fraction of the potential that is available. Automating an existing operation is also more difficult than designing an operation from scratch, because entrenched relationships in the workplace and the fear of displacement will act as a brake on progress in the former case.

Plan Personnel Costs Before Technology Costs

Investments in human capital and in the other expenses of reorganization will exceed the costs of any information technology over its lifetime. The largest cost of an information system comes from installing it, not from designing it.

Insist on a comprehensive assessment of the expenses for training, for gaining user acceptance, for organizational learning, and for ongoing support before acquiring any technology. The technical choices should be determined by people costs rather than the other way around.

Insist on Plans

Successful technology investments have sharply and simply stated objectives and clearly defined performance goals. Detailed schedules and implementation procedures are not plans, merely the mechanics for tracking events. A good systems plan will specify how people will operate after the technology is installed. It will be phrased in terms of the expected results. It will state how actual achievements can be measured and verified. The major characteristic of a good systems plan is that it can be given to everyone who will be affected by the technology. The plan must therefore be brief, understandable, and acceptable. Everyone will have to identify with it and be committed to its success.

Each successful systems project must also be viewed as only an incremental step towards the realization of more comprehensive goals. Therefore, each project plan must not only show how it will achieve its own objective, but also how it fits into a long-range progression. These matters are not to be taken lightly—by covering them informally at the conclusion of a flip-chart presentation, for example. The overall architectural design of the information flows for an enterprise must be documented in the most meticulous form. When one builds a house, one can always improvise kitchen details. But first, the foundation must be laid properly.

Use Information Technology to Improve Communications

The ultimate goal of information technology is to improve the sharing of knowledge among people. Buying isolated office automation products, computer processing, and personal computers without also obtaining the means of communication among them is like buying a truck to haul a load around the backyard. How information will flow to and from the information-processing devices deserves full executive attention. It does not matter whether the means for conveying the information is electronic or paper. Productivity of organizations improves primarily as a result of people having the tools needed to use the same information.

Organization of people is the basis of all value added. Communication is the basis of all organization. Information technology provides the means for superior communication. These three principles constitute the basis of management guidance for the electronic age and for securing the payoff from information technology.

Do Not Invest in Technology That Limits Growth

Choose only information technology that allows the user to expand the scope of his work. Productivity gains rarely come from a mere acceleration of the work tempo. People improve their productivity by increasing their capacity to handle diversity. The technology chosen should be sufficiently enticing so as to place no limits on the user's initiative in improving his performance.

Get Information Technologists to "Join the Company"

More often than not, information technologists are employed by an organization without really making a career commitment to the company. This distancing and lack of interest on the part of valuable employees acts as the largest hindrance to productivity gains from information-technology investments. The way to avoid this is to give the technical staff good reason to see their careers linked with the health of the firm. They should get business training and spend a great deal of time in learning about the firm's products and services; they should know at least some of the firm's customers. If special expertise is needed, it can always be purchased on a consulting basis. The technical staff should always include operations people who have diversified their training to manage technology.

Clarify the Role of the Experts

The new information technologies permit a widespread distribution of control over the uses of hardware and software. The experts usually view themselves in the role of custodians who prevent unknowing and untrained users of information technology from harming the enterprise. They display a strong sense of professional accountability when trying to prevent users from creating chaos by their uncoordinated technical choices. However, there is always an element of self-seeking and self-righteousness present when the experts pose as the guardians of all propriety.

When confronted with the clash between the opinions of experts and the need to stimulate the personal involvement and initiative of all employees to use information technology, the wise executive should abstain from making case-by-case, Solomon-like decisions between disagreeing factions. The burden of proof should always be on the experts to declare precisely what overall objectives and standards they are pursuing. The experts possess the necessary privileges and know-how to document, in reasoned detail, the limits of the enterprise's information architecture. Specifically, the experts must spell out where the imposition of uniformity prevents chaos and where initiative and innovation may occur. Where this equilibrium between experts and users finally rests will vary from company to company. It is one of the primary roles of the executive in charge to see that equilibrium is not achieved by simply negotiating compromises between factions. Good information architecture is arrived at by pursuing an overall, well-thought-out design which demonstrably supports the fundamental principles and strategies of the business.

Take Advantage of Vendors' Specialized Knowledge

Whenever possible, go for competitive procurement. If vendors are listened to carefully, they provide an excellent learning opportunity for the organization to explore the various purchasing options. With the enormous diversification of the information industry, there are now numerous channels through which one can procure the desired result. When considering a major new investment, a turnkey systems supplier should always be included as one of the potential solutions. Hardware and software vendors have invested tens of billions of dollars in application and installation know-how for products and services which they price at marginal cost. Don't buy just equipment. Tap into the vendor's accumulated reservoir of experience to obtain complete solutions.

Avoid Dabbling

It is not necessary to understand VLSI, CMOS, VTAM, BASIC, MS–DOS, CP/M, or any other computer language to manage the introduction of information technology effectively. The executive should concentrate on transforming the structure of organizational relationships that will ultimately take advantage of the new technology. Taking up programming or running an electronic spreadsheet analysis should be seen as an optional activity, useful perhaps to improve one's subconscious understanding of the electronic environment. It is a nice thing to do, but if taken too seriously it will interfere with management's job of integrating computers into the organization. Amateur programmers who hold high executive positions should not presume to make choices which are better left to experienced professionals. The best thing an executive can do in this context is to find useful computer applications for his own job. In this way he can serve as a model for others to follow.

Institute the Pricing of Overhead Activities

All services of information workers presently budgeted as overhead costs should be evaluated against competitive alternatives. Even if no changes are made in the way information workers do their jobs, this approach will deliver a much-improved understanding of how effectively they are employed. The concept of pricing for services should definitely be applied to the consumption of all information technology. Cost accountability at the user level is critical for success. Without it, there is no way of telling how effective an investment has been. On-line transaction processing is ideally suited for the inauguration of a competitively priced internal marketplace for information services.

Measure Productivity

Consistently reported productivity measurements should be included in all operating reports and should be explicitly integrated with published financial reporting. Productivity measures should also be applied to:

1. Guiding further productivity improvement efforts
2. Justifying further wage and salary increases
3. Awarding bonuses and incentive payments
4. Explaining the accomplishments of the firm in easily understood terms

Productivity is simply a measure of value added for each unit of resources, such as labor or capital. This approach should be applied to measure the contribution of information workers in achieving overall productivity targets.

Measure Quality of Information Services

Productivity measures should be supplemented by collecting subjective ratings from recipients of the information worker's services. The qualitative ratings should be obtained on a continuous basis. With a properly designed sampling process, valid conclusions can be drawn even from an extremely small number of interviews. The subjective ratings should include the client's perceptions about the usefulness, responsiveness, and timeliness of services. This done, testing the information payoff can be concluded.

15

Summary

Information technology provides a new means for our society to continue its development towards higher levels of prosperity and wealth. Everyone has a role to play in unlocking this potential. It is the task of our leadership to rethink the values of our industrial culture and to devise new organizations, new roles for people, new economic relationships, and new ways of communicating. A service-based society that maximizes the value of its people's skills is just ahead of us.

This book has suggested a number of insights that may be useful in reducing the learning time needed to cope with a changed environment. These ideas are summarized below.

1. The cost of information work, rather than the number of "white collar workers," determines what can be accomplished by information technology. More and more information work is being done directly by the consumer, while less is being allocated to the increasingly expensive office environment. Growth in the number of information workers comes largely from internal information-processing needs rather than from customer demand. Increase in the number of small service organizations stimulates growth of the information workers. Such small enter-

242

prises multiply as large organizations decrease their dependence on costly in-house information-worker staffs.

2. Job design based on excessive specialization is a major cause of unproductive information-handling work. If the specialist can be converted into a generalist capable of serving all or most customer needs, coordinators and administrators can be given jobs that contribute to value rather than add to overhead. Industrial engineering techniques based on the measurement of efficiency have limited value in guiding investments in information technology. A more useful criterion is that of organizational effectiveness, which includes, but is not subsumed, under the category of efficiency. Efficiency is an individualistic category; effectiveness is a matter of team performance.

3. The amount of office work done in a bureaucracy is determined by organizational design. However, the closer one examines the details of office work the less understandable it becomes. Office work reflects the way power is distributed. Automation can be used to increase the autonomy of individuals or to strengthen the control of the hierarchy. Office automation should be attempted only after work has been simplified to respond to customer needs. Productivity is improved by simplifying organizations rather than by speeding up work.

4. The principal challenge of information technology is how to deal with unpredictable office work. A flowchart is largely useless for understanding the activities of productive information workers.

5. Successful office automation projects deliver the greatest gains through enlargement of work roles. The most rewarding benefit from office automation comes from improved quality of customer care.

6. The electronic message changes the contents and the form of office communications; for one thing, it permits office work to be organized more simply.

7. The successful adoption of information technology requires agents of change—the high-performance individuals—who lead an organization in accepting a transformed workplace. Training of users should be the first priority of any information technology project. Technical choices are secondary and should be determined by the users' full labor costs.

8. Rapidly declining costs of information technology are not decisive in realizing the payoff from investments. The attainment of promised benefits is the key to success. In fact, information technology costs make up only a small fraction of total office-automation expenses. The people using the technology are the dominant cost element. That is, conventional (low-tech) expenses make up a large share of the

costs. But the office is not a factory: techniques found successful in the factory will not work well in the office.

9. Every system design should be made to fit the diversity of people using it rather than standardize the people to assure conformity. Successful office automation alters the composition of office work outputs as well as inputs. Therefore, conventional measures of efficiency do not apply. As already mentioned, *effectiveness* is the key target.

10. The effectiveness of information work can be measured by its value added to the total output of the organization. In the electronic age, work design is reoriented towards maximizing the value added by people rather than by machines. Benefits to the society are maximized through cooperation in eliminating low value-added jobs and in upgrading people into high value-added jobs.

11. Only a paying customer can determine the value of information. The presence of a market mechanism is essential for making large productive investments in information technology.

12. An individual's unique personal workstation is the central artifact of the electronic age. Information technology permits the shifting of information work from synchronous to asynchronous activities, with a corresponding gain in effectiveness and ease of coordination.

13. The economic influence of computers on organizations can be determined by the same statistical techniques as those employed in epidemiological evaluations of the effects of pharmaceuticals on groups of patients. There does not seem to be any direct causal relationship between information technology costs and management productivity. The economic value of management can be measured by finding out what is left after everyone else has been paid.

14. The "industrial culture" and the "service culture" can be characterized by their different assumptions about the nature of work. In the service-based economy, distribution logistics rather than production costs determine the cost of information included in the price of all products. The post-industrial society is not an "information society." Information will continue to be primarily a means for supporting production and distribution rather than an item of consumption. The electronic work environment makes it possible to substitute low-cost, customized products and services for low-cost, mass-produced products and services.

15. Information technology permits a simplification of the structure of entire industries and not just of individual organizations. The technical design of information systems should be guided by the needs

of the business strategy and should determine organizational design. The business executive is the key to linking information technology investments with the strategic goals of the enterprise. This linkage cannot be compromised or delegated if the full potential for productivity improvement is to be realized.

16. The electronic age will be characterized by a major restructuring of existing work-roles. People will perform tasks previously done by their bosses. The information worker in the current organization is primarily a specialist. In the future he will be primarily a generalist. Information workers, as a percentage of the overall workforce, will increase. Professional and technical workers will become the largest occupational group. The principal asset of the economy will be their accumulated experience.

17. Technological priorities should never get ahead of the abilities of users to apply computers. Technology costs can always be contained. Ineffective use of people has practically no limit when it comes to the waste of resources.

18. The coming of the future service society, based on knowledge, is not inevitable. It is, however, a desirable option to increase the standard of living. The organizing principle of a society based on services is global cooperation based on sharing of knowledge. All institutions will be shaped by questions of ownership and control of knowledge.

19. The level of employment is a matter of aggregate output. To increase output levels while increasing income per capita requires a steady gain in productivity. A gain in income per capita implies a shortage of skilled labor. The next long-term economic cycle will be characterized by investments in the appreciation of human capital. In the information age people are assets: it is machines and buildings that should be counted as expenses.

20. The coming of the "paperless office" is a myth. Visual displays are complementary to paper, both of which will continue to play vital roles in office work. The electronic medium will not substitute directly for existing uses of the spoken, written, and visual media. It should be viewed primarily as a new means, one to be applied to new uses.

21. The essence of the new electronic message is its universality— which should not be confused with standardization. The uniform central control and hierarchical structure of the totalitarian state is contradicted by the inherent need for autonomy and decentralization of the effective electronic workplace. The prospect of a workable Orwellian

state is, in any case, as yet remote on account of presently excessive costs and incompetence entailed by gargantuan, monolithic control structures.

————————

The above ideas summarize some of the more important insights discussed in this book. They provide a glimpse of the new world, based on my exploration of various vistas in that world, and refined by comparison and contrast with what others have seen. From the perspective of an advance visitor, I am pleased to report that even though the new lands may not offer us milk and honey, they are nevertheless a desirable destination. Work will be transformed in the electronic age. Equipped with a better understanding of what to expect from a workplace primarily occupied with information work, the reader will be in a superior position to benefit from the payoffs offered by this new environment. He should therefore be able to help steer this transformation with a fuller grasp of the enormous forces already at work, forces which will become increasingly powerful as we approach a new millennium.

Notes

Preface (pp. xiii–xix)

1. The idea that multiple views are most helpful in comprehending complex socio-technological changes comes from Linstone's pioneering paper: Harold A. Linstone et al., "The Multiple Perspective Concept," *Technological Forecasting and Social Change* 20 (1981), pp. 275–325.

Chapter 1: Working in the Office (pp. 3–28)

1. Here are the information worker percentages, obtained from a variety of sources, for selected countries:

Australia	39% (1966)	46% (1976)	47% (1981)
Brazil	34% (1960)	37% (1970)	40% (1980)
N. Zealand	36% (1961)	41% (1971)	43% (1981)
Sweden	30% (1970)	36% (1980)	39% (1990, estimate)

The consistency of the definitions used by different nations in determining their figures is questionable. However, the trends are consistent and the reported percentages of information workers are sufficiently large to demonstrate their dominance as an employment category.

2. The distinction between information work and production work becomes blurred when robotics is introduced. I expect it to generate a great deal of dispute. I define as production workers those individuals whose minds and limbs are directly and continually occupied with getting physical work accomplished. As an example, the truck driver's eyesight and hands are directly linked to the act of steering a truck. This person is integral to providing the necessary feedback for driving to take place. The alarm bell, the quick glance at the spindle, and the fingers that tie a knot are directly linked in the continuous operation of a textile loom. Both examples illustrate the operational feedback necessary for the performance of production.

By contrast, the information workers' minds are external to the feedback mechanism that does the work. Robots and computers have already been programmed with their own controls that correct practically all known error conditions and do not rely on continuous operator intervention to function. The human interferes with the machine only on those rare occasions when the error control mechanism itself needs correcting. If a worker is directly involved as part of the operational feedback sequence, that worker is a production worker. If the worker only manages the error control adjustments by means of corrections that provide new information to the machine which will in turn change the operational feedback sequence, that worker is an information worker.

To illustrate these distinctions let us examine what persons controlling robots actually do. Generally one finds them sitting in a comfortable chair. Occasionally they enter data by means of a keyboard. A computer terminal displays responses from various preprogrammed software routines. The connection between the physical motions of the robot and the operator's actions is mediated by many layers of software logic in the form of data and text. This makes the robotics operator virtually indistinguishable from computer operators. The operators of computer-sequenced robots are engaged in information work, in contrast with operators of automated welding equipment, drill presses or lathes, who manually change all sorts of machine settings to make sure that the production process proceeds as expected.

The above can be restated in the form of a principle: if the machine is an extension of a worker's limbs, this person is a production worker. If the machine is an extension of this person's mind, he is an information worker.

These distinctions are not just a pedantic quibble about names and labels. Occupational classifications often become controversial, especially when they concern matters of labor relations or of regulatory jurisdiction. There are also employment forecasts which are politically important. For instance, an important economist has projected a decline in the growth rate of the number of information workers. Measuring information work rather than information workers will lead to opposite conclusions—and to a different approach to employment policy by government. On the declining *numbers* of information workers, see Charles Jonscher, "Information Resources and Economic Productivity" in *Information Economics and Policy* 1 (1983), pp. 13–35.

3. The dollar-weighing method of determining the cost of information work is perhaps the closest approximation to reality. It makes a 15% allowance for sales workers' time as delivery people and a 20% allowance for service workers' time as information-handlers. A conservative estimate presumes that 15% of the time of production and craft workers is devoted to filling out forms, attending meetings, etc., and that 10% of the time of operations, laborer and farm workers' time is taken out of direct production while receiving or generating information.

4. It is interesting to note that even the most highly automated segment of the economy—banking—shows more rapid increases in employment than in output. The following indices for the United States banking industry are based on 1977–100%:

Year	Output	Output/hr	Employment
1967	52.2	83.8	63.0
1970	64.5	85.5	76.6
1975	84.6	90.0	94.2
1980	106.1	92.7	115.7

Source: U.S. Bureau of Labor Statistics, "The Impact of Technology on Labor," Bulletin 2137, December 1982.

5. The breakdown of occupations in the United States into "information worker" and "other worker" groups as of January, 1983:

	Total (millions)	Percent of Total
Information workers:		
Executive and managerial	10.7	11
Professional	12.7	13
Technical workers	3.0	3
Sales workers	11.3	12
Clerical support, secretarial	16.4	17
Subtotal	54.1 million	56%
Non-information workers:		
Service occupations	13.3	14
Production and craft workers	11.6	12
Operators and laborers	15.2	15
Farmers, foresters and fishermen	3.1	3
Subtotal	43.2 million	44%
Total employment	97.3 million	100%

Source: Summarized from tables in U.S. Department of Labor, *Employment and Earnings* 30:2 (February 1983).

6. The percentage composition of the major occupational groups in the United States information workforce has changed as follows during the last two decades:

Occupational Group	1960	1970	1983
Executives, managers	10.7	10.5	11.6
Professionals	11.4	14.2	17.3
Sales, administrative, support	21.3	23.6	25.2
Total Information Workers	43.4%	48.3%	54.0%

Source: Summarized from tables in: U.S. Department of Labor, *Employment and Earnings* 30:2 (February 1983).

7. During the severe recession from July 1982 through January 1983, professional and technical employment actually increased by 3.5%, while the employment of all non-information workers decreased by 9.4%. Except for a 1% decline in the "sales and support workers," information workers as a group gained in employment, while the total workforce declined by a total of 4.2%. See U.S. Department of Labor, *Employment and Earnings* 30:2 (February 1983), A–21.

8. What follows is a highly condensed scenario of events for the example mentioned in the text.

1. Meeting to discuss the proposed policy. Finance, accounting, sales compensation, field marketing, auditing, personnel, legal, customer relations, customer administration, and data processing representatives are invited. (Ten workhours and three days are needed to set up the meetings, twenty phone calls are made to schedule and reschedule. This segment requires ten to twenty office transactions.)

2. Minutes of the meeting are drafted. Responsibility for writing the policy is delegated to a three-person subcommittee. The text of the minutes is distributed, reviewed by recipients, and filed. (Sixteen workhours and three days: Forty office transactions are required if nobody objects to the text of the minutes. Otherwise the time required increases by 50%.)

3. One person starts working on the policy draft. The actual hours of writing the text of the policy are relatively trivial in comparison with the efforts invested in coordination and in consultation. (This requires twenty-five phone calls, three meetings, six file searches, two or three dictated drafts, and a letter of transmittal. The initial effort to get the draft ready consumes twenty workhours in the course of four days, and necessitates at least sixty photocopies. Altogether sixty to eighty office transactions are involved.)

4. The policy draft, bearing several signatures, is next distributed to the meeting attendees, to the division's legal staff, to the group pricing staff, to the corporate pricing staff, to the division, group, and corporate controller's office, to five regional sales management offices, and to the division's planning office. Most of the recipients review the text, record the request for internal

follow-up, and make additional copies for handling by their respective staff assistants, who in turn make phone calls requesting further clarification. A small number of the staff people prepare written comments which are passed back along the same route from whence they came. (This involves more than 200 workhours, 140 phone calls, consumes fifteen working days, and requires four computer runs for analysis. Six hundred photocopies are produced and well over 300 office transactions are necessary just to handle this paperwork. In case anyone takes exception to the proposal, additional time and effort—amounting to at least one quarter of the total initial effort— must be added for every exception seriously considered.)

5. A new meeting is then called to consider the latest version of the policy letter as well as any changes that may have taken place in the month since the entire action began. (This process necessitates twenty-four workhours, seven days of elapsed time, a revised draft, and copies of all the comments. Altogether 360 photocopies and sixty phone calls are made. Fifty office transactions are involved.) In case participants at the new meeting cannot agree on the recommendations, the entire procedure begins again— which requires at least 20% additional work on top of what has been done so far.

6. The policy is released for final management approval, for legal signoff, for inclusion of its effects in a revised budget, for implementation of changes by the data processing department, for audit follow-up, for inclusion in all sorts of field management communications, for publication and distribution to all affected personnel, and for instructions on how to deal with customers. (Here we are dealing with 1,000 workhours, forty-five days elapsed time, 2,000 office transactions, 8,000 photocopies, 300 phone calls, and thirty meetings.)

7. Over 350 copies of the policy bulletin are finally mailed out to holders of the policy manual. About 200 sets are merely filed. Only a few of the recipients pay any attention to the contents of the bulletin. Everybody else relies on some staff unit to institute appropriate controls to make sure the policy is actually implemented. A new and permanent additional task is added for someone to administer. A new, nine-page, monthly computer report is generated to keep track of the changes and to reconcile new information with old data. In due course, a microcomputer is purchased as a cost reduction measure so that the monthly computer report can be eliminated and the administrative work connected with monitoring the policy can be cut back.

9. John L. Neuman, "Making Overhead Cuts That Last," *Harvard Business Review,* May–June 1975.

10. It is difficult to estimate what portion of office transactions is fully definable by means of procedures. However, I was involved in one detailed study which found that an office could account for only 12% of all transactions within a formal system. Only this small fraction of office events was fully defined by means of computer programs or procedural instructions that explained what needed to be done. Some 53% of all transactions were part of a formal system but required a great deal of discretion, training, and experience if the employee was to perform tolerably well. We also discovered that 35% of transactions—including some which were of the highest importance from a customer standpoint—were not systematized at all and required a great deal of initiative and personal skill for completion. The results of this study have been shown to experienced managers. They agreed that the categories of work were fairly representative of small offices. Central office staff operations are likely to show an even larger portion of totally unsystematized office tasks.

One of the best discussions about informality in the office environment can be found in comments by the anthropologist Lucy Suchman in "The Role of Common Sense in the Process of Interface Design," in *Highlights of the International Conference on Office Work and New Technology* (Cleveland: Working Women Education Fund, 1983), p. 97:

> Several years ago I did a fairly concentrated observational study of what goes on in offices, and I made the following not very surprising observation. People don't actually carry out procedures. That is, the work that people do is not the same as the execution of a step-wise sequence of instructions. That observation is not surprising because anyone who has spent any time at all in an office knows that what people actually do is not identical with the procedural specifications. In deference to the theory of how office work should operate, people usually report their experiences of this fact either in the form of apologies, or complaints to the effect that, while the procedures sound nice, to the extent that they fail to really take into account the complexity of the actual cases, they don't actually tell you what to do. So office work is about making non-procedural events accountable to administrative procedures.

11. An interesting insight into the degree of informality observed in the office environment can be found in Wilbert O. Galitz, "Human Factors in Office Automation" (Atlanta: Life Office Management Assn., 1980), p. 43. When employees of an insurance firm received customer inquiries, they first turned to the following sources of information:

Recall from memory: 19%
Ask a colleague: 15%
Searched own files: 13%
Access to departmental files: 6%

Less than 50% of the needed information was available in the company's standard reference material. It should be noted that the insurance industry is notorious for its insistence on formal procedures and policies, so that one presumes to find here the highest levels of predefined formality. The survey results showed that even in this case, informal and semiformal documentation contained only 50% of the data that was searched for. Formal documentation could deal completely only with 9% of the inquiries.

Anyone seriously considering a detailed measurement effort in the office
will have to contend with the enormous proliferation of types of office activities. For instance, one attempt to measure office work notes the following
categories of standard "office measurement processes." The numbers in par-
entheses indicate how many separate types of measurement are necessary
in order to properly account for the variety of work done in each category:

Calculating (4)
Copying (3)
Distributing (7)
Errands (7)
Personnel-related (9)
Record-keeping (11)
Research and analysis (8)
Review and follow-up (3)
Scheduling (7)
Appointments (4)
Travel arrangements (8)
Mail handling (17)
Transmit (4)
Filing (12)

Source: M. A. Lieberman et al., *Office Automation—A Manager's Guide for Improved Productivity*
(New York: John Wiley, 1982), Table 6–1.

The profile obtained as a result of such minute measurements is characteristic not only of the particular office work that was examined, but also of
the measurement methods, the attitudes of management, and the attitudes
of the office workers. I am sceptical about the validity of such analyses. A
typical office activity profile would provide a percentage breakdown of activities such as:

Activity	*Percent of total time*
Receive and send information	21
Meetings	1
Calculations	13
Editing	4
Type	17
File	8
Enter into keyboard	11
Read	17
Organize	4
Follow-up	4
	100%

I have observed the above distribution of time in an engineering organization after the introduction of office automation. The breakdown of total time reflects the ways in which people were asked to report about their time and how they chose to classify it. A similar engineering organization would have a great deal of difficulty applying these results to their own operations since they would not be able to replicate the way the data was gathered.

12. See, for example, Russell L. Ackoff, *A Concept of Corporate Planning* (New York: Wiley Interscience, 1970), and Stafford Beer, *The Heart of Enterprise* (New York: John Wiley, 1979).

Chapter 2: Findings from Experiments with Office Automation (pp. 29–40)

1. See Paul A. Strassmann, "Forecasting Considerations in Design of Management Information Systems," *Bulletin of the National Association of Accountants,* February 1965.

2. The pilot vs. control results for record management:

	Control Group	Pilot Group
Progress report	186 min	75 min
Trip report	156 min	60 min
Memorandum	144 min	60 min
Transparencies	8 hrs	2 hrs
Graphic charts	10 hrs	4 hrs
Forms design	80 hrs	16 hrs
Sales notebook	10 days	5 days
Annual report	5 days	3 days
Executive program summary	4 days	2 days
Teaching text, lesson plan	5 days	2 days
Instruction manual	40 days	23 days

3. Carver Mead and Lynn Conway, *Introduction to VLSI Systems* (Reading, Mass.: Addison–Wesley, 1980).

4. In the public agency case, the following summarizes the work time expended in preparing a budget proposal before and after the introduction of comprehensive office automation:

Process Step	Before	After	Percent Change
Organize process	1.1 hrs	2.6 hrs	−135%
Analyze and write	12.6 hrs	9.3 hrs	+36%
Draft	1.4 hrs	3.8 hrs	−168%
Edit	5.6 hrs	1.1 hrs	+81%
Meet	1.1 hrs	1.0 hrs	+10%
Complete	9.3 hrs	2.6 hrs	+72%
Type	.7 hrs	1.5 hrs	−99%
Distribute	.9 hrs	.1 hrs	+88%
Total	32.7 hrs	21.9 hrs	+33%

Chapter 3: How Information Technology Changes Work (pp. 41–63)

1. I use the term "VDU," for Visual Display Unit, instead of the more frequent "CRT" designation (for Cathode Ray Tube). CRTs are just one of many ways of electronically displaying visual information. With plasma screens and liquid crystal plates we will be seeing a new variety of devices for looking at electronically formed information.

2. According to Walter Kiechel's *Fortune* article (November 14, 1983) on "Why Executives Don't Compute," academic studies of what managers actually do support this perception. Executives much prefer the spoken word to the written. Kiechel quotes Harvard's Kotter, who summarized his exhaustive observation of executive behavior thus: "Most executives don't spend much time dealing with routine, highly verifiable facts, but rather with ambiguities. How do you check out the validity of ambiguous information? By listening to the voice of the person relating it to you, probing away, looking for what's really soft. Much of the information that executives deal with is a form of power. Executives know that if it's written down somewhere, they can't restrict access to it."

But even the coming of the electronic in-box probably won't have as much effect on executive behavior as will the spread of computers to people lower down in the organization. While it's still too early to say for sure what form this indirect effect will take, there are interesting speculations. Consider, for example, the scenario in which people lower in the organization take over much of the manager's work in integrating information—pulling it together, getting consensus on what it means. As a result, executives will have to contend with less information than before, and they will be forced to spend more of their time honing their interpersonal skills, motivating people, and, in short, acting like leaders.

3. National Research Council, Panel on Impact of Video Viewing on

Vision of Workers, *Video Displays, Work, and Vision* (Washington, D.C.: National Academy Press, 1983).

4. B. G. F. Cohen et al., "Psychosocial Factors Contributing to Job Stress of Clerical VDT Operators," in *Proceedings of the 1982 Office Automation Conference* (Arlington, Va.: American Federation of Information Processing Societies, 1982).

5. Karen Nussbaum, "Office Automation: Jekyll or Hyde?" in *Highlights of the International Conference on Office Work and New Technology,* ed. by Daniel Marschall and Judith Gregory (Cleveland: Working Women Education Fund, 1983), pp. 15–21.

6. Gutek and Bikson's work shows the results computer patterns observed among advanced systems users. I would call such a profile similar to what I have observed with typical, leading-edge customers. In due course, perhaps five to ten years from now, we may find similar patterns a common occurrence. The Gutek/Bikson survey shows that among executives a relatively high proportion—36%—currently use their office system personally. Only 18% do not expect to ever use the computer. The comparable ratios for managers are 71% and 3% respectively; for professionals they are 79% and 3% respectively; for technical people 81% and 1%, and for secretarial personnel a surprisingly low 64%, with 13% never expecting to use computers. This profile indicates that managerial, professional, and technical workers will be the future mainstay of the automated office.

The same survey also contains interesting data about the prior qualifications of users of advanced systems; 54% of them had no prior experience whatsoever. Only 22% had frequent prior experience. This sheds an interesting light on the often-heard assertion that somehow a new generation of people is needed before computers can penetrate the workplace. That does not seem to be the case for these advanced users.

This survey also points out the importance of typing skills. A surprising 49% of all advanced systems users had good–to–excellent typing skills. Only 1% had no prior typing skills at all. At least 17% were able to type quickly using just a few fingers. See B. A. Gutek and T. K. Bikson, "Advanced Office Systems: An Empirical Look at Utilization and Satisfaction" (Santa Monica: RAND Corp., 1983).

There are other surveys which show very favorable attitudes toward office automation. One of the most complete studies is a Minolta Corporation report revealing overwhelmingly positive reactions to the introduction of office automation by secretaries from the standpoint of work enrichment—but also negative opinions about office equipment from the standpoint of the physical environment such as illumination, furniture, stress and fatigue. See Minolta Corporation, *The Evolving Role of the Secretary in the Information Age* (Ramsey, N.J.: Minolta Business Equipment Division, 1983).

Another survey, based on interviews with 1,263 secretaries, found that a substantial proportion of respondents felt that the use of word-processing equipment could result in health problems. The worst of these problems were thought to be eyestrain and backstrain. Eight out of ten secretaries called for better lighting for those who spend time at automated machines and for added rest breaks. Many also commented on the fact that management seldom consulted office staff on the design of work space or the structuring of the work day to improve working conditions and minimize stress. See Verbatim Corporation, "Office Worker Views and Perceptions of New Technology in the Workplace" (Sunnyvale, Cal.: Verbatim Corp., 1983).

7. Gutek, "Advanced Office Systems."

8. Charles Rubin, "Some People Should Be Afraid of Computers," *Personal Computing,* August 1983.

Chapter 4: The High-Performance Individual (pp. 64–76)

1. M. H. Olson and H. C. Lucas, Jr., "The Impact of Office Automation on the Organization: Some Implications for Research and Practice," *Communications of the ACM* 25:11 (November 1982).

2. A good example of how to use computerized measurement in a non-threatening way is described in Brita Tornquist and Svea Hermansson, "Automation and the Quality of Work Life at the Swedish Telephone Company," *Highlights of the International Conference on Office Work and New Technology* (Cleveland: Working Women Education Fund, 1983), pp. 82–83:

We make measurements for the whole group of data equipment service and information service, and then we know hour by hour how many operators have to work in that hour. So the operators themselves make a schedule. No supervisors tell them. When they come to the job, they look at the schedule and say: "I will sit there, and I will sit there. . . ." And there you have a job rotation.

The result of an inquiry with 116 operators after the installation of data equipment was that 95.7% found it easier and better to work with data terminals than with paper and directories. The reasons were: less strain on arms and shoulders, no heavy books to lift, faster and more detailed information, better total environment, etc. The negative effects were visual strain, headache, etc.; reflections, wrong color on the screen background and the letters; dazzling effects, static electricity, etc. It was irritating too when the computer broke down and you had to wait for an answer from the computer memory. The short average operating time, 35 seconds, makes the work intensive and causes visual strains. To get rid of that, we have to have more breaks than before, now 15 minutes after every two hours, and have instituted gym breaks once a day; there are also information and productivity group meetings for solving working problems and making proposals for better working methods and environment. It's not the most difficult thing to improve all these negative effects.

Chapter 5: The Economics of Office Work (pp. 79–99)

1. This comment is from a talk by Dr. Sidney Schoeffler, at the 1983 Annual Meeting of the Strategic Planning Institute.

2. Our industrial-age culture has acquired intuitive presumptions about how value, prices, and economics relate to each other. I call these ideas "product-based" concepts. They apply to tangible, specific, readily identifiable objects and commodities. Information has economic characteristics which totally differ from industrial-age concepts of value.

For instance, tangible products are costly to replicate. Each additional item costs roughly the same amount. Information is extremely cheap to replicate by means of printing, broadcasting, and other forms of telecommunication. Assets generally depreciate with usage. Unused information has hardly any value, whereas frequently-used information is generally among the most valuable. Multiple ownership of information is possible, that is, the same software program or equation may be simultaneously owned by many persons: the same product usually may not. Legal ownership of information is also much more difficult to prove and to protect than ownership of tangible assets.

3. The emphasis on reporting only the identifiable costs of technology can be seen in the way organizations evaluate their computer spending. The most frequently used ratio for evaluating computer expenditures is data-processing dollars spent, divided by the firm's revenues. Incidentally, this ratio is becoming less meaningful as the users' direct involvement in performing traditional data-processing tasks grows. Aside from that, the ratio is almost useless because different organizations have completely different ways to deploy their information labor. The latest survey results listing the "Data Processing as a Percentage of Revenue" numbers show a great range in ratios among different industries. The results do not reveal that within each industrial category the variations are equally large. For instance, firms in the same industry differ significantly in the quantity of purchases for each dollar of revenue. Percentages-of-revenue methods will therefore not answer the question whether too much or too little technology is used, because few of the ratios will be genuinely comparable:

Advertising, printing, publishing	1.23%
Banking	2.49
Engineering, construction	0.09
Government	0.50
Health care	1.08
Retail sales	0.47
Data processing services	52.28
Electrical manufacturing	1.01
Chemicals, petroleum	0.62
Metal producing and fabricating	1.45

Source: Infosystems Editors, "25th Annual Survey of DP Budgets," *Infosystems*, June 1983.

4. Some of the most useful information about the structure of information costs in the U.S. economy has been prepared by the firm of Booz Allen &

Hamilton. Estimates of the technology/labor cost ratios can be found in their studies (in 1981 dollars):

Technology costs	$103 billion
Information labor costs, including allocations	$967 billion
Technology/Information labor costs:	
Managers ($399 billion)	4%
Administrators, professionals ($403 billion)	3%
Clerical ($268 billion)	37%

Source: Booz Allen & Hamilton, "Strategic Implications for Office Automation Products and Markets," (New York: Booz Allen & Hamilton, 1980).

5. Caroline E. Mayer, "A.T.&T. Contract Hailed as Landmark," *Washington Post,* August 24, 1983.

6. T. J. Peters and R. H. Waterman, *In Search of Excellence* (New York: Harper and Row, 1982), p. 63.

Chapter 6: The Efficiency Approach to Productivity (pp. 100–115)

1. American Productivity Center, Computer Conference on Information Workers, *A Final Report for the White House Conference on Productivity* (Houston: American Productivity Center, 1983), pp. 14–15.

2. White House Conference on Productivity, *Report of the Preparatory Conference on Private Sector Initiatives—Information Worker Productivity* (Washington, D.C.: GPO, 1983), pp. 11–16.

3. Some delightful advice on the subject of measurement:

Step 1: Measure whatever can be easily measured. (That is OK as far as it goes.)
Step 2: Disregard that which cannot be measured, or, give it an arbitrary quantitative value. (This is misleading, but impressive.)
Step 3: Presume what cannot be measured really is not very important. (This is blindness.)
Step 4: Conclude that what cannot be easily measured really does not exist. (This is suicide.)

Source: Daniel Yankelovich, quoted in Adam Smith, *Supermoney* (New York: Random House, 1972), p. 271.

Misapplications of the techniques described in this chapter are easily classified in terms of the above categories.

4. P. Chinloy, *Sources of Productivity Growth at the Firm Level: The Bell System 1947–1978* (Washington, D.C.: AFL–CIO, 1981).

An interesting commentary on the inadequacy of efficiency measurement comes from the Nobel Prize winner in economics, Professor Leontief:

> This . . . relationship is usually measured by the "productivity" of labor. This is the total output divided by the number of workers or, even better, by the number of manhours required for its production. Thus 30 years ago it took several thousand switchboard operators to handle a million long-distance telephone calls; 10 years later it took several hundred operators, and now, with automatic switchboards linked automatically to other automatic switchboards, only a few dozen are needed. Plainly the productivity of labor—that is, the number of calls completed per operator—has been increasing by leaps and bounds. Simple arithmetic shows that it will reach its highest level when only one operator remains and will become incalculable on the day that operator is discharged.

Source: Wassily W. Leontief, "The Distribution of Work and Income," *Scientific American,* September 1982.

5. The most frequent examples of efficiency–productivity measurements in the published literature are obtained from a close analysis of secretarial work, especially of typing efficiency realized after installing word-processing equipment. It may be worth considering that this activity accounts for less than 1.2% of "white collar" labor costs in the United States. For a discussion of the relative importance of various components of office labor expense see Ronald P. Uhlig, David J. Farber, and James H. Bair, *The Office of the Future* (Amsterdam: Elsevier–North Holland Publ. Co., 1981), pp. 352–355.

6. The following samples of productivity computations—showing productivity improvement in an invoicing department, on a unit basis—are drawn from my own work:

	1979	1980	Change
Output: Invoices	854,000	942,564	+10.4%
Input: Manhours	27,450	28,340	+3.2%
Productivity:	31.11	33.26	+6.9%

7. Productivity computations showing improvement in an invoicing department, on a dollar basis:

	1979	1980	Change
Output: Invoices	854,000	942,564	+10.4%
Input: Salaries	$251,167	$325,910	+29.7%
Technology	$555,100	$570,200	+2.7%
Productivity:	1.05920	1.05184	−0.7%

8. Productivity computations showing improvement in an invoicing department, on a total cost and benefit basis:

	1979	1980	Change
Output (*in thousands of dollars*):			
Receivables, cost	2,983	1,350	−55%
Writeoffs, cost	156	49	−69%
Sales time	4,250	682	−84%
Lost business	2,000	400	−80%
Input (*in thousands of dollars*):			
Salaries	251	326	+30%
Training	—	48	N/A
Technology	555	570	+3%
Productivity:	11.645	2.627	+77%

9. Frantz Edelman, "Managers, Computers and Productivity," *MIS Quarterly* 5:3 (September 1981).

10. Paul A. Strassmann, "Managing the Costs of Information," *Harvard Business Review,* September–October 1976, pp. 134–36.

11. David L. Conway, "Common Staffing System," in Robert N. Lehrer, ed., *White Collar Productivity* (New York: McGraw–Hill, 1983).

12. James D. Schlumpf and Kenneth A. Charon, "IBM's Common Staffing System: How to Measure Productivity of the Indirect Workforce," *Management Review* 70:8 (1981).

13. The interest in Operations/Management staff ratios can be traced back to the Bible, 2 Chron. 2:2. There it is written "Solomon resolved to build a house. . . . He engaged seventy thousand hauliers and eighty thousand quarrymen, and three thousand six hundred men to superintend them." All things considered, this was not a bad ratio. The span of control was 1:42. Although a United States corporation is likely to average a supervisory span of control of less than 1:5, Solomon's men were not necessarily ten times better managers. The only way to test this proposition would be to reconstruct the Temple under contemporary construction management, observing how many would be needed to manage the project and how many to build it.

14. Calvin H. P. Pava, *Managing New Office Technology* (New York: The Free Press, 1983), p. 52.

15. Time–motion standards for office motions are represented by this example: *Job Step:* To envelope; *Standard Move Code:* R14D; *Time Allowed:* 0.156 seconds. Similar allowances are made for standard "motions" such as: move opener to table; let go; move fingers to envelope; move envelope to trash. See Bruce Payne, "Productivity Gains with New Office Technology," *The Office,* September 1983.

16. Some of the most frequently applied industrial-engineering methods adapted to office work are: *Clerical Standard Data* by Bruce Payne Associates; *Master Clerical Data,* developed by the Serge A. Birn Company; *Universal Office Controls,* developed by the H. B. Maynard Company; *Modular Arrangement of Predetermined Time Standards,* developed in the late 1960s by Chris

Heyde at Unilever in Australia and available through Price Waterhouse and Peat Marwick & Mitchell; *Motion Time Values,* developed in the '60s by Booz Allen & Hamilton; *Methods–Time Measurement—Clerical,* developed by a consortium of Motion Time Management Association members and available from the MTM Association for Standards and Research; *Advanced Office Controls,* by Robert E. Nolan Company of Simsbury, Conn.; and the *Mulligan System,* using motion-picture analysis, developed by the Paul B. Mulligan Company.

A fuller discussion of these methods is to be found in Robert E. Nolan, "Work Measurement," in Robert N. Lehrer, ed., *White Collar Productivity* (New York: McGraw–Hill, 1983).

17. An example of how to compute productivity on the departmental level has been provided by Bruce Payne in his article on "Productivity Gains" cited in note 15 above:

Activity covered by standards: 75%
Average staff performance: 85%
Employee utilization: 69%

A synthetic number of "standard hours" allowed is then computed, based on the above factors. In the example given, the figure turned out to be 409.1 hours. The problem with this number is that it disguises assumptions about what people do for the 25% of their time not covered by standards, and why 85% "average staff performance" should be an acceptable benchmark to define what work needs to be done. Even taking account of these hidden factors, the final computation conveys a high degree of confidence regarding what should be the staffing levels:

Effective number of people, actual: 14.5
Effective number of people, required: 12.4

Thus, overstaffing by 2.1 people is indicated in this case.

18. Another case, also cited by Bruce Payne and derived from a consulting practice, uses a separately derived standard to measure the "efficiency" of a professional worker as follows:

Chargeable hours	36.5 hours
Non-chargeable hours	0.5 hours
Total actual time	37.0 hours
Standard allowed time	15.7 hours
Performance	43% hours

Again, the usefulness of the entire computation hinges on techniques for determining "standard allowed time" for a professional worker. Such calculations assume that a reliable quantitative measure of the number of expected tasks was established to begin with.

19. During the White House Conference on Productivity, I received an anonymous inquiry:

> I am trying to come up with a definition of productivity for a professional services firm—law, accounting, or in my own case, consulting. We currently measure productivity as a ratio between billings and salary. This measure has the advantage of factoring our inflation. There are a number of disadvantages: 1. It ignores the quality of the service provided. 2. The more efficiently (faster) one works, the lower the billings generated for any given volume of tasks. Automation also can have a negative impact on the measure while reducing the cost to the client. What measures of productivity apply in environments where people bill based on the amount of time spent on a client's work?

I noted that productivity was expressed as a percentage of allowable time. My response was to the following effect: When the client's bill from the consultant is computed entirely according to the time spent on the client's work, then measurable "productivity" does not enter the picture at all. The only variable at the consultant's level would be manpower utilization, which is a percentage of billable time. This approach can easily become counter-productive, since it may mean excess time spent on the client's account. Cost-plus billing does not lend itself to computation of productivity at the consultant's level, since the consultant is, in effect, "retained," not unlike the organization's own management. The consultant's services add to the client's own overhead costs and can be evaluated only in the client's own productivity computations. For the consultant's productivity to be definable, there must be present in the transaction some sort of a bargain or risk. This might involve increased revenue from increasing the scope of his market, economies of scale, and higher profit margins due to the consultant's ability to deliver services at ever-lower costs. In other words, to measure the productivity of its consultants a consulting firm would have to change its billing practice to one involving fixed fees. Customization of standard services would be essential so that the customer could make intelligent choices among alternatives.

If the consultant can reduce prices and improve the delivery system for serving the client (while cutting support costs due to clever uses of information technology), productivity measurement becomes possible.

20. Carl G. Thor provides a sample technique to compute the composite measure of productivity for professionals in his chapter, "Productivity Measurement in White Collar Groups," Robert N. Lehrer, ed., *White Collar Productivity* (New York: McGraw–Hill, 1983), pp. 29–42.

21. D. L. Rowe, in "How Westinghouse Measures Productivity," *Management Review,* November 1981, describes an extreme case of indiscriminate weighting of unrelated variables, based on an instance taken from the standard procedure manual of a manufacturing company. The composite productivity index is computed by adding adjusted shop orders, division return on investment, machine downtime, counts of customer complaints, and many other indicators. Aside from the fact that customer complaints receive only scant attention in such reckonings, I doubt that any measurement which is a composite of so many totally unrelated indicators could be of much value. One can imagine the kind of negotiations that must have taken place in order to assign numerical weights to totally unrelated factors. It is as if one put a fancy smorgasbord dinner through a blender. The result might serve some purpose, but would certainly not be an optimal use of the ingredients.

22. The total-productivity index technique requires a procedure for scaling all input variables according to a common, deflated base. To avoid determining some absolute level of productivity, a prior year or an average of base years is customarily computed. Carl Thor gives us a good example of this method in Carl G. Thor, "Productivity Measurement," Chapter 15B, in the *Corporate Controller's Manual* (New York: Warren, Gorham & Lamont, 1982).

23. The following quotation from an editorial on productivity may serve as an indication of the type of analysis that is commonplace:

> Over the years, IBM's staff has grown steadily, although not as fast as its sales because, as the graph on this page shows [i.e., a rise of sales per employee from $50,000 in 1975 to $82,000 in 1981], every employee becomes more productive from year to year. . . . Of the top 10 U.S.-based electronics companies that derive all their revenue from the manufacture of electronic products, none is as productive as IBM.

Source: Alberto Socolovsky, "Robots Must Join the Team, Not Replace It," *Electronic Business,* February 1983.

My reply, in a subsequent "Letters to the Editor" column of *Electronic Business,* emphasized that sales per employee may not necessarily be a particularly trustworthy indicator of productivity:

> The claims about IBM's productivity, as measured in terms of rising sales per employee, could stand some further examination. The sales per employee increase from 1975 to 1981 are, indeed, compounded at 8.5% per annum. However, during the same period worldwide inflationary wage increases exceeded 8.5% by a wide margin. Furthermore, IBM during the same period followed a number of policies which makes its superior productivity performance even less impressive. IBM increased its net equity per employee from $39,546 to $51,166. Consequently, a portion of their improvement in the revenue per employee ratio should be attributed not to labor productivity but to the increased role of assets in generating revenues. This subtracts about .5% from the presumed labor productivity achievement. IBM has also decreased its level of vertical integration by materially increasing the amount of outside purchases of components, subassemblies, and peripherals. I estimate that this further subtracts another .5% from presumed labor productivity. The net effect of the inflationary wage increases, of the increased use of equity capital, and of the increased costs of purchases is that IBM's labor productivity, expressed in dollar terms, is negative. It should not be used as an example of excellence in productivity achievement.

Chapter 7: The Effectiveness Approach to Productivity (pp. 116–135)

1. In the critique of current methods for evaluating the productivity of information work, I agree with professor Michael Hammer, who also makes a very careful distinction between efficiency and effectiveness. See Michael Hammer, "Improving Business Performance: The Real Objective of Office Automation," *Digest of 1982 Office Automation Conference* (Arlington, Va.: American Federation of Information Processing Societies, 1982).

2. The idea that business relationships can be defined by a simple inequality comes from Renn Zaphiropoulos, president of Versatec.

3. The article "Casting Executives as Consultants" (*Business Week,* August 30, 1982) gave an early indication of how corporate staff specialists might be employed in the future:

> London-based Rank Xerox Ltd. has launched a program to encourage middle managers in such areas as purchasing, personnel, pensions, and planning to quit and sign on as outside consultants. The program is limited to specialists in support functions whose presence at headquarters is unnecessary. Instead, participants are linked to Rank Xerox via microcomputers, marking one of the most ambitious attempts to utilize home computers in such a fashion. So far, eleven have accepted the two-year renewable contract that Rank Xerox is offering. An additional ten to fifteen employees will join the program by year-end. And the company expects that as many as 150—or 25% of the corporate management staff—could become consulting "networkers" by the end of 1983. That would enable Rank Xerox to reduce headquarters costs by 8% to 10%.

Chapter 8: Value-Added Productivity Measurement (pp. 136–150)

1. Peter Drucker, as quoted by B. J. van Loggerrenberg in *Proceedings of Business Week Conference on Productivity—October 1–2, 1981* (New York: *Business Week,* 1981).

2. I am strongly inclined to value the cost of equity capital much higher than is usual for investment analysis in most corporations. In this regard I have been influenced by the convincing argument that calculation of the real cost of business investments depends not only on the cost of funds, but must also reflect increases in the cost of assets due to inflation, benefits derived from tax credits, depreciation allowances, technological obsolescence, and so forth. How assets are deployed in terms of inventories, receivables, fixed assets, and land, and what portion of liabilities are either debt or equity may have a decisive effect on how the cost of capital is evaluated. See George N. Hatsopoulos, *The High Cost of Capital* (Washington, D.C.: American Business Conference, 1983).

3. See Christos N. Athanasopoulos, "Corporate Productivity Atlas: Gross Corporate Product Measures 1982–1978" [sic] (Lincoln, Mass.: Delphi Research Center, 1983); William A. Ruch and William B. Werther, "Productivity Strategies at TRW," *National Productivity Review* (Spring 1983); Ithiel de Sola Pool, "Tracking the Flow of Information," *Science* 221 (August 12, 1983).

4. The Westinghouse Corporation is one of the most publicized companies to compute value added per employee as a key productivity indicator. Materials costs are subtracted from revenue to compute value added. Insofar as energy purchases and purchased services are significant, the productivity ratio may be distorted. Most importantly, the division of value added by the number of employees fails to take into account adjustments for labor mix, wage inflation, and capital costs. Despite these deficiencies, Westinghouse has found its productivity ratio calculation superior to other, previously used methods. See Rowe, "Westinghouse Measures Productivity."

Value-added productivity is defined as revenue minus purchases divided by dollar payroll costs in the "Rucker Plan of Group Incentives" scheme, which I consider to be one of the best approaches to sharing productivity gains in the workplace. This same approach has been successfully applied by the leaders in productivity management: TRW and the Upjohn Company. For the "Rucker Plan," see corresponding entry in *The Encyclopedia of Management* (New York: Van Nostrand Reinhold, 1982). On TRW: Ruch, "Productivity Strategies"; on Upjohn: H. L. Dahl and K. S. Morgan, "Return on Investment in Human Resources," in Robert N. Lehrer, ed., *White Collar Productivity* (New York: McGraw–Hill, 1983), p. 279.

5. Here is an example of top-down computation of labor productivity I prepared in reviewing a customer's office automation program:

Output (in thousands of dollars):	
Revenue	$9,411
Less purchases	6,961
Value added	2,450
Less cost of capital	472
Labor value added	1,978
Input (in thousands of dollars):	
Labor costs	1,499
Labor productivity:	1.32

In this case labor productivity was not extraordinary, as claimed by the customer's staff. What kept labor productivity down were substantial non-wage labor costs, which included social insurance, holidays, pension allowances, and many other benefits.

Failure to include the non-wage costs makes labor productivity comparisons between different branches of a multinational firm meaningless. According to the London *Economist* (December 18, 1982, p. 78), the variation in these costs ranges from 15.0% of total wages in Japan to 44.8% of total wages in France.

6. The frequently quoted statistics about the scarcity of invested capital per information worker are greatly influenced by the way enormous capital investments for the telephone system have always been reflected as a business expense rather than as part of the user's capital. Until recently, even business telephone instruments and on-site telephone switching equipment were always shown as an equipment rental cost. To a lesser extent, capital assets for information technology were reflected on the balance sheets of IBM and Xerox, rather than on those of their customers. I estimate that there is at least $5,000 in capital investment, per information worker, of telephone plant and other technology which remain as a supplier's asset. As companies begin exercising a much greater range of buy- vs. lease- vs. rent options, the distinction among owned, leased, and rented equipment, or bundled services must be accounted for in separate cost categories. Simple ratios of information-technology budgets to revenue, which show only the expenses and not the capital or services involved, can distort the picture of what is happening. I know of a case where the chief computer executive was very proud of his steadily declining computer expense-to-company revenue ratio, and the steadily declining computer employee-to-total company employee ratio. Upon closer examination it became apparent that the mix of expenses was really not comparable and that the ostensible declines were a result of the accounting technique used in reporting. Large amounts of computer equipment were purchased and retained on the headquarters balance sheet, thus never showing up as a part of the budgeting process.

7. Labor productivity can also be calculated from elements of the conventional financial statement. Here is an example of a bottom-up computation for the customer case mentioned in note 5 above:

Output (*in thousands of dollars*):	
Wages and salaries, including benefits	1,499
Depreciation	153
Interest expense	73
Income taxes	330
Profits, after tax	383
Value added	2,428
Less cost of capital	472
Labor value added	1,966
Input (*in thousands of dollars*):	
Labor costs	1,499
Labor productivity:	1.31

The technique for computing year-to-year labor productivity changes is as follows:

	1980	1979	1978
Output (in thousands of dollars):			
Labor value added	1,966	1,989	1,662
Input (in thousands of dollars):			
Labor costs	1,499	1,513	1,251
Labor productivity:	1.31	1.3146	1.3285
Productivity change:		−0.24%	−1.05%

The revelation that labor productivity was actually declining while heavy automation investments were made came as a surprise and formed the basis for a critical examination of the direction of office-automation projects.

8. There is considerable merit to the idea of treating taxes as purchases rather than as a part of management's value added. The effective rate of corporate taxation varies so enormously, depending on tax treatment and on allowances, that taxes can be viewed as an expense under management's control. This point is supported by the fact that the tax rates effective in 1982 on new depreciable assets for selected United States industries range from −11.3% for motor vehicles to +37.1% for services and trade. See J. W. Kendrick, "Interindustry Differences in Productivity Growth" (Washington, D.C.: American Enterprise Institute, 1983), Table 13.

It is interesting to note that the rapidly growing sectors, such as services and trade, where most of the jobs are being created, are taxed heavily, whereas investments in declining industries are taxed at a very low rate or are, in effect, subsidized. Such a policy goes counter to Peter Drucker's advice on how to succeed in business: "Feed your successes and starve your failures."

9. In the case previously noted, the method of calculating management productivity is illustrated by the following procedure:

	1980	1979	1978
Output (in thousands of dollars):			
Labor value added	1,966	1,989	1,662
Less operations	719	756	650
Management value added	1,247	1,233	1,012
Input (in thousands of dollars):			
Management costs	780	757	601
Management productivity	1.598	1.628	1.684
Productivity change:		−1.8%	−3.3%

This productivity computation revealed the depressive effect of indirect costs in the overall decline of labor productivity.

10. In the case under consideration ·the following illustrates a general approach to computing the relationship between information technology and management's value added:

	1980	1979	1978
Output (in thousands of dollars):			
Management value added	1,247	1,233	1,012
Input (in thousands of dollars):			
Technology costs	9.4	9.8	8.5
Relative productivity of			
information technology:	132.66	125.82	119.06
Productivity change:		+5.4%	+5.7%

As this analysis shows, the growth in information technology costs has not contributed to the relative decrease in overall productivity in this instance.

11. Viewing information technology as a strategic investment rather than as an operating expense is steadily gaining favor. Parsons cogently points out the broad spectrum of impact that information technology may have on the level of output in an industry, on the way a firm may be able to compete, and on how strategic leadership can be gained. Reducing product costs as well as increasing product differentiation can increasingly be achieved by means of imaginative uses of information technology. Gregory L. Parsons, "Information Technology: A New Competitive Weapon," *Sloan Management Review* 25:1 (1983).

12. The most frequently used measure of the intensity of computerization is computer expense as a percent of sales. Unfortunately, this ratio makes it impossible to compare relative levels of cost except where the organizations are almost identical in every respect. For instance, this ratio can decline without any information systems contribution at all if the corporation decreases its vertical integration during an inflationary period.

13. Subtracting the costs of wages and salaries from total revenues is an approximation of the relative size of purchases and capital costs. Labor costs, as a percentual share of total business revenues, range from 25.2% in the petroleum industry to 96.6% in the construction industry. Such a ratio is nevertheless useful in making productivity estimates based on value added. See John W. Kendrick and D. Creamer, "Measuring Company Productivity—A Handbook with Case Studies," *Studies in Business Economics* 89 (New York: National Industrial Conference Board, 1965).

The industries with the smallest labor share of total revenues, such as petroleum, tobacco, utilities, and communications have traditionally taken the lead in productivity gains. This augurs well for the economic future which is already upon us.

CHAPTER 9: Investment Profitability (pp. 151–164)

1. Capital expenditures for basic industrial equipment have been reduced from 25% of all capital spending in the 1960s to present levels of less than

13% of all capital spending. Meanwhile, spending for high-tech equipment rose from 12% in the 1960s to present levels of more than 30% of all capital spending.

Annual investment per worker in basic industry has increased from $689 in 1960 to $851 in 1982. The corresponding investment levels for high-tech industry, expressed in 1972 dollars, are up from only $263 per worker in 1960 to $932 in 1982. This shift in investment patterns is reflected in the total amounts of capital stock per worker, defined in terms of constant 1972 dollars. In 1960 basic industrial capital stock was $5,426, whereas high-tech capital stock per worker was only $2,060. In 1982 the capital levels were approaching parity. Workers in basic industries operated with $8,325 of capital each, while workers in high-tech enterprises were rapidly catching up: they already had $5,336 of capital stock at their disposal. See Stephen S. Roach, "Productivity, Investment, and the Information Economy," *Economic Perspectives* (New York: Morgan Stanley & Co., 1984), p. 10.

2. 1980 U.S. capital stock for basic industry, expressed in constant 1972 dollars ($243 billion), equalled capital invested in high-tech industries ($244 billion). However, the growth rates differed remarkably. Capital stock in basic industry grew at only 1.0% per annum during the decade of the 1970s, while high-technology industries compounded growth at 9.4% per annum. Within high-tech industries the largest gains were shown by the computer industry (with capital stock of $50 billion), growing at the astounding rate of 16.7% per annum during the decade. Faith in the profitability of investments in the computer industry can be contrasted with the sceptical attitude toward other key industries, such as energy. During the last decade even the energy crisis could stimulate only a 3.0% compound growth rate in capital stock. See Stephen S. Roach, "The Industrialization of the Information Economy," *Special Economic Study* (New York: Morgan Stanley & Co., 1984), pp. 7–8.

3. Employment in the computer and business equipment industry accounts only for about 470,000 jobs. In the period between 1960 and 1982, employment in the industry increased by 318,000. This amounts to an annual growth of 5.3%, which compares favorably with the 2.3% growth rate for all nonfarm jobs, but is certainly not spectacular as compared with the growth rate in output of the industry. Computer and Business Equipment Manufacturer's Association, *The Computer and Business Equipment Industry Marketing Data Book* (Washington, D.C.: CBEMA, 1983), Table 3–4.

The computer industry is frequently criticized for not providing enough new jobs to make up for employment losses in declining industries. Such criticism does not give adequate consideration to the following:

1. The largest consumer of labor in the computer business is now in distribution, not in manufacturing. Dealers, distributors, retails stores, computer schools, etc. have changed the structure of the computer business.

2. Another large employer of labor is among users, rather than among suppliers. In terms of application development and application support large commitments of additional manpower have been made by users in order to install low-cost information technology. For instance, the 1982 total employment in occupational categories such as systems analysts, programmers, computer operators, and computer service technicians was 1.5 million, showing a recent compound growth of 10.3%. (See CBEMA, *Marketing Data Book,* Table 3–5.)

3. Increasing proportions of total value added for computer equipment is provided by suppliers of components not classified as "computer makers," such as plastic manufacturers (for the enclosures), media manufacturers (of floppy disks, e.g.) and software providers. Employment gains by computer manufacturers is an inadequate indication of the full employment impact of the computer industry.

4. The subject of the adequacy of capital investments in the office was highlighted in a recent *Fortune* article:

> Vendors have pounded a theme: offices are unproductive because business has backed up each office worker with only about $2,500 in capital investment vs. around ten times that amount for each factory worker. Therefore, claim the vendors, business should make massive new investments in automation. That argument has major flaws, beginning with the numbers. Michael D. Zisman, president of Integrated Technologies, an office-systems consulting firm, is often cited as the source of the investment figure for office workers, which he used in a 1978 article for the *Sloan Management Review,* published by MIT's business school. Zisman now says, "I relied on that number because it was the received wisdom, but I've since found out it's plain folklore. Investment looks low because companies expense their office-related costs instead of capitalizing them. If you capitalize actual expense streams for the office, you'll find companies have already invested $15,000 to $20,000 per office worker, which is pretty damned high. . . .

Source: Bro Uttal, "What's Detaining the Office of the Future," *Fortune,* May 3, 1982.

To this observation I would add that the discussion concerning capital investment per office worker almost never considers the extremely high cost of the real estate necessary to accommodate information workers on the job. I estimate this to range from $5,000 to $15,000 per person.

5. CBEMA, *Marketing Data Book,* p. 14.

6. The Quantum Sciences 1982 Annual Report estimates U.S. end-user expenditures for computers, in current billions of dollars at $163.3 for 1982 and $268.7 for 1985.

7. An estimate of worldwide office information technology gives a good overview of the current investment rate, reckoned in billions of 1983 dollars per year:

	1985	1990
Workstations	$ 26	$ 51
Data processing	78	95
Communications	13	17
Software	23	68
Other	42	63
Total	$182	$294

It is also interesting to see how this worldwide estimate is distributed by geography:

	1985	1990
USA and Canada	49%	45%
Western Europe	31%	34%
Japan	12%	14%
Other	8%	7%

Source: Charles Jonscher, "Information Technology: Investment Needs and Opportunities," *Proceedings of an International Investment Symposium Sponsored by Fidelity International and Nikko Securities* (Cambridge, Eng.: Jesus College, 1983).

The dominance of the North American, Western European, and Japanese markets in the development of information technology is overwhelming. Many of the conclusions of this book will have to be reexamined before they can be applied to conditions outside of these three markets.

8. William L. Cron and Marion G. Sobol, "The Relationship Between Computerization and Performance: A Strategy for Maximizing the Economic Benefits of Computerization," *Information and Management* 6 (1983).

9. Ibid., p. 9.

10. Bradley T. Gale, "Can More Capital Buy Higher Productivity?" *Harvard Business Review,* July–August 1980, p. 78.

11. The lack of correlation between management productivity and information technology should not be surprising if one accepts the premise that only excellent companies will benefit from computers and that poorly performing companies may actually suffer if they spend too much money on information technology. The Strategic Planning Institute's recent study of 171 businesses evaluated what fraction of businesses were operating at what fraction of their full potential, as defined by their discounted market value:

Percent of Full Potential	Percent of Businesses
Under 25%	47%
25–50%	29%
50–75%	13%
75–100%	5%
Over 100%	6%

If many businesses operate at less than 50% of full potential one cannot expect that information-technology investments would result in much higher value added by management. Other effects would have a much greater influence than computers.

All of the findings reported as "pilot program results" have been developed and compiled by the staff of the Strategic Planning Institute under the direction of M. C. A. van Nievelt, Program Director of the Management Productivity and Information Technology Program, whose contribution is gratefully acknowledged.

12. Productivity growth in private businesses:

	1948–1973	1973–1981
Labor output per hour	+2.9%	+1.5%
Capital output	+0.6%	−2.6%
Weighted total productivity	+2.2%	+0.4%

Source: U.S. Bureau of Labor Statistics, Publication 83–153, 1983.

13. The current crisis in manufacturing industries is largely due to the fact that productive capacity in steel, fertilizers, petrochemicals, rayon, etc., has been running well ahead of the market's ability to absorb output. This shows up in the increased capital/output ratio—which is a measure of how much plant and equipment is available for producing a unit of output. This ratio has been steadily rising over the last twenty years, despite the warning signs that profitability was declining. Such a situation is characteristic of the general tendency to overinvest in new assets based on past productivity trends rather than on anticipated future productivity gains.

14. Productivity of labor and capital in the finance and insurance industry (1975 = 100%):

	1970	1975	1980
Labor productivity	96.6%	99.9%	96.4%
Capital productivity	150.8%	111.8%	85.6%
Weighted total	100.1%	100.0%	95.2%
Capital/labor ratio	64.0%	89.3%	112.5%

Source: E. S. Grossman and G. E. Sadler, *Comparative Productivity Dynamics* (Houston, Tex.: American Productivity Center, 1982).

15. U.S. Department of Labor, Bureau of Labor Statistics, *A BLS Reader on Productivity,* Bulletin 2171 (Washington, D.C.: GPO, 1983), pp. 58–66.

16. Productivity of banking (1977 output levels = 100%):

	Output	Output/hr	Employment
1967	52.2%	83.8%	63.0%
1970	64.5%	85.5%	76.6%
1975	84.6%	90.0%	94.2%
1980	106.1%	92.7%	115.7%

Source: BLS Reader on Productivity, p. 60.

17. Reluctant management can choose from a long catalogue of standard excuses why not to invest in information technology. This list is a summary and adaptation of an incisive article by Louis Nauges:

1. Do not know how to justify investment.
2. Office work cannot be measured. How can it then be improved?
3. It's not for me. It is for the other, inefficient people.
4. Cannot decide who should be responsible. Management does not know enough to make decisions.
5. Cannot do anything in the absence of a good overall plan.
6. We are still tied up with old data-processing backlogs.
7. Our people are not adequately educated. Have to wait for a new generation.
8. Do not want managers to do any typing or technical work.
9. Electronic workstations will be misused for playing games.
10. Do not know what to do with the time saved. We cannot lay off any people.
11. Cannot reduce the number of employees. They are needed for unexpected demands.
12. Machines will be cheaper next year. Have to wait for fully integrated systems.

Source: Louis M. Nauges, "Office Automation Alibis," *Datamation,* November 1983.

18. Imposition of cumbersome, phased-program management methods on information technology projects—intended as an added safeguard—may actually harm rather than improve investment analysis. Elaborate techniques for controlling investments, originally borrowed from the defense industry, may provide satisfactory levels of documentation, but will by no means assure success. Only one study is known in which a careful evaluation has been made of comparable projects conducted with and without the benefit of formal feasibility studies. In each case the economic justification of selecting a standard accounting package was examined. The users who ended up most satisfied with the selected software went through the least rigorous feasibility studies. Such a finding is counter to commonly held beliefs that formal project studies are necessary to assure the success of a computer investment. See R. H. Edmundson and D. R. Jeffery, "A Preliminary Investigation into the Impact of Requirements Analysis upon User Satisfaction with Packaged Accounting Software," unpublished research report, University of New South Wales, Kensington, Australia, 1983.

CHAPTER 10: The Paperless Office (pp.165–177)

1. F. W. Lancaster, *Toward Paperless Information Systems* (New York: Academic Press, 1978).

2. See John H. Dessauer, *My Years with Xerox—The Billions Nobody Wanted* (New York: Doubleday, 1981).

3. National Research Council, Panel on Impact of Video Viewing on Vision Workers, *Video Displays, Work, and Vision* (Washington, D.C.: National Academy Press, 1983), pp. 18–26.

4. As a participant in this United States government-sponsored conference in 1982 I extracted these comments from various messages.

CHAPTER 11: Technology, Structure, and Strategy (pp. 181–202)

1. In small establishments (with fifty employees or less) the number of "information workers" is over 30% of the total workforce, while the number of "managers" is more than 11.5%. These percentages decrease as the size of the establishment increases. For establishments with over 1,000 employees in size, the respective percentages are 23% and 5.9%. A great deal of information about the demographics of information workers can be found in the wealth of tabular data contained in Hearst Business Communications, *The Office/Business Market—A Pragmatic Analysis by Industry Segment and Job Function* (Garden City, N.Y.: Hearst, 1981).

2. When comparing the *Fortune* 500 with a large group of midsize companies, the following indicators show that the smaller enterprises delivered superior all-around performance for the period from 1975–80:

	Fortune 500	Midsize Companies
Sales growth	14%	21%
Income growth	18%	27%
Return on equity	14%	18%
Asset growth	14%	20%
Employment growth	2.8%	8.6%
Growth in federal taxes	13.4%	27.5%
Growth in capital expense	17.7%	34.1%

Source: American Business Conference, "The Winning Performance of Mid-sized Growth Companies" (New York: McKinsey & Co., 1983).

The disparity in growth between larger and smaller organizations also seems to apply outside of the United States. According to the Indivers Research Organization, quoted in the *Economist,* the average annual employment change for manufacturing industries from 1967 to 1976 has favored smaller establishments. For companies with less than 10 workers, employment grew by 2% in the United States and 2.5% in Japan and in Britain. For companies with 10 to 100 workers, employment averaged a 0.5% compound growth rate in the United States, and no growth in Japan. For companies with 100 to 200 workers, the U.S. compound growth was 1%, whereas in Japan employment in this segment *decreased* 1.5% (in Britain it decreased 0.5%).

The startling fact is that for companies with employment in excess of 200, U.S. employment decreased 1.5%, Japan's employment decreased more than 2% and U.K. employment decreased 1.5%. This indicates a consistent trend away from large organizational units. *Where* the growth takes place has a significant influence on the way in which information technology contributes to productivity. The rapid lowering of the costs of hardware and software will give the same advantages to small enterprises as have so far been enjoyed only by large organizations. There are many more small organizations than large organizations, as noted in a special report by the Gartner Group in "Office Information Systems—Solutions for the Office of Today," Special Supplement to *Forbes,* November 1983. For instance, there are only one thousand firms in the United States with employment in excess of 5,000, whereas there are 3.4 million firms with employment of less than 50.

3. The negative relationship between the size of a market and its profitability, based on research by the Strategic Planning Institute, was also quoted in American Business Conference, "Midsized Growth Companies." According to this analysis, smaller market segments—those under $50 million—were almost three times as profitable as large market segments—in excess of $1 billion.

4. Information workers make up a much higher proportion of the total workforce in the service industries as compared with manufacturing industries. In services, the percentage ranges from 49% of the total workforce (for firms with fewer than 20 employees) to 23% (for firms with more than 1,000 employees). In manufacturing, the corresponding ratios range from the high of 27% to the low of 18%. See Hearst Business Communications, *Office/Business Market.*

5. The ratio of managers follows a similar pattern as that observed in the case of information workers. In services, their percentage ranges from 12.7% of the total workforce (for firms with fewer than 20 employees) to 6.3% (for firms with more than 1,000 employees). In manufacturing, the corresponding ratios range from the high of 14% to the low of only 4.2%. Hearst Business Communications, *Office/Business Market.*

6. The "Production Sector" of the United States economy is defined as

including: agriculture, mining, construction, and manufacturing. It accounts
for 27% of total employment and 33% of the GNP. The "Services Sector"
includes: distributive services (transportation, communication, utilities,
wholesale- and retail trade); consumer services (lodging, repairs, amusements);
health and education; government; producer services (finance, insurance, real
estate, legal-, professional-, and business services). The "underground services"—among the fastest growing—are almost entirely classifiable in the
services sector.

Sectors of the U.S. economy have experienced large differences in their
growth rates. Here are the growth rates for individual sectors of the economy:
raw materials, 22%; manufacturing, 37%; construction, 4%; distribution
services, 34%; consumer services, 49%; health and education, 50%; government, 15%; producer services, 61%. See *Forbes,* April 1, 1983.

The growth in distribution services and producer services greatly exceeds
the growth in raw materials and manufacturing, the traditional mainstays
of an industrial economy. This confirms my conclusion that the transition
from the industrial to the service economy is really a transformation in channels of distribution, not a change in the method of production. It is also
interesting to note that construction, which has the least efficient distribution
system, is reported to be the mainstay of the legitimate "underground" service
sector.

7. The proportion of information workers, as a percentage of total sector
employment, varies a great deal. It ranges from 8% in agriculture and 24%
in construction to 63% in trade and 92% in finance and insurance.

8. Jonscher, "Models of Economic Organizations."

9. Jonscher, ibid.

10. Jonscher pursued the subject of information-sector productivity in
a follow-up paper which assessed the effects of increasing information-capital
investment on employment. The growth in the number of information workers
was seen as due to "differential rates of technological progress in the production and information sectors." Jonscher, "Information Resources."

In other words, as the productivity of the production sector increased,
less labor was needed to produce the same amount of physical goods. At
the same time, the declining productivity of the information sector absorbed
more and more labor. An equation was written to explain employment levels
in terms of the relative productivity of each sector. The decisive ratio is
that of information workers to the total workforce, estimated at 44.5% in
1960, 50.5% in 1980, and projected to decline to 45.7% by the year 2000.
The future ratio is derived from a projected growth of information-sector
productivity from 0.6% per annum (in 1960) to 5.1% (in 2000). If that
analysis is correct, the relative growth of information workers in the United
States peaked in 1980. Given a continuation of such low levels of productivity
in the production sector, any future gains in employment would have to
take place in production jobs. This entire employment forecast, then, hinges

on the ability to achieve 5% productivity gains in the information sector.

As noted in prior chapters, large productivity gains can be achieved through work simplification. Efficiency studies at the individual level of analysis show that the 5% annual productivity target is relatively easy to attain. The question remains, however, whether the institutional, organizational, and social barriers to productivity gains can be removed so that the 5% improvement potential will be realized in the form of overall economic growth. As shown in Chapter 9, technology does not by itself guarantee such growth. As a matter of fact, hierarchically-administered computer centers may actually inhibit the ability of organizations to adapt to a changing environment. I suspect that many large institutions find themselves in such a situation right now. Market forces do not as yet adequately discipline the propensity of large information-sector organizations to accumulate layers upon layers of unproductive information capital. Evidence for this can be seen in recent employment trends in the information workforce. There has been no change in the long-term trend to increase the proportion of information workers as a fraction of the total workforce. For instance, between January of 1982 and January of 1984, information employment grew by 7% despite a severe recession that provided every incentive to reduce overhead costs through productivity improvements. Incidentally, this period was also remarkable in that it showed an acceleration in shipments of information technology, which is presumed to increase productivity and decrease information-sector employment. If Jonscher's equations are correct, productivity gains have been revealed by the reduced fraction of information workers in the total workforce. So far, this is not the case.

11. See Paul A. Strassmann, "Managing Costs of Information." *Harvard Business Review,* September–October 1976.

12. A most revealing case study of the impact of technology on labor is contained in Bulletin 2137 from the U. S. Department of Labor. For the study period of over ten years, the following changes were shown for the printing and publishing industry:

Occupation	Percent of Total Employment	Percent Change
Professional, technical	14.8%	+18%
Managers, executives	9.8%	+8%
Sales personnel	9.7%	+29%
Clerical	21.3%	+4%
Trade, craft	24.9%	−4%
Operators	11.6%	−5%
Service workers	1.1%	−38%
Laborers	1.6%	−21%

The printing and publishing industry was one of the earliest to be heavily affected by automation. Yet large percentage losses in employment there are to be found only among service workers and laborers—accounting for less than 3% of total personnel, and a much smaller fraction of wages and salaries at that. Service- and labor losses were more than compensated for by marked increases in professional, technical, and sales employment. There is no evidence that automation may have had a devastating effect on overall employment, although it is clear that the industry had to restructure its jobs.

I regret very much the paucity of factual studies on employment changes dealing with the introduction of information technology. In view of proposed legislation on the presumed effects of such technology, there is very little solid evidence at the industry- or firm level to provide an understanding of what has actually occurred.

13. The Computer Business Manufacturer's Association recently completed a survey of salary distributions in its industry. The study was made in response to frequently voiced charges that high-tech industry is creating a workforce with only highly paid technologists at the top and underpaid assembly workers at the bottom. The total number of employees in the survey was 608,000—certainly a very large sample. The computer industry shows a relatively egalitarian compensation structure. Twenty-five percent of all employees were compensated at or near the mean for all the salaries involved. The distribution then dropped sharply. Only 10% of employees received 40% below the mean income. Only 2% of all employees received incomes 60% below the mean or 100% above the mean. I was surprised to see such an even clustering of all incomes around the middle. There was not even a hint that the income was polarized between the haves and the have-nots. The U.S. computer industry has every characteristic needed for being the stronghold of a well-paid middle class.

CHAPTER 12: Information and Societal Productivity
(pp. 203–219)

1. A forecast of future incomes per capita can be made by examination of historical productivity trends. The following shows U.S. productivity gains.

Years	Labor Productivity Gain/Yr
1909–1929	1.6%
1929–1947	2.9%
1947–1965	3.4%
1965–1973	2.4%
1973–1982	0.9%

Source: U.S. Department of Labor, *Productivity and the Economy—A Chartbook,* Bulletin 2171, (Washington, D.C.: GPO, 1983), p. 2.

A gain of 3% in labor productivity, which would compensate for the stagnation of the last decade, is achievable. Assuming a 3% annual productivity growth, I estimate that the following real per capita income could be produced:

Year	Real per Capita Income Potential
1983	$12,000 (actual)
1990	$14,760
2000	$19,800
2010	$26,700

Real per capita incomes in excess of $60,000 per annum can be attained in about fifty years. The awareness that low productivity growth has caused a loss of jobs and of income is well illustrated by the following comment:

> If the economy had been able to sustain its old 3% trend rate of productivity growth through the 1970's, the private sector's total output in 1981 would have been 20% greater than it turned out to be. That comes to $234 billion in 1972 dollars. . . . Conservative estimates put the permanent loss of jobs in smokestack industries such as autos and steel at 2 million.

Source: "The Revival of Productivity," *Business Week,* February 13, 1984, p. 94.

2. Herbert A. Simon, "Prometheus or Pandora: The Influence of Automation on Society," *IEEE Computer Journal,* November 1981, pp. 69–74.

3. The importance of computer investments in the economy is highlighted by the following:

	Computer Share of Total		
	1965	1972	1982
Producer's durable equipment	6.6%	22.8%	33.4%

Source: CBEMA, *Marketing Data Book,* p. 14.

4. Anthony P. Carnevale and Harold Goldstein, *Employee Training: Its Changing Role and An Analysis of New Data* (Washington, D.C.: American Society for Training and Development, 1983), pp. 34–35.

CHAPTER 13: Information and the Media (pp. 220–231)

1. John P. Kotter, "What Effective Managers Really Do," *Harvard Business Review* (December 1983); H. Mintzberg, "The Manager's Job: Folklore and Fact," *Harvard Business Review* (July 1975); id., "Managerial Work:

Analysis from Observation," *Management Science* (October 1971); id., "Structural Observation as a Method to Study Managerial Work," *Journal of Management Studies* 7 (1970).

2. Starr Roxanne Hiltz and Murry Turoff, *The Network Nation—Human Communication via Computer* (Reading, Mass.: Addison–Wesley Publishing, 1978), p. 7–39.

Bibliography

ACKOFF, RUSSELL L. *A Concept of Corporate Planning.* New York: Wiley Interscience, 1970.

American Business Conference, "The Winning Performance of the Midsized Growth Companies." Private report published by McKinsey & Co., New York, 1983.

American Productivity Center, Computer Conference on Information Workers. *A Final Report for the White House Conference on Productivity.* Houston: American Productivity Center, 1983.

ARTHUR ANDERSEN & CO. "Cost of Government Regulation Study," Chicago: Arthur Andersen, 1979.

ATHANASOPOULOS, CHRISTOS N. "Corporate Productivity Atlas: Gross Corporate Product Measures 1982–1978 [sic]." Lincoln, Mass.: Delphi Research Center, 1983.

BAIR, JAMES H. "Productivity Assessment of Office Automation Systems." A SRI International Report for the National Archives and Records Service. Menlo Park, Cal., March 1979.

BEER, STAFFORD. *The Heart of Enterprise.* New York: John Wiley, 1979.

BOOZ ALLEN & HAMILTON. "Strategic Implications for Office Automation Products and Markets." New York: Booz Allen & Hamilton, 1980.

Business Week Editors. "Casting Executives as Consultants." *Business Week,* August 30, 1982.

———. "The Revival of Productivity," *Business Week,* February 13, 1984.

CARNEVALE, ANTHONY P. AND HAROLD GOLDSTEIN. *Employee Training: Its Changing Role and An Analysis of New Data.* Washington, D.C.: American Society for Training and Development, 1983.

CETRON, MARVIN J. "Getting Ready for the Jobs of the Future," *The Futurist,* June 1983.

CHINLOY, P. *Sources of Productivity Growth at the Firm Level: The Bell System 1947–1978.* Washington, D.C.: Communications Workers of America, AFL–CIO, 1981.

COHEN, B. G. F., M. J. SMITH, AND L. W. STAMMERJOHN. "Psychosocial Factors Contributing to Job Stress of Clerical VDT Operators." *Proceedings of the 1982 Office Automation Conference.* Arlington, Va.: American Federation of Information Processing Societies, 1982.

Computer and Business Equipment Manufacturer's Association. *The Computer and Business Equipment Industry Marketing Data Book.* Washington, D.C.: CBEMA, 1983.

CONWAY, DAVID L. "Common Staffing System." *White Collar Productivity.* Edited by Robert N. Lehrer. New York: McGraw–Hill, 1983.

CRON, WILLIAM L., AND MARION G. SOBOL. "The Relationship Between Computerization and Performance: A Strategy for Maximizing the Economic Benefits of Computerization," *Information and Management* 6 (1983).

DAHL, H. L., AND K. S. MORGAN. "Return on Investment in Human Resources." *White Collar Productivity.* Edited by Robert N. Lehrer. New York: McGraw–Hill, 1983.

DE SOLA POOL, ITHIEL. *See* Sola Pool, Ithiel de.

DESSAUER, JOHN H. *My Years with Xerox—The Billions Nobody Wanted.* New York: Doubleday, 1971.

DRUCKER, PETER. Quoted by B. J. van Loggerenberg in *Proceedings of Business Week Conference on Productivity—New York, October 1–2, 1981.* New York: Business Week, 1981.

EDELMAN, FRANTZ. "Managers, Computers and Productivity." *MIS Quarterly* 5:3 (September 1981).

EDMUNDSON, R. H., AND D. R. JEFFERY. "A Preliminary Investigation into the Impact of Requirements Analysis upon User Satisfaction with Packaged Accounting Software." Unpublished research report, University of New South Wales, Kensington, Australia, 1983.

FIKES, R. E. "A Commitment-Based Framework for Describing Informal Cooperative Work. *Cognitive Science* 6:331 (1982).

FISKE, EDWARD B. "Americans in Electronic Era Are Reading as Much as Ever." *New York Times,* September 8, 1983.

FOX, JOHN. "Fear and Loathing of Office Automation." *Management Information Systems Week,* August 3, 1983.

GALE, BRADLEY T. "Can More Capital Buy Higher Productivity?" *Harvard Business Review,* July–August 1980.

GALITZ, WILBERT O. "Human Factors in Office Automation." Atlanta: Life Office Management Assn., 1980.

GARTNER GROUP. "Office Information Systems—Solutions for the Office of Today," *Forbes* special supplement, November 1983.

GROSSMAN, E. S., AND G. E. SADLER. *Comparative Productivity Dynamics.* Houston: American Productivity Center, 1982.

GUTEK, B. A., AND T. K. BIKSON. "Advanced Office Systems: An Empirical Look at Utilization and Satisfaction." Santa Monica: RAND Corp., 1983.

HAMMER, MICHAEL. "Improving Business Performance: The Real Objective of Office Automation." *Digest of 1982 Office Automation Conference.* Arlington, Va.: American Federation of Information Processing Societies, 1982.

HATSOPOULOS, GEORGE N. *The High Cost of Capital.* Washington, D.C.: American Business Conference, 1983.

Hearst Business Communications, *The Office/Business Market—A Pragmatic Analysis By Industry Segment and Job Function.* Garden City, N.Y.: Hearst, 1981.

HILTZ, STARR ROXANNE, AND MURRAY TUROFF. *The Network Nation— Human Communication via Computer.* Reading, Mass.: Addison–Wesley, 1978.

HODGES, PARKER. "Fear of Automation—Do Computers Give You the Willies?" *Output,* 1980.

Infosystems Editors. "25th Annual Survey of DP Budgets," *Infosystems,* June 1983.

JOHNSON, R. A. "Organizational Analysis by the INTROSPECT Process." *White Collar Productivity.* Edited by Robert N. Lehrer. New York: McGraw–Hill, 1983.

JONSCHER, CHARLES. "Models of Economic Organizations." Ph.D. thesis, Harvard University, Cambridge, Mass., 1980.

———. "Information Resources and Economic Productivity." *Information Economics and Policy* 1 (1983): pp. 13–35.

———. "Information Technology: Investment Needs and Opportunities." *Proceedings of an International Investment Symposium Sponsored by Fidelity International and Nikko Securities.* Cambridge, Eng.: Jesus College, 1983.

KENDRICK, J. W., "Interindustry Differences in Productivity Growth." Washington, D.C.: American Enterprise Institute, 1983.

KENDRICK, JOHN W., AND D. CREAMER. "Measuring Company Productivity—A Handbook with Case Studies." *Studies in Business Economics* 89, New York: National Industrial Conference Board, 1965.

KIECHEL, WALTER. "Why Executives Don't Compute." *Fortune,* November 14, 1983.

KIRCHNER, ENGELBERT. "At the Mercy of Machines." *Datamation,* September 1982, pp. 252–261.

KOTTER, JOHN P. "What Effective Managers Really Do." *Harvard Business Review,* December 1982.

LANCASTER, F. W. *Toward Paperless Information Systems.* New York: Academic Press, 1978.

LEONTIEF, WASSILY W. "The Distribution of Work and Income." *Scientific American,* September 1982.

LEVIN, HENRY, AND RUSSELL RUMBERGER. "The Educational Implications of High Technology." Stanford, Cal.: Stanford University Institute for Research on Education, Finance, and Governance, 1983.

LIEBERMAN, M. A., G. J. SELIG, AND J. J. WALSH. *Office Automation—A Manager's Guide for Improved Productivity.* New York: John Wiley, 1982.

LINSTONE, HAROLD A., et al. "The Multiple Perspective Concept." *Technological Forecasting and Social Change* 20 (1981) pp. 275–325.

MACKINTOSH, IAN M., AND TOM JACOBS. "The Impact of New Technology on Employment." Manchester, England: Manchester Statistical Society, January 15, 1980.

MAIN, JEREMY. "Work Won't Be the Same Again." *Fortune,* June 28, 1982.

MAYER, CAROLINE E. "AT&T Contract Hailed as Landmark." *Washington Post,* August 24, 1983.

MEAD, CARVER, AND LYNN CONWAY. *Introduction to VLSI Systems.* Reading, Mass.: Addison–Wesley, 1980.

MINOLTA CORPORATION. *The Evolving Role of the Secretary in the Information Age.* Ramsey, N.J.: Minolta Business Equipment Division, 1983.

MINTZBERG, H. "Structured Observation as a Method to Study Managerial Work." *Journal of Management Studies,* 7 (1970).

———. "Managerial Work: Analysis from Observation." *Management Science,* October 1971.

———. *The Nature of Managerial Work.* New York: Harper & Row, 1973.

———. "The Manager's Job: Folklore and Fact." *Harvard Business Review,* July 1975.

MORF, MARTIN. "Eight Scenarios for Work in the Future." *The Futurist,* June 1983.

MUNDEL, M. E. *Measuring and Enhancing The Productivity of Service and Government Organizations.* Tokyo: Asian Productivity Organization, 1975.

――――. "Work-Unit Analysis." *White Collar Productivity.* Edited by Robert N. Lehrer. McGraw–Hill, 1983.

NAISBITT, JOHN. *Megatrends.* New York: Warner Books, 1982.

National Research Council, Panel on Impact of Video Viewing on Vision of Workers. *Video Displays, Work, and Vision.* Washington, D.C.: National Academy Press, 1983.

NAUGES, LOUIS M. "Office Automation Alibis." *Datamation,* November 1983.

NELSON, T. "Literary Machines." Swarthmore, Pa.: Nelson Publishing, 1981.

NEUMAN, JOHN L. "Making Overhead Cuts That Last. *Harvard Business Review,* May–June 1975.

――――. "Make Overhead Cuts That Last." *White Collar Productivity.* Edited by Robert N. Lehrer. New York: McGraw–Hill, 1983.

NOLAN, ROBERT E. "Work Measurement." In *White Collar Productivity.* Edited by Robert N. Lehrer. New York: McGraw–Hill, 1983.

NUSSBAUM, KAREN. "Office Automation: Jekyll or Hyde?" In *Highlights of the International Conference on Office Work and New Technology.* Edited by Daniel Marschall and Judith Gregory. Cleveland: Working Women Education Fund, 1983.

OLSON, M. H., AND H. C. LUCAS, JR. "The Impact of Office Automation on the Organization: Some Implications for Research and Practice." *Communications of the ACM* 25:11 (November 1982).

OMAN, R. C. "Comparing the Benefits and Costs of Electric Typewriters and Word Processors." *The Office,* June 1977.

PARKINSON, C. NORTHCOTE. *Parkinson's Law and Other Studies in Administration.* Boston: Houghton Mifflin, 1957.

PARSONS, GREGORY L. "Information Technology: A New Competitive Weapon." *Sloan Management Review* 25:1 (1983).

PATRI, P. "The Impact of Systems on Office Design." *Proceedings of the AFIPS Office Automation Conference.* Arlington, Va.: AFIPS Press, 1982.

PAVA, CALVIN H. P. *Managing New Office Technology.* New York: The Free Press, 1983.

PAYNE, BRUCE. "Productivity Gains with New Office Technology." *The Office,* September 1983.

PETERS, THOMAS J. AND ROBERT H. WATERMAN, JR. *In Search of Excellence.* New York: Harper & Row, 1982.

POOL, ITHIEL DE SOLA: *See* Sola Pool, Ithiel de.

POWER, KEVIN P. "Now We Can Move Office Work Offshore to Enhance Output." *Wall Street Journal,* June 9, 1983.

ROACH, STEVEN S. "The Industrialization of the Information Economy." Special Economic Study. New York: Morgan Stanley & Co., 1984.

――――. "Productivity, Investment, and the Information Economy." *Economic Perspectives,* New York: Morgan Stanley & Co., 1984.

ROCKHOLD, ALAN. "White Collar Productivity—Top Management Doesn't Know What It Wants." *Infosystems,* April 1982.

ROWE, D. L. "How Westinghouse Measures Productivity." *Management Review,* November 1981.

RUBIN, CHARLES. "Some People Should Be Afraid of Computers." *Personal Computing,* August 1983.

RUCH, WILLIAM A., AND WILLIAM B. WERTHER. "Productivity Strategies at TRW." *National Productivity Review,* Spring 1983.

"Rucker Plan of Group Incentives." *The Encyclopedia of Management.* New York: Van Nostrand Reinhold, 1982.

SALMANS, SANDRA. "The Debate over the Electronic Office." *New York Times,* November 14, 1982.

SCHLUMPF, JAMES D., AND KENNETH A. CHARON. "IBM's Common Staffing System: How to Measure Productivity of the Indirect Workforce." *Management Review* 70:8 (1981).

SENTRY INSURANCE COMPANY. "Perspectives on Productivity." A public opinion survey conducted by Louis Harris & Associates. Stevens Point, Wis.: Sentry Insurance Company, 1981.

SIMON, HERBERT A., "Prometheus or Pandora: The Influence of Automation on Society." *IEEE Computer Journal,* November 1981.

SMITH, H. T. "The Office Revolution." Willow Grove, Pa.: Administrative Management Society Foundation, 1983.

SOCOLOVSKY, ALBERTO. "Robots Must Join the Team, Not Replace It." *Electronic Business,* February 1983.

SOLA POOL, ITHIEL DE. "Tracking the Flow of Information." *Science* 221 (August 12, 1983).

STRASSMANN, PAUL A. "A Plant–Warehouse System with Variable Lead-Times and Variable Re-order Levels." *Management Technology Journal,* August 1962.

――――. "Forecasting Considerations in Design of Management Information Systems." *Bulletin of the National Association of Accountants,* February 1965.

――――. "Management of White Collar Productivity Programs." Proceedings of the *Frontiers in Knowledge* lecture series, Manhattan College, School of Business, Riverdale, N.Y., 1975.

――――. "The Future Direction of Information Services to Impact the Bottom Line." Proceedings of the Eighth Annual Conference of the Society for Management Information Systems, September, 1976.

———. "Managing the Costs of Information." *Harvard Business Review,* September–October 1976.

———. "Stages of Growth in Information Systems." *Datamation,* October 1976.

———. "Organizational Productivity—The Role of Information Technology." Proceedings of the Congress of the International Federation of Information Processing Societies, Toronto, 1977.

———. "Ten Thousand Years of Recorded Information." A Xerox Corporation exhibit catalogue, Stamford, Connecticut, 1979.

———. "The Office of the Future: Information Management for the New Age." *Technology Review,* December/January 1980.

———. "Information Technology and Organisations." A presentation of the IT '82 Conference, London, December 1982.

———. "Information Systems and Literacy." In *Literacy for Life,* edited by R. W. Bailey and R. M. Fosheim. New York: The Modern Language Association of America, 1983.

STRASSMANN, PAUL A. AND RICHARD HESPOS. "Stochastic Decision Trees for the Analysis of Investment Decisions." *Management Science,* August, 1965.

Strategic Planning Institute (Cambridge, Mass.). "PIMS Survey on the State of the Planning Function." PIMS Annual Conference, Boston, 1983.

———. "Management Productivity and Information Technology—Results and Conclusions from the Pilot Program." 1984.

SUCHMAN, LUCY. "The Role of Common Sense in the Process of Interface Design." *Highlights of the International Conference on Office Work and New Technology.* Cleveland: Working Women Education Fund, 1983.

THOR, CARL G. "Productivity Measurement." In *Corporate Controller's Manual.* New York: Warren, Gorham & Lamont, 1982.

———. "Productivity Measurement in White Collar Groups." *White Collar Productivity.* Edited by Robert N. Lehrer. New York: McGraw–Hill, 1983.

TOFFLER, ALVIN. *Future Shock.* New York: Random House, 1970.

———. *The Third Wave.* New York: William Morrow and Co., 1980.

TORNQVIST, BRITA, AND SVEA HERMANSSON. "Automation and the Quality of Work Life at the Swedish Telephone Company." *Highlights of the International Conference on Office Work and New Technology.* Cleveland: Working Women Education Fund, 1983.

UHLIG, RONALD P., DAVID J. FARBER, AND JAMES H. BAIR. *The Office of the Future.* Amsterdam: Elsevier–North Holland, 1981.

U.S. Bureau of Labor Statistics. *The Impact of Technology on Labor.* Bulletin 2137, December 1982.

————. *A BLS Reader on Productivity.* Bulletin 2171, June 1983.

U.S. Congress, Office of Technology Assessment. *Automation and the Workplace.* Washington, D.C.: GPO, 1983.

U.S. DEPARTMENT OF LABOR. *Productivity and the Economy. A Chartbook.* Washington, D.C.: GPO, 1983.

————. *Employment and Earnings* 30:2 (February 1983).

U.S. General Accounting Office. *Productivity Sharing Programs: Can They Contribute to Productivity Improvement?* Publication AFMD–81–22. Gaithersburg, Md.: U. S. General Accounting Office, 1981.

UTTAL, BRO. "What's Detaining the Office of the Future." *Fortune,* May 3, 1982.

Verbatim Corporation. "Office Worker Views and Perceptions of New Technology in the Workplace." Sunnyvale, Cal.: Verbatim Corp., 1983.

WEIL, ULRIC. *Information Systems in the 80's.* New York: Prentice–Hall, 1982.

WEIZER, NORMAN, AND LEON JACKSON. "The U. S. Office Automation Market; The Evolution Toward Integrated Information Processing." Cambridge, Mass.: A. D. Little Decision Resources Report 830703, July 1983.

Western Behavioral Sciences Institute. "Final Report, United States Department of Commerce Teleconference on Productivity." La Jolla, Cal., October 20, 1983.

White House Conference on Productivity. *Report of the Preparatory Conference on Private Sector Initiatives—Information Worker Productivity.* Washington, D.C.: GPO, 1983.

Index